HERMAN MELVILLE

J. O. Eaton, pinx.

HERMAN MELVILLE

HERMAN MELVILLE

LEWIS MUMFORD

NEW YORK
THE LITERARY GUILD OF AMERICA
1929

PRINTED IN THE UNITED STATES OF AMERICA
BY QUINN & BODEN COMPANY, INC., RAHWAY, N. J.
TYPOGRAPHY BY ROBERT S. JOSEPHY

PREFACE

THIS is a study of Herman Melville's life and thought. In interpreting Melville's life I have relied primarily on his own writings, including his letters, some of which are still unpublished, and his notebooks. There are occasional blank spaces in Melville's history, but the record is singularly complete in that part of Melville which most matters: his ideas, his feelings, his urges, his vision of life. I have verified and corrected these data by the use of every available piece of independent evidence; and I must express my hearty thanks to Mrs. Frances Thomas, Melville's surviving daughter, for answering my written questions, and to his granddaughter, Mrs. Eleanor Melville Metcalf, for giving me the benefit of her own memories and family tradition, as well as her courtesy and hospitality in placing at my disposal Melville's manuscripts. I am likewise indebted to Miss Caroline W. Stewart, an old friend of the Melville family, for her impressions of the Melville household during the later period of his life.

These pages could not have been written without Mr. Raymond Weaver's pioneer work on Melville. Mr. Weaver not merely brought to light much important data and cleared up relationships that concerned Melville's objective life: he also, through Mrs. Metcalf, discovered Melville's unpublished manuscripts and included them in a definitive edition of his work. For this, he has placed every admirer of Melville in his debt. In addition to acknowledging this great service, I must thank him for the scholarly generosity with which he gave me the benefit of his intimate knowledge of Melville's remains, and his copies of Melville's notebooks. Mr. Weaver's generosity is equalled only by that of Dr. Henry A. Murray, Jr., who shared with me his knowledge of certain Melville letters otherwise inaccessible—an act of pure chivalry, since Dr. Murray is himself at work on a biography of Herman Melville. Such deeds sweeten one's notions of human conduct: they give one not so much a feeling of gratitude as a renewed sense of human dignity, and I warmly place them on record.

In describing Melville's experience and his state of mind, I have taken the liberty of using his own language wherever possible; and I have done this so freely that, except where I have quoted whole passages, I have omitted quotation marks. In condensing and paraphrasing the notebooks of Melville's travels, I have usually employed Melville's own words; for it would be a vain biographer who did not make full use of Melville's sharp descriptions and striking epithets. If I have been frank and unreserved in dealing with the difficult parts of Melville's life, I have been no more so than I think he would have wished, nor more candid than he himself was in treating Pierre. "In reserves," he wrote, "men build imposing characters." Melville's worth, as a man and a poet, has no need for a reputation so created. My purpose has not been to embalm Melville but to bring him to life; and one cannot know or sympathize with the man unless one shares his vicissitudes as well as his triumphs.

Certain portions of this book have appeared, with slight changes and abbreviations, in The New Republic, The American Mercury, and The Saturday Review of Literature.

LEWIS MUMFORD.

CONTENTS

YOUR zodiac here is the life of man in one round chapter; and now I'll read it off, straight out of the book. Come, Almanack! To begin: there's Aries, or the Ram—lecherous dog, he begets us; then Taurus, or the Bull—he bumps us the first thing; then Gemini, or the Twins—that is Virtue and Vice; we try to reach Virtue when lo! comes Cancer the Crab and drags us back; and here, going from Virtue, Leo, a roaring lion, lies in the path—he gives a few fierce bites and surly dabs with his paw; we escape and hail Virgo, the Virgin; that's our first love; we marry and think to be happy for aye, when pop comes Libra or the Scales—happiness weighed and found wanting! and while we are very sad about that Lord! how we suddenly jump as Scorpio or the Scorpion stings us in the rear; we are curing the wound when whang come the arrows all round; Sagittarius, or the Archer, is amusing himself. As we pluck the shafts, stand aside! here's the battering ram, Capricornus or the Goat, full tilt, he comes rushing, and headlong we are tossed; when Aquarius, or the Water-bearer, pours out his whole deluge and drowns us; and to wind up with Pisces or the Fish we sleep.

MOBY-DICK.

PROLOGUE

PROLOGUE

WHEN Herman Melville died in 1891, the literary journal of the day, The Critic, did not even know who he was. The editors rose bravely to the occasion and copied a paragraph about him from a compendium of American literature; and in the weeks that followed they reprinted various commentaries on Melville and his work that were carried in the correspondence columns of the New York newspapers.

The older generation remembered that Herman Melville had once been famous. He had adventured in the South Seas on a whaler; he had lived among the cannibals; and in Typee and Omoo he had made a romantic pastiche of his experiences. On these books Mr. Melville's fame had been founded: it was a pity he had not done more in this line; for his later books, obscure books, crowded books, books that could be called neither fiction nor poetry nor philosophy nor downright useful information, forfeited the interest of a public that liked to take its pleasures methodically. Both the fame and the later absence of recognition, Mr. Melville's commentators agreed, were deserved. By his interest in Sir Thomas Browne and metaphysics, Mr. Melville had carried his readers into a realm much too remote, and an air too rarefied: a flirtation with a South Sea maiden, warm, brown, palpable, was one thing: but the shark that glides white through the sulphurous sea was quite another. In Moby-Dick, so criticism went, Melville had become obscure: and this literary failure condemned him to personal obscurity.

The writer about whom all these sage banalities were

3

written shares with Walt Whitman, I think, the distinction of being the greatest imaginative writer that America has produced: his epic, Moby-Dick, is one of the supreme poetic monuments of the English language: and in depth of experience and religious insight there is scarcely any one in the nineteenth century, with the exception of Dostoyevsky, who can be placed beside him. To his contemporaries, the greatness of Melville was an enigma: they valued him for those lesser virtues in which he more closely resembled themselves. They had no place, on their matter-of-fact plane, with its confident flat-footed science, and its many odd and useful inventions, for the crosslights of Melville's imagination, for his oblique revelations, for his habit of questioning the foundations upon which their vast superstructure of comfort and complacency was erected. "What we want, sir, is facts!"—and though Melville gave them facts, they resented his white vision, because it froze the facts into a state that defied their easy assimilation. When they charged Melville with obscurity, they did not realize, perhaps, that sight demands not merely an object that can be seen, but an eye that is capable of seeing; and it never occurred to them, with all their doubts about Melville, that the defective vision might be their own.

In a great degree, Herman Melville's life and work were one. A biography of Melville implies criticism; and no final criticism of his work is possible that does not bring to it an understanding of his personal development. The exotic elements in Melville's experience have usually been overstressed; the fatality and completeness of his withdrawal from the contemporary scene have been exaggerated; the incidental rocks and rapids and whirlpools have diverted the critic's attention from the flow of the stream itself. It is with Herman Melville's strength and energy on the spiritual plane that I shall chiefly deal. He lives for us not because he painted South Sea rainbows, or rectified abuses in authority in the United States Navy: he lives because he grappled with certain great dilemmas in man's spiritual life, and in seeking to answer them, sounded bottom. He left the clothed and carpeted world of convention, and faced the nakedness of life, death, energy, evil, love, eternity: he drew back the cosy hangings of Victorian parlours, and disclosed the black night outside, dimly lighted with the lights of ancient stars. Had he been a romantic, he would have lived a happy life, buttering his bread with feeble dreams, and swallowing down his regrets with consolatory port: he who wishes to escape the elemental stings of existence need only grasp the outstretched hands of his contemporaries, accept the subterfuge goals they call success in business or journalism, and shrink by means of a padded physical apparatus from the cold reality of the universe itself.

But Melville was a realist, in the sense that the great religious teachers are realists. He saw that horsehair stuffing did not make the universe kinder, and that the oblivion of drink did not make the thing that was forgotten more palatable. His perplexities, his defiances, his torments, his questions, even his failures, all have a meaning for us: whether we renounce the world, as Buddha did, affirm a future transcendence, as Christ did, or, like Whitman, embrace its mingled good-and-evilness, our choice cannot be called enlightened until it has faced the gritty, unassimilable substratum Melville explored. Melville, like Buddha, left a happy and successful career behind him, and plunged into those cold black depths, the depths of the sunless ocean, the blackness of interstellar space; and though he proved that life could not be lived under those conditions, he brought back into the petty triumphs of the age the one element that it completely lacked: the tragic sense of life: the sense that the highest human flight is sustained over an unconquered and perhaps an unconquerable abyss. On the peak of Melville's vision, a man stands poised as on the spur of a glacier:

nature offers no shelter, and humanity does not succour him: he is alone. Will he live or die? One cannot say. But if he returns to the warm valleys and the friendly villages he will be another man; and a part of him, a precious part, will forever remain alone, impregnable.

OLYMPIAN

CHAPTER ONE: BITTER MORNING

THE SOCIETY into which Herman Melville was born was in the fullest sense of the word a provincial one. His heritage and his work united him with that society; and when its occupations were undermined and its customs effaced by the great tide of destruction that marked the Civil War, he himself was intimately involved in its ruin.

By a provincial society I mean one which finds its sources and motives within its own region, and that achieves a certain balance and continuity by a restricted development. To understand Melville's background, one must think back to a time when New York was only one of a number of Atlantic ports that claimed the commerce of the seas and the wealth that it brought: Salem was almost as important: so were Boston and Baltimore and Charleston: it was little more than the accident of a regular sailing packet line that made New York take the lead in attracting population, that, and the opening of a direct water-route into mid-America, via the Erie Canal, which was still a-building in 1819, the year that Herman Melville was born.

The United States, except as an abstract political entity, scarcely existed. There were eagles on the furniture: there were eagles on the dollars: there were flags and martial birds on mirrors and bedspreads and glass and china: but a good part of the community, certainly in the older, more settled regions, was hardly yet political-minded, still less conscious of a mystic relation with the other parts. During the War of 1812 New England, threatened with economic ruin, was on the point of breaking loose from the political union:

and though the national government coined money in quarter dollars, people still referred to such coins as two shillings. If Rip van Winkle was surprised at the changes that had taken place during his long nap, a modern observer of that provincial society would be even more astounded at the lack of them. Whitman, writing a whole generation later, and loathing the notion of secession, still had a consciousness of the individuality and independence of the separate states which the strongest defender of states' rights never expressed after the Civil War.

This provincial society had its own economic foundations, its own locus, its own seat of authority: it differed in a marked way from that which was developing on the frontier: the drama of one of Cooper's best books, The Pioneers, is chiefly concerned with that contrast. The frontier society was a flowing and moving one: the only thing that united it was the common flag that waved over it and the Constitution, to which its officers paid their superficial respect. Its members came from anywhere, got a living anyhow, and pushed on, in an uneasy, restless search for more fertile land, wilder creatures, greater distance from their neighbours—or merely, from the habit of locomotion. It was strenuous, uncertain, heroic; but once the settlement was effected, once the town was founded and the building-lots divided and the outlaws rounded up, it was unbearably tame: the excitements of civilized life, the clash of ideas, the conflict of cultures, the absorption of experience, did not occupy the pioneer: even when he adopted the external habits of the red man, his weapons, his tools, his maize and dried meat, he avoided the inner content of his culture. In provincial society we are nearer to Europe, that is, nearer to a settled life, to order, authority, tradition. In every colony there was an historic mixture of nationalities and stocks, and that peculiar to New York, English and Dutch, with a dash of French Huguenots, had at last begun to bubble and ferment: presently a Whitman, a Melville, came out of it.

In provincial society, the family was still a prime reality; and in New York it was not less so, certainly, because of the fact that the Dutch had founded great landed proprietorships, like those of the Gansevoorts to whom Herman Melville belonged on his maternal side. Two hundred years of inherited wealth create family pride and all the futile snobberies of caste: they also create a firm sense of self-possession. Washington Irving, who was one of the conquering English, might laugh at these Dutch burghers and patroons: but from their manorial seats along the Hudson and the Mohawk, the Van Rensselaers and the Schuylers and the Gansevoorts could view this mockery with sleepy disdain. They had only to sit tight to be eminent; as the population grew, the value of the land doubled and quadrupled, and in spite of rent wars and the abolition of feudal privileges, the landed families rose to the top like cream.

The Dutch throve in this expansive environment, on farms that stretched from hilltop to hilltop, as they throve by intensive activity in the lowlands by the Zuyder Zee: if their old canals were covered over and filled up in New Amsterdam, they still had their commodious stone or brick houses in the country; there was one such at Gansevoort, where the Gansevoorts lived, not far from Saratoga. The fine arts did not find disciples among these great families: the Copleys, Trumbulls, Stuarts, Peales had English names: but the crafts were cultivated in great variety: the architecture was straightforward and in minor matters, like the horizontal windows and the peculiar gambrel roof, original: the landscape was well treated; and above all, there was food, wild pigeon and grouse and deer, well-fed beef and succulent ducks and geese and great handsome cheeses. When Herman is a little boy his mother will remember Uncle Peter Gansevoort, at Albany, with a tub of five hundred pickled oysters.

"A thoroughly developed gentleman is always robust and

11

healthy." When Melville wrote these words he was thinking of the great gentlemen between whose legs he had walked as a little boy, and particularly, perhaps, of one he used to hear about, that grandest of old fellows, General Peter Gansevoort, a mighty soldier during the Revolution and a great figure among men. He had died but seven years before Melville was born; many of his remains, including a portrait by Stuart, were still visible; and his legend stayed on the tongues of those who had known him. Six foot four he was, with an appetite and a digestion fit to keep that colossal frame in motion. Now, among all the pleasures of life, positive health—not mere freedom from disorder and disease— is surely the first: living needs no extra justification when the blood is clear and all the juices are flowing harmoniously. In Melville's youth even a city lad could sail a boat, tramp into the country, shoot game, experience the active, outdoor life which has always been the mainstay of the aristocracy, and which doubtless explains its ability to conquer and control the urban populace, habituated to the ledger, the bench, the desk, and the foul air thereof. Melville had scarcely reached maturity before some of these natural pleasures were curtailed in the city of his birth, so that, to preserve them, William Cullen Bryant launched the campaign to create Central Park.

"Too often," Melville wrote in 1852, "the American that himself makes a fortune, builds him a great metropolitan house, in the most metropolitan street, of the most metropolitan town. Whereas, a European of the same sort would thereupon migrate into the country. That herein the European hath the better of it, no poet, no philosopher, and no aristocrat will deny." Melville's ancestors had kept close to the country: Grandfather Peter and Uncle Herman at Gansevoort, Uncle Peter at Albany, little more than a country town, Great Uncle Thomas Melville on his farm, eastward in the Berkshires. Although Melville was born in New York, he was nourished by the agricultural experience of the back-country: when he idealized his early life in Pierre, he gave his hero a twenty-mile ride or a ten-mile walk every day, a turn at felling a hemlock in the forest, or boxing or fencing or boating. That was something like a foundation, and it resembled Melville's own. When we come to a later period of Melville's life we will not be tempted, if we remember these things, to overstress his doldrums or his adolescent uncertainties: for we shall not forget that he became a magnificently healthy animal—and healthy animals itch to use their energies and test their muscles.

2

Against the vigorous, fleshy life of the provincial countryside, the immediate environment in which Melville was born must seem a little petty and painful around the neck; and it was. Herman's father, Allan Melville, was by trade an importer of French goods, and by every evidence of physiognomy, notebook, and letter a trivial but not uncultivated man. The portrait of Allan as a young man that survives is cruel in its exposure of Allan's simpering elegance: his lip is weak and his eye has a vacuous leer, and when one puts these qualities alongside the careful pedanticism of his letters, one is left with a mixture of odious characteristics.

Allan was completely given to the outward amenities of life. He valued name: he was not unconscious of this, perhaps, when he married a Gansevoort, nor was he less so the year before Herman was born, when he visited his titled Scotch cousins at the original Melville seat. Deportment and modest behaviour were only less in Allan's eyes than wifely name and beauty: when he married Maria he made sure, remembering it may be a disturbing levity in Napoleonic France, which he had known as a young man, that she saw eye to eye with him on every point. He was the sort of man from whom one expects prudence without imagination. He doubtless had passionate adventures before he married, for he was thirty-two when that happened: but he was circum-spect in all things, and if the adventures left any tell-tale traces, we have no better reason for thinking so than the fact that Melville confronted his hero with such a crack in his father's image, in his novel, Pierre. Such a man may do very well in business, so long as no unforeseen circum-stances occur: not doing the wrong thing will suffice in many occupations for actually doing the right thing—and one may be sure that Allan Melville had a sense of gentlemanly correctness in all his dealings. Business was not yet a ruth-less obsession: one expected to retire from it into a more cultivated existence; indeed, such an early withdrawal was the capital mark of success.

Maria Melville, born Gansevoort, seems to have been Allan's counterpart in many ways: each carried the same tune in a different register. Like Mrs. Glendinning, in Pierre, she was a noble creature, but "formed chiefly for the gilded prosperities of life, bred and expanded in all devel-opments under the sole influence of hereditary forms and world-usages." She was correct, formal, proud; she valued a high station in life, to which her maiden name, at least, entitled her; she valued good food, low voices, courteous servants, correct manners. An only girl in a family of boys, preening herself with a sense of her family's importance, does not profit by sufficient chastenings of pride: Maria, unfortunately, was such a girl; and to the last she wore her pride in station like a crest.

Maria had stooped a little to marry a mere trader like Allan, although he, too, came of good English stock which sided with the colonies in the Revolutionary War; still, she stooped; and she never quite recovered from the painful crick in her back. She must have attributed the misfortunes that followed in her middle age to this original mistake; at all events, one cannot imagine a woman with such traits as she left behind in the memory of her contemporaries, taking any disaster to her station in life or her income with

14

resignation or becoming meekness. Christianity, for a Gansevoort, meant a prominent pew in church, not an equal place in heaven; and to deprive her of the world's goods was to deprive her of everything she valued.

Both Melville's father and his mother were monsters; but it took him a long time to discover this, because they were correct and meritorious members of society, and it is difficult to believe that the image of God can err, if it be repeated often enough. In the New York of the early nineteenth century, Mr. and Mrs. Allan Melville can be duplicated many times over. Their correctness, their pettiness, their shallowness, were the correctness and shallowness of a venial society whose pretensions to culture and civilization were, on the whole, pretty thin. It was an agreeable society, make no doubt, and Mr. and Mrs. Melville were just the sort of people to persuade one to accept its conventions as the very acme of human desire. One visited: one left one's card; one entertained at dinner; occasionally one went to the theatre, or to one of those miscellaneous exhibitions of forgeries and bad copies and minor masterpieces that served to introduce art into America: one might even descend a little to that prodigious educational spectacle, the Cosmorama, or Picture of the World, at Scudder's Museum.

It was not London or Paris, of course. Allan had seen the paintings in the Louvre and doubtless knew better than some of his contemporaries: but it was the outward activity of a great city, with none of the inner effort that sustained it in Europe. No one in New York, up to 1819, had dedicated himself to the creative life; and whether one is conscious of it or not, a great poem, an original thought, an effective piece of scientific investigation, subtly affect the spirit and tempo of a place. New York was the counterfeit of a great metropolis, just as the pictures it looked at were the counterfeits of great painting, just as the exhibition of a Cosmorama was a counterfeit of a voyage around the world. Pigs snouted in the gutters; the waterfront had be-

come a jumble of shipping; the old docks had begun to
splinter up and decay; the Collect Pond was being filled
up to make real estate for the growing city, and later a site
for the Tombs; in the vacant fields on the outskirts of the
town, squatters settled in little hovels that reminded one of
a misery and want not yet wholly native to America: in
short, over a vast welter of miscellaneous activities there
was only the most transparent film of a civilized life.

As long as one remained on the surface one could manage
one's time agreeably; and the refined, fastidious people who
constituted Melville's social class were unaware of the fact
that their provincial shell was becoming more and more
hollow, as the organism within it died part by part and
shrivelled up. The Erie Canal and the general starvation
and impoverishment of Europe after the Napoleonic wars
would draw vast masses of needy men across the Atlantic:
the city itself would lose its waterfronts and pleasances: the
trees would make way for cobblestones and hitching-posts:
the area around its little villages would be broken up into
building lots, and it would have to convert its Potter's Fields
into parks in order to recapture a little open space: by 1835,
dingy-looking tenements, newly built, and made-over "tenant houses," abandoned by the original merchants, would
spread around and engulf the neat provincial city. In the
twenties, from the overcrowded slums and the insanitary
backyard wells, fever came forth, year after year: a little
later, a wave of cholera caused almost a general exodus.
Eventually, the noses of the respectable would detect the
change and tilt upward in pained appreciation of it; but
that the ugliness and misery and disease were in any way
connected with the sources of their incomes, they would of
course indignantly have denied.

3

Allan Melville was not a rich man; but when Herman
Melville was born, on August 1, 1819, Allan Melville was

doing well in a modest way: the family lived at Number Six, Pearl Street, and Herman was the second son and the third child of this agreeable union. When Herman was a year old, Allan noted in a letter that he had hired a cook and a nurse, and wanted only a waiter; and one may take for granted, I think, that such a household already has its complement of maids, linen, silver, sherry, port, brocades, and books.

To awake in a home surrounded by the decencies of life must mollify an infant's indignation at having to enter the world at all; and in Herman Melville's earliest years, nothing ever conveyed a sense of danger or physical stress. In the even decorum of the days, meals ebbed and flowed like the tides; the sheets were as white as the tops of wind-whipt waves off the Battery; clothes sprang into existence out of the sewing-room as naturally as feathers cover a robin's back: little boys had handkerchiefs to blow their noses in and pillows to cuddle into when they fell asleep in their cribs; in the obscure world that crowded around little Herman, there were convivial discussions between his father and strange gentlemen in the library, when he might do no more than linger in the shadows of the hall or hush his breath at a crack in the partly opened door; there were visits to relatives and a few select friends that were as sociable as a regimental inspection in the army, when he might not get his pinafore mussed, nor bunk up against the furniture, nor tease his older sister, nor rub shyly into his mother's neatly disposed dress, visits with every one sitting upright, stiff, the spine imitating the rigid line of the chairs, just blossoming "deportment."

On the whole, in spite of its high-chokered formalities, it was a kind world that Melville found himself in: shallow men are not obstacles to little boys, and as for Mrs. Melville, she had all the affection for her children that natural instinct and the graces of society prompted her to have, not a great deal, one suspects, for children, like servants, are only subordinate ministers to the ego—and one cannot take pride in satisfying society's minimal requirements. She was, however, an intelligent and capable mother: all her eight children grew to maturity, and that was no little feat, even for an upper-class family, in the early nineteenth century. Herman must have been a little starved of affection, I think; for in Pierre he gives his hero no sisters or brothers, so that Pierre may absorb all his mother's warmth for himself; and his hungry claims for sympathy and caresses were no doubt put off by Mrs. Melville's aloof rectitude, her concern to keep part of her energy and sweetness for her husband, and her manifest partiality to the younger children, when they arrived. Herman stood as in a cold room before an open fire: one side of him was toasted, and another side was chilled. That chilliness remained; and in the parts of his emotional frame that were affected, circulation was never quite restored.

When Herman was five the family moved two miles up-town, to a house in Bleecker Street which combined the advantages of town and country. It was good for Herman that the change was made. He had been ill and had not regained his health fully: he looked, his father reported then, pale, thin, and dejected; but the new house had a vacant lot where children could play; and not far away the farms began to stretch on each side of the Albany turnpike: despite the activity of the City Planning Commissioners in laying out rectangular blocks over the hills and dales and streams and swamps and ponds of the island, the farms themselves were retreating slowly. Life, for little Herman, was no longer a matter of sitting and staring at the furniture: he went to school: he found that c-a-t and d-o-g were a new way of playing with a dog and a cat: when he was bored he could always practise tricks on Gansevoort, who was older and more considerate and could not legitimately hit back.

Still, Herman did not thrive quite as well as he should have. Winter drew a black curtain between him and all the pleasant things one could see or find or do in the country: darkness fell much too soon after school: November's rains confined him to the house and March's snows and slush did the same: as the winter progressed his cheeks would grow paler and his small blue eyes more wan. His father shook his head doubtfully and grieved over little Herman's melancholy situation. As a result of these stops and gaps in his life Herman "is backward in speech and somewhat slow in comprehension, but"—so Allan reports to the Albany Gansevoorts, when Herman in the summer of 1826 is sent to them on a visit—"you will find him, as far as he understands men and things, both solid and profound and of a docile and amiable disposition."

One is grateful to Allan for using such unusual words as "solid" and "profound" to describe a child of six: there must have been something in Herman's attitude or attack that warranted them: one cannot altogether lay those adjectives to pompous speech or parental pride. Is one going back too far if one finds the beginnings of Melville's reflective turn in these juvenile illnesses and confinements? The periods of solitude in bed, the lassitude of recovery, the slow, patient hours undistracted by physical activity, the rehearsing in the mind of things done and things seen—these limitations make content and docile little boys. John Ruskin amused himself, in an enforced confinement without toys, by tracing minutely the patterns of the parlour carpet: in such dull, quiet states is the beginning of a meditative life.

A year later Herman was sent to his Great Uncle Thomas Melville at Broadhall, near Pittsfield. Uncle Peter, at Albany, was still something of a countryman: Uncle Thomas was a different sort, more fine, more polished, with a touch of the old beau about him perhaps and no little of the courtliness of aristocratic Paris: he had brought home a French wife, and the undercurrent of French between the old fellow and his spouse, when Herman was present and not supposed to understand, must have teased him like a glimpse of a foreign port. Uncle Thomas had nothing of the boor about him; his manners were mild and kindly, "with a faded brocade of old French breeding" and a certain daintiness of gesture, as when he would drop his rake and pause for a pinch of snuff, that brought the reminder of a society less angular and impetuous than that which jostled little boys in the streets of Manhattan. It was a little pathetic, too, to see this fine old gentleman handling a rake or patiently feeding a cow: he was so manifestly cut out for more urbane companionship.

In the galaxy of uncles and grandparents and aunts, the patrician element was dominant: every one of them knew what it was to be well bred and cultivated in the arts and able to command men. There was Grandfather Thomas at Boston, he whom Oliver Wendell Holmes poked a little fun at in the trivial piece of verse called The Last Leaf: he had been a major, too: he had fought well in the Revolution, too: a dried-apple sort of man who had lost his juices and perhaps his sweetness: let the times change as they would, he kept his shape, and to define it, he wore cocked hat and knee-breeches up to the day of his death: the eighteenth century was good enough for him. Then there was Uncle John de Wulf, who dropped in miraculously one day to see Herman's father: an old man with hair as white as the pin-feathers on a swan's breast, and face as red as a cranberry: he used to sail to a place called Archangel, and, more marvellous still, he had crossed Russia with Captain Langsdorff, starting from the Sea of Okhotsk in Asia and going to St. Petersburg, drawn by large dogs in a sled. What a hearty old fellow he was! His clothes almost had the smell of the far-off places he had visited. Ever memorable was that June day when his father and Uncle John took Herman over to Staten Island, and they explored the ruin of a fort that had been hastily erected by Governor Tompkins to defend the city against the British in 1812. Uncle John was a mystery: the crumbling walls of the fort were a mystery: but the sky above was as blue and benign as the blue eyes of Herman's mother, and in the still air of noon, there was no sound but the twitter of birds, and a great shout of delight and happiness in the little boy's heart.

But Manhattan was always full of mysterious strangers and sunburnt men with a rolling walk and a sea-bag or a chest jauntily carried on one shoulder. New York did this for Herman Melville: it taught him to be discontented with New York. There was Liverpool: there was London, Havre, Paris. The trim little packets down at the docks went back and forth between Liverpool and New York as regularly as clockwork, or very nearly: the swift ones could make the journey, with a little luck, in fifteen or sixteen days, and the best record for a sailing vessel was considerably under this: they took away wheat and furs and passengers, and they brought back cloth from the Midlands and carpets from Brussels and gloves from Paris and knives from Sheffield and cheap gewgaws from Birmingham and china from Burslem, or even from China itself—and more passengers. One simply could not forget the wideness of the world in this wide harbour, edged with green banks and feathery trees. Even some of the furniture in the house had been made in Europe: Herman looked at it again and again, wondering where the mahogany grew and whether the workmen who made the furniture were still alive, and what they might be doing with themselves now. His papa had been a great traveller; in a score of years, as he methodically noted down, he had travelled "by land 24,425 miles, by water 48,460 miles" and had been 643 days at sea; and once Allan had lived two whole years in Paris. Every stone, every mast, every stick of furniture, every print had a message for Herman: Travel!

How the books and prints Allan had brought home fomented Herman's dreams! There were prints of French men-of-war, of French fishing boats, with "high French-like land in one corner and a gray lighthouse surmounting

21

it. The waves were toasted brown and the whole picture looked mellow and old. Perhaps a piece of it would taste good." On Saturdays, when school didn't keep, and the rain imprisoned the children in the house, Augusta and Gansevoort would take out a French portfolio of coloured prints. More romance! Versailles: grand drawing-rooms: fountains where writhing Tritons spouted gleefully: rural scenes: shepherd boys and cottages: above all, there was a picture of a great whale, as big as a ship, stuck full of harpoons, and three boats sailing after it as fast as they could fly. Then, too, there was a tall brown bookcase in the hall; behind its glass doors one might see long rows of old books that had been printed in Paris and London and Leipsic. There was the Spectator in six volumes with "London" on the title page: there was a copy of D'Alembert in the language Uncle Thomas used to speak to Tante Marie.

Some day Herman would grow up too: he would see the world and have stories to tell about it: he would confront these marvellous pictures and find out how real they were. How snug Herman felt on a winter evening by the old sea-coal fire in Bleecker Street, when his father would tell the children of monstrous waves at sea, waves mountain-high and masts bending like twigs. Herman's stomach curdled pleasantly at the thought of it, or the equally dizzy but in some ways more marvellous thought of looking over London from the ball of St. Paul's, and picking out the Monument and London Bridge and Blackfriars and St. Dunstan's crown, and Southwark, where Shakespeare used to act, across the Thames. One would risk waves as high as mountains if one had some assurance of reaching eventually this fine old land, full of cathedrals and churches that were built before Columbus sailed to America, and narrow, crooked streets without sidewalks, and fields and woods that were as tidy as an American garden. That would be Albany or Gansevoort, prodigiously magnified by age and association. How hard to remember that little boys went to school in

Europe, too, and were punished if they didn't learn their lessons. Did they study geography, grammar, writing, speaking, and spelling there? Did they wear their shirt collars turned over and tied with a black ribbon; and did their papas allow them to wear boots, nice manly boots, instead of shoes? A long breath; a sense of choking anticipation. The days pass so slowly. Herman will be quite old—he may be twenty or twenty-five at this rate, before he goes there!

4

In 1828 Allan's position in society ballooned a little. He moved to a house on Broadway, with a lot two hundred feet deep, and doubtless more commodious rooms, for the rent was almost double that of his old quarters; but whether he was losing hold of his prudence or miscalculating, or whether circumstances that lay beyond his view were altering his position as an importer, one does not quite know. It is possible that, without being fully aware of his losses, he was shaken by the financial crisis of 1826, or it may be that his importations became inept, and the old lines were giving out. At all events, his business became so bad that he moved to Albany in 1830, so that, perhaps, he might take advantage of the Gansevoort connections. But he moved too late. He became a bankrupt. In 1832, when Herman Melville was only thirteen years old, his father gave up the struggle and died.

One suspects from the look of Allan's portrait that he was a fair-weather sailor and did not know what to do when the winds began to blow adversely. He left his loving wife with eight children, and only the family name to support them. No thanks to Allan that part of the family name was Gansevoort; but although that name certainly was an asset, and although Uncle Peter and his wife doubtless did all that they felt was in their power to make things easier for the proud widow and her orphans, the morals of bourgeois society are meant, like Allan's character, for smooth sailing, and when hardship overtakes one branch of the family there is usually no such general sharing round among the surviving groups as there is among the poor, who know shipwreck perpetually. Herman was going to the Albany Academy when his father died; he probably knew only by hints and murmurs and brooding faces that a calamity was approaching—and he suddenly found himself a half-orphan, with only the dear mild image of his father to comfort him.

This death before Herman had reached intellectual penetration did Allan a kindness: he became "a shrine in the fresh-foliaged heart of [his son] up to which he ascended by many tableted steps of remembrance; and around which annually he . . . hung fresh wreaths of a sweet holy affection. In the shrine stood the perfect marble form of his departed father, without blemish, unclouded, snow-white, serene . . . fond personification of perfect human goodness and virtue." But this did Herman himself an ill turn, for instead of permitting the august image of his father to experience the vicissitudes of the weather, and ripen into the natural disillusion that greets a son when he finds his deity one in flesh with himself, equally mortal, equally fallible—instead of this, the image became fixed, and when Herman outgrew his father, he did not simply leave him behind: he rose up and annihilated him, revenging himself upon the actual Allan for the perfect marble shadow he had carried in his heart. In the asperities of fortune, Mrs. Melville, with a hard row of her own to hoe, doubtless fell in Herman's heart because she had to face comparison with the marble portrait of his father: even the best of mothers, under such circumstances, would seem a little harsh and unkind, beside him who had by his bankruptcy and his death escaped the dilemmas of both his creditors and his family. At all events, Herman found himself at thirteen in the midst of a hard-hearted world; and the shock of that transposition left him breathless and weak.

The aunts and uncles were kind, of course; but they had

cares and interests of their own ; and it needed dire extremity to move them to action. Herman's cousins continued to go to school: the cousins had butter on their bread and cream on their porridge; but the Melvilles must have known that sinking feeling that comes to a big family at table when the eye takes in the bowl of stew or the little roast and the nine plates that wait for it, and knows instantly that no thinning of slices or spreading of gravy will make the portions large enough to satisfy a healthy appetite. The summers in the country, the long, lazy summers, were over: it was winter all the year round. Gansevoort, dogged, patient, resourceful fellow that he was, opened a hat store on Market Street, and as soon as Herman was fifteen, he got a job as clerk in the New York State Bank, of which Uncle Peter was one of the trustees: a year later, Herman shifted over to the hat store, where Gansevoort now needed an extra clerk.

This was not the way, Herman doubtless felt, that one's adolescence should open. The son of a gentleman can, it is true, remain a gentleman, even when he adds figures or sells hats: in America, thank Heaven, every trade is an honorable trade; but there is something wrong with a world that gives the young Gansevoorts all that their hearts ask for, and that draws the Melvilles up sharply wherever they turn. All Herman's ambitions, to go to college, to become an orator, like Patrick Henry, to become a great traveller, like Uncle John or Papa, or to become a great general, like Grandfather Peter, to live in Paris, like Uncle Thomas, to make the name of Melville somehow glorious—all these dreams were like great bonfires suddenly drenched by cold rain. He was as unambitious as a man of sixty. Such careers do not begin in a hat shop. The stream of life had suddenly stopped; its margins became stagnant; there was no way out; one might add columns or sell hats forever. One's uncles and cousins didn't care. One's friends only said they cared. Cold, bitter cold as December, the world seemed to young Melville.

Fifteen years later, he still felt the bitterness and sting. He had only a lonely pride to wrap around him; and the world, not seeing any money in the pockets of that garment, smiled a little scornfully, and wondered whether it might not be just as well to leave such wrappings off!

At fifteen a lad can do little more than earn his keep; there was no question of Herman's helping to support the family, as Gansevoort patiently did. Some one must have observed that things were not going well with Herman in the hat shop; or perhaps there were not enough hats to be sold to make his presence necessary; in the summer of 1836 he lived with his Uncle Thomas at Broadhall, helping in the hayfields; and when autumn came he taught school—one needed muscle rather than letters for teaching school in those days—in the Sykes district, near by. He spent the winter in the shadow of Washington Mountain, and when spring came, and his pupils were needed in the fields, he himself felt a desperate longing to see his mother and his sisters again, and Gansevoort and young Allan and little Tom; so, presently, he went back to Lansingburgh, a little river village just outside of Albany, where his mother had moved. Scarcely had the welcome worn off before he realized that his existence was a problem: he was another mouth to feed! What was he going to do? Perhaps Uncle Peter would get him another chance at the bank. Not that? Well, what then? Gansevoort is doing bravely: Allan is already thinking of the law: every one must help.

Young Melville felt the world closing in on him. He had no answer to the major problem of civilization, namely, how to get a living without losing all the other things that make life joyful and significant. Herman's contemporaries, with all their factories and mines and new-fangled machinery and speeding ships, were perhaps as far from solving this problem as any civilization has yet been: the only people who were contented with the current solution were those whose narrow aims and limited personalities were completely fulfilled by the business routine itself. Herman was not of that cast, so he must invent an alternative. If he cannot go to college, he must at least have that other advantage of an education: the Grand Tour. He will be his own tutor, guide, philosopher, and friend. Why should he not ship for a trip to Europe? He would not merely earn his keep; but at the end of his voyage he might have a little to spare. Europe itself was at least a goal, or the promise of a goal; not a dead-end, like the bank.

Herman had not spent his early years in Manhattan for nothing. He doubtless knew, up in the fresh waters of Albany, the nostalgia of desiring just a whiff of salt-laden wind: when he looked at the little glass ship in the square case that stood on the claw-footed Dutch table in one corner of the sitting-room, that admirable ship, with masts, yards, ropes, all of glass, and little glass sailors on the rigging, and a glass figurehead, and a glass captain smoking a glass cigar and looking at the world with a glassy eye, all his desires somehow crystallized into a sudden overwhelming passion to be on the sea, and to wake up some early moonlit morning in a distant port, with dawn breaking over strange roofs. His father's books reinforced his dreams; and he was still bound by his father's heroic image and wanted to follow it, ancient guidebook in hand, through the streets of Liverpool. That would somehow establish a connection with those better and happier times before bankruptcy, death, penurious circumstances, had cut like flint through the soles of paper boots. In England, he might recapture his magnificent ambitions; or, if not that, he would at least return to Lansingburgh with a badge of cosmopolitan distinction: his sisters, Fanny, Helen, Kate, Augusta, would be proud of him; and people might say when he passed: Do you know that Herman Melville has been to Europe? Yes, and he's only seventeen!

It sounded daring and adventurous; but there was a brackish taste in the going. At the outset of the journey, on the boat to New York, he did not have enough fare for the trip and had to brazen his poverty out: his sole wealth was a fowling-piece his brother had given him, to sell in New York for spending-money; with the gun and a dollar and his brother's cast-off shooting-jacket, he set out to face the world. He felt himself driven out into the desert, an infant Ishmael, without a maternal Hagar to accompany him and give him comfort. Riches and poverty stared at him at his very first venture alone beyond the family nest: the jovial party in the saloon, gay, flushed over wine, crackers, cheese, cigars—and himself on deck, collar up, outcast, facing the rain! "Talk not of the bitterness of middle-age and after life," exclaimed Melville in Redburn, "a boy can feel all that, and much more, when upon his young soul the mildew has fallen; and the fruit, which with others is only blasted after ripeness, with him is nipped in the first blossom and bud. And never again can such blights be made good; they strike in too deep, and leave such a scar that the air of Paradise might not erase it."

Melville's downheartedness was deepened by contrast with the natural expectations which he had formed in the balmier period of his childhood, and which people somehow kept up, for form, to go with the family name. His sisters told all inquiring friends that Herman had gone abroad, as if just for his health and education with no expense spared; and when he applied for a place on ship, under the tutelage of a young family friend, his friend's high talk about Melville's name and connections enabled the sly captain to withhold an advance in pay—because the family would attend to that! The pretensions were shabby ones; they brought Herman nothing but an insufficient supply of clothes and an empty stomach in the day that elapsed between his saying good-bye to his friend and leaving port. That was the irony of having a proud name and a poor purse, of following in his father's footsteps and sleeping in the forecastle instead of a stateroom.

Thirty days on the water will take the wind out of these pretensions. Herman will forget that he is a Melville and a Gansevoort and a pupil of the Albany Academy and a relative of a regent and a general, and a reader of books, and a member of the Juvenile Total Abstinence Association and the Anti-smoking Society; he will lose many of the little refinements of birth and breeding; but the loss will not leave him destitute. In exchange, he will learn the ropes, and find out what men are like in the rough.

5

Every boat is a little world, every ship a Noah's ark; but the vessel on which Melville worked his way contained more than its share, perhaps, of the battered and unvarnished furniture of human society, from Captain Riga himself, sleek, bland, affable, cunning, a lap-dog in port and a mastiff at sea, to Jackson, the depraved wreck of a man who, not through any physical strength, but through a sort of Satanic energy, ruled the forecastle.

The contrast between the sisterly society of Lansingburgh, clean and very chaste, and the ugly, dirty, promiscuously vile company of the forecastle was as acute as the difference between the feather-beds of his home and the hard, bug-ridden planks on which he was forced to sleep. A greenhorn in men, a greenhorn in work, Herman met face to face the uncouth cruelty of men whose own hides had been blackened by hardship and mean living, and who flayed every new comer until he was equally able to stand the misery and depression.

With the exception of Jackson, these men were not innately unkind: they had simply been brutalized. The Greenlander brought Herman Jamaica rum the first time he was seasick, helping him to recover and incidentally making him break his pledge of total abstinence; and though they resented his nice language and his earnest moralizings, which marked him off as a member of that inimical social

class out of which captains are hewn, they gradually learned
to tolerate him when they found that he was ready to work
with a will and tumble out of his bunk at call. But, at best,
it was hard for Melville to get the hang of the ship's ways:
climbing aloft was terrifying at first; and slushing down the
masts and spars with old grease was disgusting. He would
have liked to chat with Captain Riga in a friendly way and
discuss his prospects in the world and what one might find
at Liverpool: surely, a gentleman would appreciate the
plight of a gentleman's son, and perhaps he would even
cozen Herman with something tasty to eat, as an offset to
the hogwash and hard-tack of the forecastle: Herman was
a little surprised when he dolled himself up for a sociable
call to find the mate stamping with astonished outrage when
he discovered Herman's purpose in time to turn him back.
What a disillusion to find that there is an impassable gulf
between skipper and crew, a gulf that even gentlemen's
sons cannot cross on any pretext!

There were few books on board: a dream-book and a copy
of the Wealth of Nations which his brother's friend had so-
licitously given Herman, for his self-improvement, on the
eve of departure; but the sailors, who had been to Gibraltar
and Canton and Valparaiso and Bombay, just as Herman
might have ventured to Coenties Slip or Hoboken, were a
complete library of Voyages and Travels around the World.
The names they uttered in such a casual way were magical;
but the world they moved in was grim and formidable; a
hand with delirium tremens jumped overboard and drowned
before the boat was much beyond the Hook: shipwreck,
mouldy bread, hard weather, mutiny, did not sound so romantic if one had been in the thick of it; and as for the
sailors' fonder recollections, these stories were as tasteless
as duff: did the bar-girl in Hamburg have blue eyes or
black: what a nice time Max the Greenlander had had with
the young ladies in Stockholm: who kept the Foul Anchor
Tavern at Portsmouth at such and such a time? They had

seen so much and taken in so little, travelling with their
bodies, not with their minds: they knew chiefly the sameness
of sailor's stews and purchased caresses, and to them one
city was like another and one girl was like another: the best
port was that which promised the longest and fullest
oblivion.

The ship itself was the strangest port of all. Pails were
buckets: pegs were plugs: floors were decks: "Yes, sir" was
"Ay, ay, sir": in addition to all these new habits and ways,
one must grasp new handles for old ones. The ropes needed
a dictionary in themselves: every knot and reef had a name.
The accent of this world was gruff: Herman had never
dreamed that a malign, cur-faced rascal like Jackson, who
swore he would swipe him off the rigging if Herman got in
his way, could exist in real life; nor could he have imagined
the uncouthness of men to whom life at its best was simply
hard work, hard words, hard fare, fornication, drunkenness
and sleep. Herman was shocked: but the sea gave him what
the sailors did not: there were good moments when the sails
were hoisted to the breeze and the ship responded: every
mast and timber seemed to have a pulse in it, and as the ship
picked up speed, he felt a wild exulting in his own heart.
"Then," says Melville, "I was first conscious of a wonderful thing in me, that responded to all the wild commotion of
the outer world and went reeling on and on with the planets
in their orbits, and was lost in one delirious throb at the
center of the All. A wild bubbling and bursting at my
heart, as if a hidden spring gushed out there. . . . But
how soon these raptures abated, when after a brief idle interval, we were again set to work, and I had a vile commission to clean out the chicken coops, and make up the beds
of the pigs in the long boats. Miserable dog's life is this of
the sea: commanded like a slave and set to work like an ass:
vulgar and brutal men lording it over me, as if I were an
African in Alabama."

What a contrast Herman Melville felt between the wholeness he felt within, in response to wind and sea and sky, and the crass deformities of the world outside, among cruel men, grasping men, lecherous men, men sick and stunted in the soul, like the strayed seeds that creep up through some cranny in the barnyard floor and become livid spindly plants, unnourished by sunlight! It was a trial; but not altogether a fruitless one. He had it in him to deal easily with life aboard ship. Ill provided with clothes, a shrinking moleskin jacket being his chief protection, his body was sound enough to furnish its own warmth. "I frequently turned into my bunk soaking wet, and turned out again piping hot and smoking like a roasted sirloin, and yet was never the worse for it; for then I bore a charmed life of youth and health, and was dangerproof to bodily ill." This testing and priming of his physical capacities was a great experience for Melville; and though in the end he was to pay a heavy penalty for excessive exposure, the confidence he achieved must have toned up his whole being.

Even dirty work and humiliation have, in retrospect, a power to sustain a man: for if one has faced the worst indignities of life, if one knows what it is to be poor and hungry and cold and friendless and beset by hostile men, nothing that lies in store can really daunt one: once one has touched the extremities of pain and misery, all the lesser tribulations of life become small. Perhaps the best proof of this fact is Melville's small concern for money or authority in later life, although it was poverty that drove him to sea, and only a position of power on ship would have lifted his lot. He never went after these things, never sought to improve his condition by their aid; and though in the end, he struggled for a living and got it dearly, he never sought for more than a living: he did not seek compensation in wealth, ease, luxury, power.

6

At last Melville and the Highlander reached Liverpool. His anxieties were at rest for six weeks: he was even freed

from the miserable pot-scrapings of the black cook, for no
fire could be lighted in the galleys while the ship was at dock;
and the whole crew dined at the Baltimore Clipper. England
at last: a guest in an English tavern!

"I examined the place attentively," writes Melville. "It
was a long, narrow little room, with one small arched window
with red curtains, looking out upon a smoky, untidy yard,
bounded by a dingy brick wall, the top of which was horrible with pieces of broken old bottles, stuck into the mortar. A dull lamp swung overhead, placed in a wooden ship
suspended from the ceiling. The walls were covered with a
paper, representing an endless succession of vessels of all
nations continually circumnavigating the apartment. By
way of a pictorial mainsail to one of these ships, a map was
hung against it. . . . From the street came a confused
uproar of ballad-singers, bawling women, babies, and
drunken sailors."—And this is England?

It is not by dreams that people are defrauded, so much
as by misplaced pictures of reality. A dream represents an
inner urge and movement; presently it may work through
to an objective manifestation; defeated in one place, it attacks in another; and though its final form may be far from
the image originally projected, it does not disappoint one
like the comparison of an actuality with some previous description. It was so with Melville in Liverpool: he eventually
visited England again and found its abbeys and its Lord
Mayors' processions; but when he followed his father's steps
in Liverpool, down to Riddough's Hotel where Allan had
once stayed, he was completely defeated: the hotel was gone,
and the city that had seemed so great and magnificent in the
guidebook, a generation before, had been swallowed up by
a vaster town: the pool itself, where ships once floated, had
been filled up; even the pretence of age was lacking, and
mid the old shops and warehouses of the waterfront, nothing
seemed nearly so venerable as the gable-pointed mansion of

the Gansevoorts, whose bricks had been brought from the Netherlands long before the Revolutionary War.

Disappointed, Melville nevertheless continued to explore the city. He went aboard an Indian merchantman, built by Indian shipwrights out of Oriental wood, manned by Malays, Burmese, and Cingalese: he visited the floating chapel: he saw the German immigrants about to depart for America: he was fascinated by the little salt droghers, with broad bows painted black, and red sails: he even ventured out into the countryside one fine morning, and got his first glimpse of the English landscape and the English country people he had dreamed of. These were the relatively bright lights in the picture: but there were ugly spots, too: the villainous brothels and doss-houses, where murders were venial sins and a stale putrid odour hung over every doorway: there were the dock-wall beggars, full of sores, misery, and monstrous deformations: worst of all, there was a narrow street, lined with cotton warehouses, where the sunniest noon became twilight, and where, in an open vault, communicating with deeper cellars, Melville came upon a motionless figure of a woman, with a dead baby at her breast, and two blue-skinned children clinging to her, slowly starving to death, starving, dying, finally passing out, with not a soul except Melville to offer succour, despite his pleas with constables and watchmen, until the stench of their dead bodies demanded their removal and the application of quicklime to the spot where they had perished. A fine, prosperous world! A great, progressive civilization!

Ironically, the city Melville had dreamt much about, London, he saw only in a baffling nocturnal glimpse, behind the draperies of a gambling-house, in the company of a new shipmate, a blade of good family, who made friends with Melville and took a last opportunity, with Herman for companion, to retrieve his fortunes. The whole journey to London brought nothing more than the tantalizing glimpses one gets from a cab—not Westminster nor Whitehall nor

Regent Street. Mr. Weaver has cast doubts on this adventure in London: he regards it as one of the few wide inventions Melville made in Redburn: but to me its very vagueness and mysteriousness smells of reality. That an unsophisticated boy should be as confused by a gambling-house as by Aladdin's palace is quite natural: and if anything else were wanted to show that the trip was real and the disappointment cutting, one need but remember that Melville treated Israel Potter to a similar experience on his first visit to Paris, although there is no foundation in Israel's story for his being confined to his room until the time comes for departure.

The six weeks that confronted Melville with all these scenes and people and apparitions were an essential part of his education. Indeed, there is no better experience for a well-prepared lad than to be thrown in a strange city, not too remote in habit and culture from his original home, with long days for exploration, experience, meditation. Melville regretted in later life that he had not encountered misery and bad fortune by degrees; and very possibly, the shock of finding himself suddenly in the midst of this bestiality, cruelty, degradation, was too much for him: the inoculation with evil was almost as bad, it may be, as the disease itself: it certainly must have cast a shadow on his innocence, and it may even explain, in some degree, the inhibitions and regressions of his own sexual life—since his first glimpse of sex was in association with these filthy dives and their rotting inmates. But, even with these allowances, such an education in men and cities is better than the non-education given by textbooks and academic treatises and unrelated "knowledge." Between the Albany Academy or the Harvard College of 1837 and Liverpool, the latter had incomparably more to offer to a lad already sufficiently used to books to make constant reference to them. If a whaling-ship proved finally to be Melville's university, Liverpool was at least an admirable preparatory school.

When the Highlander started home, it must have seemed to Melville that everything would be smooth sailing: but one of the new crew was a dead man, shipped aboard by a crimp, the ship met head winds and made no progress: malignant fever broke out in the steerage: Jackson, with the yellow skin, the snaky eyes, the projecting bones, the curse against goodness and beauty, died: and when the ship finally got to port, with Melville still in sound health, the wily Captain Riga buncoed him of his wages. Four months of this sort of thing was quite enough. Melville returned to Lansingburgh. For the next three years, he lived among the civilities, and taught school, at Greenbush, now East Albany, and at Pittsfield.

7

Melville's growth was slow, and we have little evidence of what took place during these three years. School teaching must have given him leisure, and one can infer from two prose pieces, written in 1839, and published in the Democratic Press and Lansingburgh Advertiser, that his dreams and broodings were turned, not to the wretchedness of his adventure, but to the susceptibilities and urges of adolescence.

What do we know of Melville's early sexual life? In Pierre, Melville pictures a passionate attachment between his hero and one of his boy-cousins, and describes how it undergoes the normal sublimation through erotic transfer to a person of the opposite sex: Melville's sharp observation here anticipated by many years the discoveries of the analytic psychologists. When, in Redburn, we find the youthful hero remembering the three red-cheeked maids who lived in the cottage where he was given bread and milk, we cannot doubt that he made the usual easy transition to a maturer state of sexuality. If we needed any further evidence, these surviving clippings would be sufficient: he pictures himself, beautiful as Apollo, "dressed in a style which would extort admiration from a Brummel, belted round with self-esteem, and sallying in dizzy triumph among the ladies —complimenting one, exchanging repartee with another, tapping this one under the chin, and clasping this one around the waist; and finally, winding up the operation by kissing round the circle."

It was a grandiose dream: under the cover of a jocose style, he tossed it off in public. "By my halidome, sir," he cries, "this same village of Lansingburgh contains within its pretty limits as fair a set of blushing damsels as one would wish to look upon on a dreamy summer day." Young Melville courted by the wholesale; he made love to the village; reluctantly, he narrowed down his vision to a paltry three girls, and dwelt for a little while upon their seraphic beauty. It was high-flown silliness; and the second Fragment from a Writing-Desk, as these pieces were called, went even further, in the manner of Thomas Moore and Edgar Poe, painting a mysterious houri whom he followed to her lair. She was properly mournful and lost in melancholy reverie —all young ladies, in Melville's day, arrayed themselves in a mysterious sorrow, as an aphrodisiac, so that the tender hand of solace might achieve in compassion what it dared not snatch by brasher methods—and one leaves Herman, brain spinning and faculties gone, kneeling before his Divinity.

This is a correct and roundabout way of announcing that he has kissed a pretty hussy—or perhaps it is a covert expression of more deeply pent-up desires; but one must remember that, when Melville was twenty, Emerson, discussing the sexual life of young men with his literary acquaintances in England, declared that the majority of young men in America were chaste before marriage; and whether he was right or not about the majority—Whitman gives us a different picture of city morals among more plebeian contemporaries—there is little reason, in the general state of morals and opinion and social censure, to doubt that Melville was abstinent sexually during his nonage.

When he wrote these pieces, woman was still a divinity to him; and, like his sisters, like his mother, she was still unapproachable.

These Fragments from a Writing-Desk do not merely throw a light upon Melville in an amorous mood; they also are full of hints about his reading and his preparation for authorship.

The manner of these essays was perfervid and exaggerated; the language was the high-flown journalese that Poe never entirely conquered in his short stories; and every word was turned before the mirror, and powdered and ribboned, before being committed to the air. He had nothing to write about except tenuous threads of dream, or rather, his disguise of their warmer reality. Thoreau, at twenty, had ideas that would not have done the man an injustice at forty; not so Melville. Melville, like Whitman, resembled a deep well: he had to pump all sorts of muddy water and stale slush to the surface before the crystal liquid began to run. He was fortunate, however, in belonging to a social class that had libraries: he alluded in these pieces to Burton, Lord Chesterfield, Milton, Byron, Shakespeare, Scott, Coleridge, and we have independent knowledge, through a letter written to a Cooper Celebration Committee, that he had read widely at this period in his best early American contemporary—whom he always valued. These mooning days by the river, and these lone nights of candlelight, were days and nights of preparation. His swollen language, his simpering allusions to beauty, his self-consciousness, were vices, but not unpromising ones: better all these flourishes, to begin with, than a wooden mould and a more definite set of limitations.

There is nothing in print between these press clippings and Melville's first book, Typee; but from the great clarification of language, and the abandonment of most of his weaknesses, it is plain that Melville must have had much practice, if not at writing, then at ample conversation and oral story-telling. Though Melville dated his growth from his twenty-fifth year, as he told Hawthorne, it actually began at an earlier period: it was self-consciousness that came into existence at twenty-five. The growth was well started with a "solid and profound" boy of six; and at twenty, the down of intellectual manhood was already thickening into a beard. Like Pierre, he was an omnivorous and lynx-eyed reader. With all these qualities leafing and budding, we shall not be surprised at an early blossom.

CHAPTER TWO: SEA-DRIFT

In 1840, Richard Henry Dana published Two Years Before the Mast. It was an account of a long voyage around the Horn, and various experiences in the Spanish settlements of California where American boats traded Yankee calico and trinkets for hides. Written from the point of view of a sailor, Dana's story gave no picture of unalloyed pleasure and adventure; but there was quite enough exotic charm in the California picture to make a healthy, adventurous lad forget about the floggings, the brutality, the heroic difficulties of rounding Cape Horn. One has no proof that Melville read Dana's book as soon as it came out; but nine years later, he referred to the author as "my friend Dana," and the chances are that Two Years Before the Mast gave Melville just the fillip he needed to determine on a wider, farther jaunt into the South Seas.

The wildness and misanthropy of Melville's joining a whaler in the depth of winter, with the certainty of having to endure a long sea-voyage, may easily be exaggerated: it would be a mistake, I think, to apply to the boyish impulse, which he shared with a thousand other mothers' sons, the dark words of the opening chapter of Moby-Dick: "With a philosophical flourish Cato throws himself upon his sword; I quietly take to the ship." In Moby-Dick Melville was supremely an artist, with an eye constantly upon the dramatic values of his story; and in the very first paragraph, no, in the first sentence, he establishes the mood in which the whole book is written. Every bit of factual material Melville uses there is bent to his purpose; and though Moby-Dick is biographic of Melville at thirty-two, in the sense that it discloses every nook and corner of his imagination—one must not make the mistake of reading back from it into the Melville of twenty-one, strapping, healthy, restless, impetuous, and blind to his deepest impulses.

The only certainly objective part of his account of himself in Moby-Dick is his announcement that he had little or no money in his purse, and nothing particular to interest him on shore. Melville was preparing himself for something; but he was not at all sure for what; and in those distracted hours before the feet are set definitely upon the road to maturity he chose the most obvious goal before him—that of adventure in the more watery part of the world. He did not run away from home: he was already disattached. He did not retreat from hard "reality": his voyage to Liverpool had taught him what to expect as a common seaman. In the light of Melville's earliest promptings and suggestions, his father's trips, his uncle's arduous voyages, his own infinite curiosities, stirred by the strange sails and sailors he had encountered in Liverpool, there is nothing mysterious in either his mood or his purpose. The "Invisible Police Officer of the Fates" knew more about the reason for Melville's voyage than he himself did.

The whale, perhaps, had already seized Melville's imagination; he hints as much in the first chapter of Moby-Dick; but one must accept this hint circumspectly; for in Redburn Melville tells how disappointed he was when he first saw whales from the Highlander. "Can these be whales? Monstrous whales such as I had heard of! . . . It was a bitter disappointment, from which one was long in recovering. I lost all respect for whales! . . . From that day whales fell greatly in my estimation." I suspect that the whale was important; but that the distant voyage mattered even more. At all events, Melville, some time in December, 1840, made his way to New Bedford, and on January 3, 1841, he left land behind him.

New Bedford, a town of twelve thousand inhabitants, was already the centre of the whaling industry, a port full of industry and piety, great columned mansions set out on lawns, and benign elms, and iron greyhounds guardedly couchant, and ship-chandler's shops and dingy little nautical inns, and a rough waterfront that was not altogether puritanic nor of New England. Spots and patches of that New Bedford remain today: the great mansions on County Street are still impressive: the iron greyhounds and deer are unabashed: even the newer streets, except around the dingy factory-slums, are lined with trees: the Seamen's Bethel is bright with new paint and elegant graining: the chowders and the fish dishes are above the average, especially in the poorer restaurants: but around these patches stretch the dismal shopping thoroughfares, and the dismaler factory districts where an impoverished population, French-Canadian, Portuguese, Italian, minds the looms of vast prison-factories, dumped by the laws of chance and political economy over a lawless landscape of dingy wooden houses.

The whale has become a memory. The gold rush of 1849 resulted in a vast secession of whaling-men, lured from the South Seas to the gold-diggings, and the discovery of petroleum in 1859 introduced a cheaper substitute for whale-oil, whilst the manufacture of spring steel took the place of whalebone for corsets. The Confederate blockade under Simms and the sinking of the Stone Whaling Fleet in Charleston Harbor, whose failure Melville was in due time mournfully to celebrate, resulted in a large loss of tonnage; and, finally, the manufacture of cotton for profit attracted capital more readily than the uncertainties of the sea. All these things heaped together, and the mechanical improvements of harpoons and harpoon guns and steam vessels and launches, could not offset them.

Melville saw the whale's day of glory; and that day was soon done. There is a real whaling-ship embedded in concrete at South Dartmouth, and an admirable reproduction on half scale in the Historical Society's museum; there are numerous prints and whaling treatises in the New Bedford Library—Moby-Dick itself is bound in whaleskin, first edition—and there is a tank labelled sperm oil on the waterfront: in the museum collections there are models, log books, trinkets, ornaments, scrimshaw work, tools, harpoons, Polynesian and African loot, and names like Pease and Coffin still survive, in positions more or less commanding, in New Bedford, and on Marthas Vineyard and Nantucket. But there are no whaling-ships in New Bedford now: the Norwegians maintain the trade; for the American masters of Leviathan abandoned their calling in the years after the Civil War. The whaler is to New Bedford what the Conestoga wagon is to Pittsburgh—a romantic compensation for a dreary and untidy and depauperate provincial life.

The vessel on which Melville shipped was the Acushnet of Fairhaven, sailing from New Bedford. The master was Valentine Pease; but one must not look for Queequeg and Tashtego and the Parsee in this boat: the motley crew of the Pequod was, perhaps, a possibility; but the actual ship list shows twenty-one Americans, three Portuguese, and one Englishman. For the first time, Herman Melville enters our vision with a definable external appearance: forgetting the beard of his later portraits, one is conscious of a small straight nose, high forehead, full, mobile, sensitive lips, and, most curious of all, remote, cold green-blue eyes, that, in this big head, below a shock of dark-brown hair, have the canny, speculative look of the whale himself. His complexion in the ship's list is given as dark—which may merely mean that he was used to the outdoors and well tanned by the sun. His height, at twenty-one, was five feet nine and a half inches.

This is the sober-hilarious lad who scanned the tablets in the Seaman's Bethel and noted all the young men who had met their death fighting weather and whales on remote seas: this is the young writer who listened to the pedantic-looking

Chaplain Mudge, and transformed him, through later acquaintance with Father Taylor of Boston, into Father Mapple in Moby-Dick: this is the secretive fellow who put down his place of residence as Fairhaven, the little village across the river where he had taken lodging. Does he sometimes look dour and grim around the mouth? Perhaps; but he is as elastic as an india-rubber ball, and he will bound back with a joke and a smile: and it will take more than a little jouncing to break down that quizzical reserve.

We leave Herman Melville in New Bedford, and we do not really pick him up again until he is in the South Seas, sailing towards the line, one of a dissatisfied company on a harsh, uncomfortable ship, under a brutal master. The ship stopped at Rio de Janeiro and at the Galapagos Islands; and probably on the coast of Peru: there he picked up sights and yarns that served him well in a later period; and in spite of the bad food, the mean-spirited crew, and the inhuman treatment of the sick, conditions about which every decent non-professional writer, like Browne and Dana, justly complained, the voyage had not been a lost one. For the man there are misfortunes, bitter ones, laming ones. For the writer, who wishes to heighten his consciousness of existence, to relive other men's lives, and to share with them the deeper realities of their experience, there are no misfortunes. Every disappointment, every trial, has its revelation. The crew of the Acushnet was an ill-fated one: ten years later Melville found out from one of them, Hubbard, what had become of them: the record is one of desertion, suicide, murder, or a miserable death from syphilis; and the ship itself foundered in the very year he wrote Moby-Dick: but this catalogue of misfortunes does not exhaust the matter.

Melville undoubtedly chafed at the monotonous routine and the salt horse and hard-tack, varied though it might occasionally be by bananas and breadfruit: in the meanwhile, however, he had jumped into boats and gone in pursuit of the whale: he had helped to dismember its carcass: he had chopped up blubber and watched the fire in the try-works: he had observed his shipmates whittling and carving in wood and in whalebone all sorts of curious tools, orna-ments, and fetiches, work that was often done with a more sure aesthetic touch than any of the contemporary arts could show in America; for these whaling implements, par-ticularly the jagging-wheels, are worthy to have a place alongside the handsome coverlets and the hooked rugs of the forties in a museum of American folk-arts. Weaving mats, with the slow methodical motion of the weaver, his thoughts would solidify into new patterns; or aloft, on look-out duty, in the bland air of the tropics, he would gaze into his own mind, still, gently heaving, fathomless, like the waters around him, and be lulled into a feeling of oneness with the circumambient world, not with the ship's crew or the captain, but that remoter world of infinite space and un-thinkable time which somehow, in these moments of solitude, seemed so much nearer to him.

These thoughts have no images and are not framed in words; Melville must wait long before, in any way, he can find word or fable to express them; but though he himself, as observer, was no more conscious of his growth than a child is conscious of the passage of stars in the sky during the daytime, these were growing-days for him. The routine of the ship was in itself a varied education: every sailor was a bit of a musician and a weaver and an artist and a rope-maker and a blacksmith and an athlete: thought, when it existed at all, had the benefit of those manual exercises and bodily rhythms which, quite literally, increase a man's grasp and range—a true gymnosophy.

"If by any possibility," Melville said in Moby-Dick, "there be any as yet undiscovered thing in me; if I shall ever deserve any real repute in that small but high hushed world which I might not unreasonably be ambitious of; if hereafter I shall do anything that, upon the whole, a man might rather

have done than have left undone; if, at my death, my
executors or more properly my creditors find any precious
MSS. in my desk, then here I prospectively ascribe all the
honour and the glory to whaling; for a whale ship was my
Yale College and my Harvard." Melville was not wide of
the mark: these broad-bottomed ships, slow, even sailers,
cut off for six months at a time from the distractions of any
port, were in truth the best of universities for a young man,
still not out of adolescence, to retire into: they were a sort
of profane cloister. The regular routine, the monastic
discipline, yes, even the restricted diet, were all favourable
to a vivid and purposive inner life—all the more so because
a lick of bad weather or a sudden chase after the whale confronted Melville peremptorily with the demands of reality,
and broke the routine sufficiently to avoid the torpor and
complacent lassitude that dogs all restricted lives.

2

As the Acushnet approached the Marquesas in order to
renew water and to procure fresh food, Melville made plans
to escape her. Conditions were intolerable, and he had
learned that there was no definite terminus to the voyage:
he had already endured a year and a half, and he might have
to hover somewhere between the tropics and the poles, if the
oil barrels did not fill up quickly enough, for three, four,
even five years. At twenty-two, he did not dare to squander
so much of his life: he had ties at home, and did not wish
to be buried in a floating coffin. Perhaps this tedious prospect determined Melville as much as the inhuman treatment;
perhaps the sight of Nukuheva itself, its bold headlands,
with the surf beating against the cliffs, its deep inlets with
thickly wooded valleys, separated by the bare spurs of
formidable mountains, made him ache for solid ground.
There is a form of homesickness one must call land-sickness,
and perhaps Melville had it. Did the naked maidens who
swam aboard when the ship came to port make the scene

seem doubly attractive to Melville and to his companion,
Toby? Was he pleasantly shocked and intoxicated by those
brown bodies, and stirred, as well as repelled, by the open
debauchery of the nights they spent aboard ship? Melville
does not tell us. The cruelty and the hardship and the tedium
and the green jungle and the abrupt mountains and the
brown maidens doubtless all played a part in the adventure
and gave heat to it: at all events, Toby and Melville made
speedy use of their shore-leave, and set out to escape for a
while into the interior, till they could make away again on
another ship. Their plans miscarried. After dire hardship,
sleeping in dank ravines, leaping from tree-trunk to tree-
top down gorges, they found themselves in the valley of a
dreaded tribe, the Typees, whose very name meant eater of
men.

Melville stayed among the Typees for four months, with
a leg that had become lamed and infected in making the
escape. The people he was thrown among were suspected
of ferocity and cannibalism; that is to say, like a good many
savage tribes, they fought a species of extravagant and
ritualistic battle with their enemies, the Happars, and re-
tired from the fray usually fit enough in flesh and limb to
fight another time. As for the cannibalism, at the very end
of his stay, Melville had reason to think that one of their
feasts was culminating in the extreme delicacy of Long Pig:
but up to that time he had had an exemplary vegetarian
diet of breadfruit and cocoanut and various fine elaborations
of these staples; and but for the anxiety of losing Toby,
who disappeared completely, after going in search of medical aid for Melville's leg, and the further anxiety of not
knowing whether he was being treated as a distinguished
visitor, entitled to the services of a young man-servant,
Kory-Kory, and royal attentions from Mehevi, the chief, or
whether he was being fattened for the sacrifice, like the god-
apparent among the Aztecs—but for these things all was
serene.

If life were merely a matter of getting a living in the physical sense, as Western Civilization had come largely to believe, then the Typees were in a higher state of civilization than New York or Paris or London had achieved. The Typees were a sort of perpetually endowed leisure class; their food fell from the trees; their water flowed at their feet; their garments, of pounded bark, tappa, were a sport to make, and with less attention than they would have to give to a fitting from a Bond Street tailor or dressmaker, they were made; their days were torpid and free from care, like those of a *rentier* with gilt-edge government bonds; and though they had ceremonial observances and religious feasts and wars, the symbol never stood between them and their physical life: they did not whine about their sins and cry to God: even in their sexual life, there was rivalry without jealousy, and marriage without physical fidelity: almost the only desire they were accustomed to repress was the typical Western desire for a little repression!

The first whaleman Melville had ever met, on his trip to Liverpool, had raised a doubt about the value of civilized society. "And what's the use of being snivelized," he used to say. "Snivelized chaps only learns the way to take on 'bout life and snivel. You don't see any Methodist chaps feelin' dreadful about their souls; you don't see any damned beggars and pesky constables in Madagasky . . . Blast Ameriky, I say." Melville could appreciate this among the Typees. "There were," he says, "none of those thousand sources of irritation that the ingenuity of civilized man has created to mar his own felicity. There were no fore-closures of mortgages, no protested notes, no bills payable, no debts of honour in Typee; no unreasonable tailors and shoemakers, perversely bent on being paid; no duns of any description; no assaults and battery attorneys to foment discord, backing their clients into a quarrel, and then knocking their heads together; no poor relations everlast-ingly occupying the spare bed-chamber and diminishing the elbow-room at the family table; no destitute widows with their children starving on the cold charities of the world; no debtors' prisons; no proud and hard-hearted nabobs in Typee; or, to sum up all in one word—No Money! That 'root of all evil' was not to be found in the valley. In this secluded abode of happiness there were no cross old women, no cruel step-dames, no withered spinsters, no lovesick maidens, no sour bachelors, no inattentive husbands, no melancholy young men, no blubbering youngsters and no squalling brats. All was mirth, fun, and high good humour. Blue devils, hypochondria, and doleful dumps went and hid themselves among the nooks and crannies of the rocks."

By this process of exclusion, Melville tells us much about his experience and the effect it had on him. "Civilization," he discovered, "does not engross all the virtues of humanity: she had not even her full share of them. . . . If truth and justice and the better principles of our nature, cannot exist unless enforced by the statute-book, how are we to account for the social condition of the Typees?" Small wonder that Melville's contemporaries in the money-warrens of the West thought that he was inventing these people out of whole cloth! But it was not by the mere absence of ugly and harassing things that the Valley of the Typees was flecked with sunlight and warm, rose-violet shadows; there were positive pleasures as well; above all things, there was beauty, the constant beauty of splendid forms, undisguised by clothes, beauty so simple and statuesque that, in later years, it gave Melville an immediate clue to Greek sculpture. There were many happy afternoons; afternoons that he spent in bathing with a parcel of brown river nymphs; afternoons when, once he had got the taboo lifted, he paddled idly in a canoe with Fayaway, a lovely girl in his household, who was his constant companion; there were evenings spent watching the dancers in the hula-hula grounds, swaying, arching, gliding, swimming, whirling in an ecstasy of sensuous enjoyment that threatened to rob this "quiet, sober-minded, modest young man" of all his studious inhibitions; and there were days of contrast, spent with masculine gravity in the company of Mehevi and his attendant warriors, feasting heavily, with no cloying reminder of the other sex. Life itself became the most beautiful of rituals: its duties were games, its necessities were pastimes. Rivalry, enmity, jealousy, hardship, violence were all transposed to the realm of art, where, instead of defeating life, they added to its enjoyment.

True: these people were simple to the point of childishness: they could become excited, young and greybeards alike, over a popgun that Melville devised; but did not the Western World have its popguns, too: did not the crowds on Broadway turn out for a fire or a soldiers' parade with the same naïve delight? It was true, too, that these islanders had taboos, whose meaning Melville could never quite understand: they seemed as capricious as the flight of a bat, and like that flight, were determined doubtless by some imperceptible fact or belief that belonged to the insect order of rationality: but the taboos did not strike many of the essential elements of life. A man might be taboo against the assaults of his enemies and so might venture among them freely as a messenger, like the good fellow who abetted Melville's final rescue, or the canoe might be taboo against women using it—a comical male reservation—but food and clothing were not made taboo to the destitute by the laws of property, nor were men and women condemned to an acrid chastity by sexual taboos which had also arisen very largely out of laws and customs connected with the succession of property. There was no theft where every one could help himself, and no vice where virtue made such simple and rational demands.

Melville had a healthy capacity to adapt himself to a situation; and he was not ill at ease, little though this life resembled the world of the United Grand Junction Ebenezer Temperance Association, which the missionaries were introducing with the help of biblical pocket-handkerchiefs, pious exhortations, cheap Manchester rags, ugly bedizenments, and the sense of bitter sin that naturally accompanies the horrors of venereal disease. Had it not been for the infection in his leg, the uncertainty as to his eventual fate, and the plain desire of some of his native friends to make a thorough Typee of him, by a spirited application of tattooing, there is no telling how long he might have stayed, or how thoroughly he might have been lulled into forgetfulness of his Western connections.

In Mardi Melville pictured Hautia, the symbol of sensual oblivion, as the constant beckoner of the hero; and Hautia must have pressed him hard in Typee. Nevertheless, Yillah, who represented the spiritual quest, had already stirred him up before he started on his voyage, and in the end, Yillah must have reminded him of activities that found no answering chord among his happy, kindly Typee captors. When that ghastly devil with his tattooing implements made advances to him, Melville felt his quintessential foreignness. People wore queer clothes in Albany, perhaps, but thank heaven, they did not permanently discolour the flesh. Fayaway was lovely to look at, lovely to court, and perhaps lovelier to possess: but no man in full command of his faculties ever looked forward to a lifetime of such possession as sufficient reason for not committing suicide. Kory-Kory, his ugly man-servant, was as faithful as Sancho Panza; King Mehevi was as gracious as Francis I; one might even say a good word about tattooing and man-eating: they were matters of taste, perhaps; but inevitably, Melville felt a little out of it; and neither love-making nor bachelor companionship could quite make up for his spiritual isolation.

The moment for escape at last came. Melville, sadly in need of medical aid, hobbled down to the shore: a boatload of tabooed Kanakas had come with presents of calico and a musket to ransom the captive. The Typees were unwilling to part with Melville, and the boat was about to pull off

without him, when, in the midst of the clamour, he broke
away and threw himself into the arms of his rescuers,
escaping only after he himself had killed a ferocious old
chief, hot in pursuit, who in a happier and more apathetic
day had been kind to him. Fayaway and Hautia's bliss lay
behind him; Fayaway clutching a piece of calico Melville
had thrown her for consolation: Yillah lay in an unfathomable distance beyond, and what stood between was a tor-
tured filthy life in a broken-down whaler, whose planks were
rotting and whose hold swarmed with cockroaches and rats.
Many a time during the next two years, Melville must have
regretted leaving Fayaway's arms! Yes: and she must have
regretted Melville, for a little later an American traveller,
Henry Augustus Wise, discovered a brown maid from the
valley of Typee, named Fayaway, working as maid-of-all-
work to the French commissary of the garrison at Nukuheva—a proper snivelized anti-climax to the unsullied
tropical summer of Melville's residence and courtship
among the Typees.

3

A harsh captain is a bad fellow to sail under, but a weak
captain is worse. When Melville came to on the Julia, a drab
little barque, with a jaunty way of catching the wind, he
found himself under the orders of an uncertain cockney
landsman from Melbourne, with a crew of discontented
scalawags, and a roving commission to hunt whales or seals
or pick up a living somehow on the South Seas. Paper Jack,
as the men called this landlubber of a captain, signed him
on for one cruise, with the stipulation that he be discharged
at the next port; and when Melville looked around him, he
discovered that between the slack disorder of the Little Jule
and the tyranny of the Acushnet he had little to choose.

The physician on board, Dr. Long Ghost, had parted
company with the captain and had made his bunk in the
forecastle. The mate, a hale, bullet-headed fellow with a

kind heart and a heavy fist, John Jermin by name, was always half-seas-over; the captain was one of those watchful, ineffectual, capriciously determined men who achieved the dignity of isolation and got the semblance of obedience by never delivering an order through his own mouth. Without any success in whaling, the ship remained at sea, lest by lying in harbour and replenishing its provisions it might incidentally lose the whole crew by desertion.

Melville was contemptuous of the captain, he admired the bluff, bustling Jermin, and he fell in with the doctor, who was an educated man, as naturally as one globule of mercury will coalesce with another as soon as they touch. The doctor was a capital fellow to finish off Melville's education and to while away the sleepy hours of the night: "he had certainly at some time or other spent money, drunk Burgundy, and associated with gentlemen. As for his learning, he quoted Virgil, and talked of Hobbes of Malmesbury, besides repeating poetry by the Canto, especially Hudibras. He was, moreover, a man who had seen the world. In the easiest possible way he could refer to an amour he had in Palermo, his lion-hunting before breakfast among the Caffres, and the quality of the coffee he had drunk in Muscat." Such a man did not merely bring authentic reports of books and conversations; he was himself a picaresque library, and he who ran with him had much to read. This was the sort of acquaintance Melville could never have picked up in Albany, nor in New York: one first must become an outcast before he can have the privilege of such company.

The captain became seriously ill; and he purposed to send his men to sea under command of Jermin while he recuperated on shore. Heartily sick of the voyage, the crew rebelled at the notion, and when the ship lay off the harbour of Papeetee, they sent a round robin to the English consul, stating their grievances and petitioning to be put ashore. Wilson, the consul, would not hear of it: to cow them into submission, he delivered them over to the French frigate,

La Reine Blanche, that lay in the harbour; and for five days and nights Melville had a chance to live on a French man-of-war and to observe the contrast between French customs and character, and the American and English ways he was used to; but the imprisonment was only a demonstration; and the ship returned so that Wilson might again utter his ultimatum to the crew. The upshot of it was that the crew was put inside the British jail, the Calabooza Beretanee, under the surveillance of a huge, brown Polynesian dignitary; and after a few weeks of their semi-confinement, the Julia went off without them; and they finally found themselves at liberty among the miscellaneous riff-raff that haunted the shores of these tropical islands.

During the next couple of months, Melville lived the life of a rover, in the company of Dr. Long Ghost, visiting among the natives, working for a brief period on a Polynesian farm, for a tall robust Yankee born in the backwoods of Maine, and finally trying, unsuccessfully, to advance their fortunes in the court of Queen Pomaree. It was a rambling, roving, thoroughly outlandish mode of life which must have had the episodic and incredible quality of a dream: there was a complete absence of pressure and direction; Melville drifted from one islet in Imeeo to another as a leaf driven by chance breezes will drift on the surface of a still pond. Thrown among the superficially converted Christians of Tahiti, Melville observed no advance over the untainted pagans of Typee; quite the contrary. "So far as mere temporal felicity was concerned, the Tahitians are far worse off now than formerly. Years ago brought to a stand, where all that is corrupt in barbarism and civilization unite, to the exclusion of the virtues of either state . . . they must here remain stationary until utterly extinct."

Away from the purlieus of the Christian "mickonaree" Melville enjoyed the lazy, savage life. The air was relaxing; but for a young American, bred in Albany and Pittsfield, the danger was that he might bless his braces, and damn his relaxes too opprobriously; so, on the whole, one must count these months of rambling and laziness and observation as good ones for Melville. Some of the dreamy, unexpected quality of them went, no doubt, into the fantasy of Mardi when he came to write it: Omoo, which records the actuality, and Mardi, which utters the dream, are the morning and night of the same day. Through it all, Melville kept his shape; he was still a quizzical, modest, slightly sentimental, sober-minded young man: when he beholds the beautiful wife of a sugar-planter, mounted gallantly on a white pony, his emotions are touched by distant adoration and curiosity, just as they might have been in Lansingburgh; and one suspects that he plagued more than one incipient brown sweetheart with a far too respectful and brotherly reserve. Five years later, Melville still remembered how the sugar planter's wife had captivated him: when he thinks back to this trivial incident he sets it apart in a chapter; and he remembers, too, the brown feminine mockery at his attempts to be sentimental. There is no likelihood that this young man will succumb to Queen Hautia: he is always on guard. If he needs any advice at this period it is that of Koheleth: Be not righteous over-much: why shouldst thou destroy thyself?

4

Whether Melville judged better of his third whaling captain, the Vineyarder, whom he finally fell in with, he does not tell: whether he tired of whaling off the coast of Japan one does not know either. One has a glimpse of him working as a clerk for four months in Honolulu, the capital of the Sandwich Islands, among the fine dwelling-houses, the hotels, the barber-shops, the offices, of the whites; and there one's knowledge ends. By the summer of 1843 he had shipped aboard the frigate, United States, upon its homeward voyage. The free, vagrant, uncertain life of the rover was over: he was in the Navy now. Melville had not done more than pick up a bare living, certainly, for when he was in Callao, about to equip himself for the terrible exposure of rounding the Horn, he could get no pea-jacket from the purser, and apparently could not afford to purchase one on shore: so he manufactured a white jacket for himself out of a white duck frock, folded and padded, cold comfort enough in dry weather, and colder comfort in wet, when the jacket was so absorbent his shipmates would cruelly stand up against him, to get rid of their own moisture.

Melville was as sick of adventure as Ulysses himself. When he heard the words, "Up anchor! Man the capstan: we're homeward bound," from the gruff boatswain, the words ran through his veins like golden wine. Now the little daily current of anxiety was over: there were a few new ropes to learn; but a strong, eager fellow, always ready to bear a hand, always prompt to spring to his post, is pretty sure of getting a good word from his immediate superiors, even though it is not an audible one; and with the big ship's company, the work itself was not so onerous but that there was time for long chats and lengthier meditations, particularly if one belonged to the maintop. Melville knew the value of height and seclusion to stimulate the inward eye: climbing a high tower, he wrote in The Encantadas, is the best way to see the country around one; and at sea, he would climb the mast: that was his watch-tower and his cloister.

The Navy of Melville's day was not unlike the Navy of today: these saurian institutions do not add to the quantity of brains in their brain-pan, nor do they change the quality of their tissue: it was bound up by red tape, precedent, a stupefying routine, and a set of regulations designed to establish and maintain the authority of those marginal officers who may have neither seamanship nor the gift of command. In addition to the abuses that still exist in the Navy, some of which are inevitable by the mere act of regimentation and by an existence that is purposeless except in terms of slaughter and bellicose action, there was in Melville's time the further iniquity of flogging. Melville's words against this institution are in bold contrast to Dana's. Dana was one of those cautious friends of a cause whose timid counsel is far harder to dispose of than the practices of its enemies: he minced and compromised, and, dealing only with merchant sailors, still recommended merely that flogging be mitigated. To Melville flogging was a degradation of humanity; if discipline could not be maintained without it, discipline was degrading; if the navy of a free community could not be maintained without it, navies were degrading: let us get rid of all these things together.

Life on the man-of-war was difficult and capricious still. Through the mere punctilio of an officer in charge, Melville was unable to give his white jacket a coat of paint; and he suffered from terrible exposure in the journey round the Horn; but after the comparative solitude of his savage Polynesian existence, with just a stray soul for company, the ship had something of the stir and variety of a metropolis: it contained people like Nord, a man of mystery and romance, who, Melville suspected sympathetically, had been bolted in the mill of adversity: and there was Lemsford, the poet, who conceived platitudes in Dionysiac ecstasy, and above all, there was Jack Chase, the captain of the maintop, a simple, hearty, beautiful soul, who gave young Melville all a father could have given him; and to whom Melville clung, at sea, and later, in memory—a starved orphan, finding in Jovian Chase all that his father's death, and his father's marble image, denied him. The hours spent with Chase on the maintop were happy hours indeed; and no less so were those that Melville spent with books, Walpole's Letters and the Jew of Malta and Volpone, as well as earlier books of travel and adventure, such as Morgan's History of Algiers, and Knox's Captivity in Ceylon. Coming as they did, after a long period of abstention and thirst, these books had a profound influence upon Melville: and they give his literary pedigree. Through his experience of life, he broke away by necessity from the weak romantics of his youth, and, seeking the nearest parallels to his own adventures and meditations and visions, he found them in the Elizabethan dramatists and the seventeenth-century travellers and literary philosophers. Melville's genius followed two separate lines of growth, which joined in Moby-Dick: one of them was that of Marlowe and Webster, with their untrammelled emotions, their stertorous vitality, and their keen transposition of dream into reality and of reality into dream —the other was that of Knox's Captivity, direct, honest, well ballasted. Had not these books been in the ship's library, Melville might have taken much longer to find himself. Jack Chase himself added to Melville's literary education: he could recite the Lusiad by heart, and Camoëns made a vivid impression on Melville. In two of his last poems he assumed Camoëns' personality.

"Mind you, White-Jacket," Jack Chase would say, "there are many great men in the world besides commodores and captains. I've that there, White-Jacket"—touching his forehead—"which under happier skies—perhaps in yon solitary star there, peeping down from those clouds—might have made a Homer of me. But Fate is Fate, White-Jacket; and we Homers who happen to be captains of the tops must write our Odes in our hearts and publish them in our heads." Did Melville smile at Chase's conceit, or was he already meditating his own odes and epics? When he wrote Typee, he explained that the incidents of it had been imprinted in his memory by being told over and over again; and one can imagine a hundred places where Melville might have found less incentive to literary activity than he found in the library and the maintop of the U. S. frigate United States.

There were three main events in the voyage. Two of these experiences involved deep personal humiliation. One was the time he was called to the mast and condemned to the scourge for being absent from his post at general quarters, a post to which he had never to his knowledge been assigned: in a panic of righteous anger, he measured the distance between himself and the captain, and had the blind impulse to rush him overboard, and end his own life, too, rather than undergo the degradation of this punishment. By a miracle, he was saved from this fate through the courageous intercession of a corporal of the marines, who spoke up in his behalf and got the order remitted. The other humiliation was the massacre of the beards, when, by the capricious order of "Captain Claret," the autocrat of the United States, even the oldest veteran, just completing his last voyage, was ordered to shave his beard; and when he would not submit to it, was flogged and put in irons. No one can feel the inner resentment occasioned by such an order who has not been subject to a similar indignity; on such occasions, the spirit boils in helpless rebellion. In civilian life, only the poor and the outcast know this experience; but in every large and regimented organization, military or commercial, such affronts to human dignity and autonomy are commonplace; they characterize the system, rather than the men who conduct it. Had Captain Claret not, on the whole, been a lenient officer, Melville would have had a hundred other occasions for this feeling. In gauging Melville's conduct at a later period, one must not forget these humiliations; their effect was cumulative.

But the crowning adventure of the voyage happened when the United States was off the capes of Virginia in a calm sea: the ship gave a sudden lurch and he was thrown from the yard-arm into the water. Let him tell the story for himself:

"With a bloody, blind film before my eyes, there was a still stranger hum in my head, as if a hornet were there; and I thought to myself Great God! this is death. Yet these thoughts were unmixed with alarm. Like frostwork that flashes and shifts its scared hues in the sun, all my braided, blended emotions were in themselves icy cold and calm. . . . As I gushed into the sea, a thunderboom sounded in my ear; my soul seemed flying from my mouth. The feeling of death

flooded over me with the billows, the blow from the sea must
have turned me, so that I sank almost feet foremost through
a soft, seething, foamy lull. Some current seemed hurrying
me away; in a trance, I yielded, and sank deeper down with
a glide. Purple and pathless was the deep calm around me,
flecked by summer lightnings in an azure afar. The horrible
nausea was gone; the bloody, blind film turned a pale green;
I wondered whether I was yet dead, or still dying. But of
a sudden some fashionless form brushed my side—some
inert coiled fish of the sea; the thrill of being alive again
tingled in my nerves, and the strong shunning of death
shocked me through. For one instant an agonizing revulsion came over me as I found myself utterly sinking. Next
moment the force of my fall was expended; and there I
hung, vibrating in the mid-deep. . . . The Life-and-death
poise soon passed; and then I found myself slowly ascending, and caught a dim glimmering of light. Quicker and
quicker I mounted; till at last I bounded up like a buoy and
my whole head was bathed in the blessed air." Melville was
rescued; but not before he had rid himself of his white
jacket forever; the ominous whiteness that he found later
in Moby-Dick was accentuated, perhaps, by his memory of
that "accursed jacket" which had delivered him up to the
elements, rather than protected him, and in the moment of
extremity, had nearly proved his shroud.

To have faced life and death, not as abstractions, but as
concrete events, when a sinew less of resolution would have
meant his extinction, in a stove boat off the coast of Japan,
at the hands of the pursuant Typees, or enveloped in the
white jacket at sea: to have thrown himself among strange
men, and to have kept his own shape, always set apart a
little by culture and breeding, but never rebuffed for a
feebleness or an unmanliness or inability to bear a hand: to
feel the wild throb of a ship in a gale, sea-wracked but magnificent, creaking, whining, wind-whistling, slapping into a
trough of wave or climbing dizzily on to a crest, and to feel

a wilder, louder, more victorious throb within: to have been
attracted by the languors and sensuous jollities of a savage
life, but still more attracted by all that civilisation had left
with him, in hints and promises, Homer and Dante and
Shakespeare and Cervantes: to have left home a boy, innocent and unspoiled, and to have returned a man, tough-
ened, bronzed, firm-fibred, and full of mixed knowledge, yet
still essentially innocent and unspoiled—all this had happened to Melville. He had left America to seek adventures.
Now he had found adventures; and he left that behind, left
the South Seas and the whaleman's joys and hardships, and
the man-of-war's settled routine, to pursue adventure farther, but on a higher plane.

There comes a time—it is the beginning of manhood or
womanhood—when one realizes that adventure is as hum-
drum as routine unless one assimilates it, unless one relates
it to a central core which grows within and gives it contour
and significance. Raw experience is empty, just as empty
in the forecastle of a whaler as in the chamber of a counting-
house; it is not what one does, but in a manifold sense, what
one *realizes*, that keeps existence from being vain and
trivial. Mankind moves about in worlds not realized: Wordsworth's phrase expresses a profound reality, and Melville
himself suggests a similar idea in Mardi, when the
philosopher points out that ages hence people may realize
more keenly what has happened today than our own contemporaries do. It is the artist, the knower, the sayer, who
realizes human experience, who takes the raw lump of ore
we find in nature, smelts it, refines it, assays it, and stamps
it into coins that can pass from hand to hand and make
every man who touches them the richer. "No man can live
for another" is a true doctrine as far as experience goes;
but it is the opposite of true in the life of realization; for
into this fuller and more durable apprehension of experience goes our whole social heritage, all the forms and symbols that have aided human expression in the past, the

cumulative effect of many cultures and many different modes of life. Those who absorb and reflect and meditate and relate, play an important part in the economy of society; and life is abrupt and incomplete when that part is not performed.

Melville had travelled far and had experienced much; he had run the gamut, or rather, the gauntlet of every sort of human experience except the normal and easy and domestic one promised him by birth and parentage. He will never be a school teacher, a professor, a ship captain, a lawyer, a political leader; however necessary these occupations, there is nothing in Melville's training or temperament that moves him in one of these directions. What is left? What is left is something he has been silently preparing himself for all along: he must become a writer. Though the society to which he returned, unlike Jack Chase and other humble listeners to Melville's yarns, regarded that function as a trivial one, compared to accomplishments in a dissociated world of action, and by its contemptuous regard and its dissociation, deprived it of sustenance and made much of it in fact trivial, here is the occupation which will gain in a hundred ways by his experiences.

Melville must have had more than a dim anticipation of this career when he stepped ashore, at Boston, in October, 1844; and had he known where it would lead him he might well have shrunk from following it further. His physical adventures were to be welcomed as romantic myths, and his mental adventures were to be denounced as blasphemies. In short, "the indefinite Navy Commissioners, so far out of sight aloft," had a mission in store for Melville that Hardy's ironic President of the Immortals might have concocted in a sinister moment.

CHAPTER THREE: TROPICAL SUMMER

In 1844, when Herman Melville landed in Boston, provincial American society was in that state of uneasy transformation which means either a vaster accomplishment or destruction; and in 1844 it was still possible to think that the result would not be, fatally, destruction. The Mexican War loomed ahead, thanks partly to the itch of Southern planters to extend the territory under cotton, abetted by the belief of men like Seward that by a process of territorial aggrandizement and conquest the conflict between Northern and Southern economic interests could be diverted. The American state had already acquired the desire to crown itself with glory and prestige by conquering one of its disordered neighbours—a process which mixed an ineffable air of virtue with the proud consciousness that we had chosen an opponent who could not possibly lick us.

Already something that aggravated the economic conflict had appeared on the horizon, a breach between the several states over the ancient metaphysical question of the one and the many, somewhat confused by doubts as to whether free institutions could flourish alongside an empire committed to slavery and expansion. These doubts must have been even more confusing to a neutral observer, since cities like Charleston and New Orleans, for all their slavery, were less depressing and barbarous than such proud emporia as New York and such dingy manufacturing hives as Philadelphia and Pittsburgh. There was so much right and wrong on both sides of Mason and Dixon's line that the question could only be decided by furious men of action, who would decisively pound their fist into one side of the scale or the other in order to make weight and register a conclusion.

If slavery showed a dark countenance, beautifully kalsomined by the most solicitous Christian hypocrisy, industrialism showed a dingy one. The little water-driven mill-wheel, which greatly lightened the domestic labour of the early nineteenth-century farm, and which served equally to operate the small mill or factory, had only a brief day of social efficiency: by 1850, Melville could encounter a factory in the Berkshire Hills, turning rags into paper, and call it a Tartarus of Maids. Mechanical instruments, so far from diminishing the amount of servile labour in the world, threatened to turn all industrial operations into a form of servitude: in this middle period, craftsmanship of the hand decayed, and craftsmanship of the machine was subjugated by the demand for the cheap, the shoddy, the ephemeral. The mills at Lowell, which Dickens described with admiration in 1837, were already huge, and it was only by contrast with Bradford or Leeds that they could be called tolerable. In the forties, the concentration of coal and iron was slowly giving Pittsburgh a pre-eminence over the old iron mines and furnaces scattered about the countryside in Connecticut, New York, and New Jersey. Railroads, first laid where capital and immediate convenience dictated, were now joining along strategic lines of communication, following coast and inland water routes: as the stage-coach disappeared, and the inns ceased to get patronage, the inner parts of the country became inaccessible and they gradually ran down: only the railroad thread prospered.

Was this a triumph or a *débâcle*, this coming of industrialism, this volcanic intrusion of new methods of living, new means of communication, new habits of work? When one thinks of the countrysides that ran down, the forests that were wantonly destroyed, the soils that were depleted, the towns that were jerry-built and burned and jerry-built again, the public lands that were thrown into the laps of speculators, the industrial population that was starved and depressed in dingy cities, one sees that there is no easy answer to this question; and certainly none of the economists has ever been impartial enough as accountant to tell whether the final result for civilization was a gain or a loss, and if so, how much was gained and how much lost, and where these things happened. But when Melville came back to America, industrialism was a value in itself: people encouraged it as the patrons of the Renaissance encouraged art, not doubting that the activity was a great one, and made for a higher civilization.

It is perhaps a little absurd to speak of such disparate things as Attica and the North Atlantic states in the same breath: but these regions, between 1820 and 1860, which coincided with Melville's birth and maturity, were in many respects in the same situation as Attica between the birth of Socrates and the death of Plato. An old provincial culture, closely bound to the land, was being overthrown by a new order based upon trade and imperialistic enterprise and military expeditions in support of the prestige of the state; and, at this moment of dissolution, the spirit fulfilled itself in a sudden outburst which expressed, in a new form, all that was valuable in the old culture, with an additional energy, derived partly from the seething activities of the new life that was inimical to it and already threatened it. The gap between Sophocles and Menander was no greater than the gap between Melville and Mark Twain: both these Americans roughed it and travelled much and gave accounts of their adventures; but their feeling and their vision belonged to different worlds.

In the America of the forties there was a sense of poignant expectation which was also a fulfilment. Emerson was giving his lectures on the Times, Thoreau was making his experiment at Walden Pond: warm spirits with thin and fantastic notions about the ideal life were discussing Fourier, welcoming the writings of Cabet, trying by a single gesture to regenerate the morals of society, to get an easier living, reform the diet, and alter the institution of matrimony—absurd, rickety people they were, no doubt, but Bronson Alcott's preference for the sun-touched fruits and vegetables has turned out not to be so fantastic in fact as it sounds in theory; and if it is possible now to eat food which does not lead inevitably to gout and indigestion, to wear clothes that do not stifle and constrict the human body, and to think candidly about institutions which were once too sacred for rational thought, we owe these improvements not a little to the passionate women who dared to wear trousers and the comical men who listened patiently to Dr. Graham's famous lecture on the benefits of bran bread and squashes.

In 1844 this mixture in society of new and old, provincial and metropolitan, free and servile, vital and mechanical, was still a turbid one: the elements had not settled; contrast and comparison were difficult; and people stood for one or the other, chiefly by intuition, while perhaps a good part of the population sought both: they wanted the old privileges of birth and the new ones of opportunity, the old stability and order, and all the new fields to conquer and the new positions to occupy. Melville belonged by temperament and shade of interest to the order that was passing, and not to the chaos and dissolution that was to come; still, in so far as he was aware of the change, he accepted it and even took a little pleasure in it, as when he anticipated from the progress of invention that fifty years hence it would be a commonplace for an American to spend the week-end in Honolulu.

2

Melville came back to this turbid spring freshet of a world, and he found that his family, too, was in the process of growth and change. Allan had become the business man of the family, a lawyer, with offices in Wall Street; young

Tom already wanted to become a sailor, not just to see new places like Herman but to master the sea as a profession; Gansevoort, who had struggled hard and become a little wan and disappointed, had gone in for a political career, and, like Henry Adams a little later, he went to join the American Legation in London in 1845 as secretary. After a little visiting among his relatives and with Chief Justice Lemuel Shaw of Massachusetts, an old friend of the family with a marriageable daughter, Melville settled down for a while in Lansingburgh: he had decided to write an account of his adventures. The lack of any other opening and the promise of some financial return were the external stimuli; but one cannot doubt that there was also an inner need. This loquacious, introspective sailor, who can so vividly hold an audience that, later, when he described for Mr. and Mrs. Hawthorne an encounter in which he had used a club, they searched the house on his departure to find the imaginary club he had left behind—this young man had reached a stage where literary expression was inevitable, necessary— indeed, good for the health.

Up to the age of twenty-five Melville had knocked around the world solely for the purpose of making the best of a bad job. At twenty-five he discovered, in writing Typee, that he actually had made the best of it: his roaming, wasted life was all to the good: its idlest moments could be salvaged; for he had come into possession of something he had not deliberately set out to find, and twenty years of sedentary labour at home would not have given him equal experiences or equal leisure to reflect upon them. The wreckage of these Polynesian years was more precious than any cargo he might have punctually guarded in New York or Boston, at some purser's job like school-teaching. The outcast came into his own; and the prodigal returned with his own fatted calf to give him welcome!

Herman Melville's first book was a narrative of his Four Months in the Marquesas among the Typees: its American title was Typee. It was at the opposite pole, at the other end of the world, from another book that was being composed during this period, Thoreau's Walden, but the similarities are no less important than the contrasts. Typee is Melville's Walden, without the philosophic reflection and without the premeditated purpose to test the benefits of a more primitive life: Walden is Thoreau's Typee without the physical derring-do and adventure.

Melville had found in the Marquesas the simplicity and directness of livelihood that Thoreau sought nearer at hand; and as for Thoreau, he treated the oak tree as if it were breadfruit, and was glad to find sweet acorns fit to eat, because they diminished the number of enemies in the universe. Both Melville and Thoreau had found out what it meant to throw off the impedimenta of civilization; and though both of them returned to the society of their own kind, they carried back to everyday American life a little contempt. Life at the core was a much simpler matter than the civilizee would admit: for civilization, which creates enjoyable forms for human activity, also creates grotesque ones, which grow up alongside the shapely forms and tend to supplant them: the accumulation of capital comes to mean more than the provision of food and shelter, and the regalia of the book of etiquette means more than friendly intercourse. The Philistines that surrounded Melville knew no more about the great forms of civilization, about the art of Shakespeare or Rembrandt or the philosophy of Spinoza and Goethe, than the naked savages: they were just as destitute in these higher essentials, and, on top of these disabilities, they lacked the savage's animal health, charm, and good nature. Melville did not set out to test these things, as Thoreau did; but unconsciously, on the mere weight of evidence, he came to the same conclusion.

Writing is not merely a process of explicating what one already knows: it is also a matter of discovering what one is not aware of: it brings to light the hidden loot in that storehouse which psychologists call the Unconscious. In the very act of writing Typee, Melville must have become conscious of his specific equipment and his gifts as a writer; for, though he had been able to make no notes of his adventures while he was undergoing them, they had sorted themselves out and formed a pattern of their own. In his first book, Melville went about his work with a sure instinct. He read up every account of the South Seas he could lay hands on, Captain Cook's voyages, missionary reports, travellers' descriptions: he discovered, what some writers find out far too late, that if one trusts to one's own experience alone, one gets something less than one's own experience, while, if the background is filled out and enriched, one's own contribution comes out more copiously. This habit of reference became characteristic of Melville in almost all his later works: Moby-Dick is full of citations, and even in a series of short sketches, like The Encantadas, he mentions as authorities Cowley, The Buccaneer, 1684; Colnet, The Whaling Ground Explorer, 1798, and Porter, The Post Captain, 1813.

It would have been hard to spoil such adventures as Melville's: he could only have done it by a weak memory or a poor gift of visualization, or, more fatal perhaps than these, a tendency to touch every event with a sentimental gloss. Melville's Typee was free from these sins. He trusted his eyes completely; he told what he saw. Did he understand everything? By no means; the taboo was a mystery, the religious observances obscure, the exact status of cannibalism hard to define: in his very failure to interpret these data, he gave an account which is still valuable to the anthropologist as a description of the South Sea Islanders in an entirely primitive and untainted state. If Melville had trusted his eyes less and his wits more he might perhaps have disclosed facts which were sealed to him: he might also have muddled and misinterpreted everything. The very limitations of Melville's descriptions give one confidence in their authenticity: this is not unvarnished truth, perhaps, because unvarnished truth with no inaccuracies and distortions and running together of separate events is impossible without a written record, promptly made; but it is still truth.

Does one want a further guarantee of Melville's accuracy in Typee? The answer is to be found in the rest of his work. While his powers of invention were not small, it was only with difficulty that he could escape the actual world and create a world sustained by his own fantasy. He tried to do this in Mardi, and he was forced back upon history and fact; by the time he reached the end of the book, he lost his grip entirely and converted his fabulous Mardians into out-and-out Europeans. He tried again in Pierre, and as we shall see, he fell back upon the stereotyped figures of conventional melodrama: he succeeded completely, in fact, only once, and he did this by an heroic effort, for which he had to pay a severe physical penalty. Like Defoe, Melville was closely chained to the document, the fact, the experience; he could endow these things with imaginative life, for all the other instruments of creative writing were at his command; but he was not given to inventive elaboration. Do we not perhaps exaggerate the possibilities of the pure imagination? The recent studies of Poe's and Coleridge's fantasies should warn us. Even in the dream, where the imagination works without any obligation to be understood or communicated, the most bizarre effects are a blowing up into a vast bubble, through the mechanism of dream-work, of some tiny drop of actual soapy water. Indeed, the highest imaginations, those of an Aeschylus or a Shakespeare or a Goethe, work upon themes already given in myth and history: they do not waste their energies upon the skeleton of fact, but take whatever lies at hand, cover it with flesh, breathe upon it, and give it life.

In Typee, then, Melville made no attempt to write a pure idyll, compounded of butterfly wings and spiderwebs and rainbows. Fayaway was interesting to him; but so, on reflection, were the misdemeanours of the missionaries in the Marquesas. The dangers of being eaten were horrid: so were the brutalities that whaling captains inflicted on the natives: so was the military overlordship of the French. Everything was told in its place, as far as everything could be told to an already Victorian public. The wonder is that Melville, in the first edition of Typee, was as frank as he was: when Dickens' Oliver Twist was published in America it was attacked for its immoral picture of Bill Sykes and Nancy, by one of the shrinkingly pure American newspapers of the time, which no doubt carried in the neighbouring columns advertisements of quack doctors, books on "sexology," and patent medicines to be used as abortifacients. Melville, who was fresh from four years of travel, wrote with easy freedom and candour, forgetting that his audience was Thackeray's, not Smollett's.

Typee belongs to the morning of the imagination—like Pickwick Papers. It is direct, fresh, free from self-consciousness, like the healthy youth who experienced these adventures and sat down to write about them. That quality is precious and irretrievable. Dickens lived a whole lifetime without again creating anything so sanative and comic as Pickwick Papers; and though Melville fared farther and pondered more deeply on life, this book and the one that followed, alone had the full bloom of youth upon them. Such books are written without a formula; their essential quality is almost beyond formulation. When one has said youth one has said almost everything. Typee is a book to make one go visiting tropical islands, a book to make one question the well-arranged career, the carefully ironed routine, the dull inevitability of the days one has chosen to lead. A scholarly boy reads Typee, and engages a berth for himself on a ship bound for Madagascar; a young architect reads the book and leaves his drawing-board for a trader's post in the Marquesas, where he becomes a specialist in Polynesian dialects; another young man reads Typee and decides to bind his Fayaway to him by the tie of marriage. One reads Typee, and life suddenly shows a new vista. Adventure is possible: Eden is real: life need not include timetables and bank accounts and exercises in physical culture. And unlike romantic fantasies Typee is not itself a narcotic, a form of escape: it suggests appropriate actions and deeds. If one person becomes a philologist through reading it, another takes to anthropology; another buys himself a sailboat; and another suddenly decides to carry out some difficult course he had resolved on and put aside again and again.

Like Pickwick Papers—but how differently!—Typee communicates its own simple health and manly confidence: its keenness, its straightforwardness, its hearty appetite for life. It is written with that skill which disarms skill, with the clarity beside which a more deliberate artifice would be clumsy. The colour of such romantic episodes may be artificially imitated: Kaloolah was such an imitation, and in a very bad light one may not at once detect the difference: but there is no imitating the down on the cheek and the clear eye—the stigmata of unspotted youth. I do not underestimate the charm of his subject; but Melville imparted to it his own candid and buoyant nature, watching this strange delicious world with intent, water-blue eyes. The subject was made for a young man to tell about—and happily the young man appeared. It was matched to this adventurous young American as the England of comfortable inns and Christmas jollity was matched to young Dickens. Melville varied the formula of wishy-washy romance by treating all romantic facts realistically, as he treated brutality and danger, and both the romance and the hard adventures profited by it.

What a contrast Typee is to Robinson Crusoe! Defoe's prose was a far richer instrument than that Melville used in Typee; but after the first few chapters of Robinson Crusoe one's mind refuses to follow that plaguy Philistine:

nobody but a classical economist would pursue his tedious moralizings and his adept contrivances on his desert island. Defoe set out to teach a lesson, and before Crusoe has his last boatload of wares stowed away, long before he has re-established himself in that middle estate in life from which he originally fled, we are asleep. Melville sets out to teach us nothing: but at every step we follow eagerly and find ourselves making notes, instituting comparisons, seeing the world in fresh perspective. Typee is a magic mirror. In Typee we hold the secret of youth, and hold the world up to its clear surface: for the first time, perhaps, we note its unhealthy complexion, its fat paunch, its jaded smile, its fatuous anxieties, its lack of even animal repose.

3

Typee, which was published in London by John Murray, in his Colonial and Home Library, quickly won a name for itself as a piece of picaresque fiction. The London Times could not believe that a common American seaman could have the style of an educated literary man; and even a friend of the family, Mr. Evert Duyckinck, could hint politely that Melville had manufactured some of his adventures; Typee, literally, seemed too good to be true. The only people who took Typee for what it was were the missionary promoters: they damned the whole account heartily as unfair to the missionaries, and a perversion of Christian teaching, since this impudent and ribald young man pictured evangelical zeal as making no particular improvement in Polynesian morality, and since he even went out of his way to comment sarcastically upon the missionaries in Honolulu, who published a journal in which the doings of the "converted" king were recorded with the unction of an official English court gazette.

Against the charge of untruth and the imputation of fiction, Melville had two answers. One was happily furnished by Richard Tobias Greene, the Toby of Typee, a resident

73

of Buffalo, who had in fact escaped from the Marquesas without being able to effect Melville's rescue, and who wrote to the Buffalo Commercial Advertiser, when Typee was published, verifying Melville's story and asking Melville to get in touch with him. Melville got from Toby an account of his adventures, and embodied them in a sequel to Typee called The Story of Toby. As for the missionaries, Melville's instinct in controversy served him well: in his next book, he returned to the misdemeanours of the pious and hit harder in the same place. He had observed that all the eulogistic reports of the missionaries were written by the missionaries themselves: their zeal to propagate Christianity was not unmixed with their concern to get money which would further that fine enterprise: against these glowing reports of conversion and grace and the introduction of shame and sin into the South Seas, Melville pitted his own acrid memories. No animus against Christianity led him to do this; for he had a strong initial bias in its favour: what spurred him was mere honesty of record, and the desire to see the Polynesians left alone in a happier state.

There is one further confirmation of Typee's verity: one cannot neglect it, though it comes at third hand. M. Philarète Chasles, in his Anglo-American Literature and Manners, translated and published in New York in 1852, quotes a "well-informed American who reported that a cousin of Melville had said: 'My cousin writes very well, except when he reproduces exactly what he has felt. . . . He could not invent the scenes which he describes. Charmed by his improvised reputation, he would be vexed, I think, to lose his reputation as an inventor. The reappearance of his companion, Toby or Richard Greene, a real personage, annoyed him to some degree. It made him descend from the pedestal of romance to the level of mere narrator. For me, who know Melville, his wild disposition, and the history of his youth— who have actually read his rough notes, now in the hands of his father-in-law, and who have talked twenty times with

Richard Greene, his fidus Achates, I laugh at the preoccupation of a public accustomed to see a lie where no lie is.' "

A strain of malice lies in this description of Melville's own reception of praise as an inventor which does not altogether lessen one's belief in its authenticity. In Redburn, Melville resented his cousins, and in Pierre he made one of his hero's cousins play the part of a callous betrayer of trust and friendship; one has reason to suspect a little bitterness on Melville's side, and a little condescension and concealed envy on the other. If the public's mistake made Melville find more easily his path as an imaginative writer, let us thank the incredulous but forever gullible public: their mistake did him service.

4

The fuss that was raised over Typee was not merely on account of its supposed lack of fidelity. It was also because it had displayed loose and immoral scenes. If people could find looseness and immorality in Melville's description of sexual customs in the South Seas, or in his anecdote of the proud South Sea queen examining with naïve pleasure the tattooing on a French sailor, and, in all innocence, raising her skirts so as to disclose her own to such a connoisseur of the art, or in the incident of the beautiful yellow-haired wife of a missionary, who was worshipped by the natives as a mysterious goddess until they stripped her of her clothes and discovered that she was even as they—if the public could feel a titillation of wickedness over these things, it must have been in a state of pathological sensitiveness; and no doubt it was, for the exposure of more than the lower part of the female ankle in society was then the mark of a wicked and abandoned woman.

This did not make it any easier for a candid fellow like Melville; and when a new edition was projected in America, the officious and correct Mr. Duyckinck must have suggested, as adviser to Wiley and Putnam, that a little judicious editing would reduce the offence and increase Melville's audience. The young must be protected; the clergy must be conciliated; just a little pruning here and there would give the book a place on every library table. Melville should not have listened to this nonsense; sooner or later a man with anything worth saying must face the world of Pimminee and be prepared to stuff its prejudices and its gentlemanly objections down its throat: if a young author does not make this stand in his first book, he will increase his difficulties with his fourth or fifth. But in 1846 Melville was still uncertain of himself: a novice in his vocation, he was not aware of all the snares that beset a man of letters: the pressure toward amiable compliance with the all too amiable Mr. Duyckinck must have been pretty stiff; all the more, perhaps, because a Duyckinck might almost be a Gansevoort, and family pressure may have played a part, too. At all events, he consented to let Typee be bowdlerized.

"The *Revised* (Expurgated?—odious word!) Edition of 'Typee' ought to be duly announced—and as the matter (in one respect) is a little delicate, I am happy that the literary tact of Mr. Duyckinck will be exerted on this occasion." So Melville wrote in the middle of 1846 to Mr. Evert Duyckinck. He grimaced a little at the dose; but unfortunately swallowed it. The anecdote about Queen Pomaree went: the anecdote about the missionary's wife went; and various other passages were underscored by elimination. What Melville said about the missionaries of the Dollar and the Cross is worth remembering, before Mr. Duyckinck runs his blue pencil through it:

"Look at Honolulu, the metropolis of the Sandwich Islands!—a community of disinterested merchants, and devoted self-exiled heralds of the Cross, located on the very spot that twenty years ago was defiled by the presence of idolatry. What a subject for an eloquent Bible-meeting orator! . . . But when these philanthropists send us such glowing accounts of one-half of their labors, why does modesty restrain them from publishing the other half of the good they have wrought?—Not until I visited Honolulu was I aware of the fact that the small remnant of the natives had been civilized into draught horses and evangelized into beasts of burden. But so it is. They have been literally broken into the traces and are harnessed to the vehicles of their spiritual instructors like so many dumb brutes."

I would not say that this bowdlerization ruins the book, or that it materially takes away from its value: that is not the point. Small and "immaterial" suppressions may have no effect upon the literary value of a work: but they cannot help having a subtly corrosive effect upon the man who has created it. As A. E. once pointed out, in discussing the matter of censorship, the spirit of the artist is a sensitive one, and in many cases it works only with great difficulty. If its wings are clipped by so much as a feather-tip, its capacity for flight may be ruined. It is perhaps impossible to say how far Melville was harmed by Mr. Duyckinck's tactful exertions, or by the hysterical denunciations that prompted them. For objective evidence, we have only the fact that sex, except in remote allusions to debauchery in Redburn or to sodomy in White-Jacket, did not enter into any of Melville's stories, until it suddenly erupted in 1852 in Pierre with the violence of long repression. Mark Twain was burdened by a similar censorship; and he took refuge in the flat obscenity of "1601." Melville's own development as a man and a writer might have been a happier one, had not sex become in his day a sanctimonious ritual, with no middle term between the licence of the brothel and the waxen purity of the home. The censorship which operated on Melville's books bore equally on his spirit: his libido turned back upon itself, and got lost for a time in the mazes of an infantile life. To take sex easily, naturally, rationally, is to subject it to the refining elements in life: to take it with a sense of unholy attraction and holy repulsion is to dissociate it com-

pletely from the normal influence of knowledge and convention and taste: in this dissociated, fragmental state, sex
rages irresponsibly like a bolt of lightning in an open field:
it may disappear into the ground, it may shatter a tree, it
may kill a human being.

Melville had carried back from the South Seas the simplicity of an essentially chaste, but, we must suppose, not
altogether inexperienced young man. This simplicity had
something valuable in it for Melville's contemporaries, just
as his appreciation of savage society must have warned them
about the absurd extravagance of acquiring dyspepsia and
hard faces and an incapacity for the arts of living by their
concentration upon money-making—and the censorship of
Typee kept this part of Melville, I think, from maturing
with reflection and experience. Sex was taboo. That element
in his growth knew no middle state between greenness and
blight. One part of life was locked for him in a dark chamber; one part will die by asphyxiation.

5

Typee was a success, and Melville soon had the consciousness of being an author. He could scarcely mention his book,
in passing, without pausing to realize how strange it
sounded. All his dispersed interests and his random purposes
were suddenly concentrated: his life had the spiritual momentum that a genuine career gives it: he was no longer
an outcast Olympian, but one of the great circle, now treated
by his elders as an equal, respected, deferred to, genially
slapped on the back, welcomed when a group of literary
men met for conversation: if an English author came to
America, as Thackeray did a little later, Melville was bound
to be the most promising younger man in the circle that
dined him and gave him welcome.

In Pierre, Melville gives his hero's sensations at suddenly
finding himself quoted in the public press, and urged by
various grave societies to lecture before them—little gratui-

ties of attention that afflicted him with a sense of his own insignificance, no matter how inflated he might seem to the world outside: and Pierre's humility was doubtless Melville's. He had grown a beard; but he did not need that symbol of years and experience to wear his new honours easily: with his reading and his miscellaneous adventure and the deep or brilliant conversation that might unexpectedly escape from him, he must have been a ready companion in any of the current literary circles: indeed, the difficulty was that, in the particular group where he moved, it was hard to single out any minds that came up to his level: the Manhattan literati of Melville's heyday were a slick and shallow parcel of journalists, with a few scholars like the learned author of the Lives of the Presidents, as makeweight.

Melville's quick entry into the literary world was partly furthered by two men who once wielded power in American letters, Messrs. George and Evert Duyckinck; George, a little thin and abstemious and given to pious reflections, Evert, more full-blooded, shrewd, worldly, an energetic hack who accumulated more than a modest competence as an editor and a compiler of ostentatious books of reference. They were busy little moles, these Duyckincks; one can scarcely utter their names or recount their ephemeral glories without smiling a little; but they gave Melville support and sympathy at a time early enough for him to profit by it; and if Melville found Evert Duyckinck worthy of his friendship there was something in the man's geniality that merited it, and it is not for us to withhold what Melville himself freely gave. Evert Duyckinck had, according to Richard Lathers, one of the choicest libraries in the state: he was literary adviser to Messrs. Wiley and Putnam, and after Charles Fenno Hoffman's brief editorship, he assumed charge of the Literary World. Until the publication of Pierre, Mr. Duyckinck was intimately associated with Melville's literary ventures. Melville trusted him the way that a foreigner may trust a native as a guide to a strange country, realizing only after many days that the man he has thrown himself in with, whose company he has enjoyed, would be the most antipathetic of companions if one met him on one's own ground. Duyckinck helped Melville to find his own depths; and when Melville had found them the two men were, by that simple fact, cut off.

It is not difficult to see how this friendship matured and withered: Duyckinck's life was devoted to those superficies that Melville dedicated his whole energies to piercing and getting beyond. Lowell hit Evert off in one of his Fables for Critics; it was not the least happy of his arrows:

Good-day, Mr. Duyckinck, I am happy to meet
With a scholar so ripe and a critic so neat,
Who through Grub Street the soul of a gentleman carries.
What news from the suburb of London and Paris?

Walt Whitman met the Duyckinck brothers: he describes them both as "gentlemanly men" and he could say no worse of any one. "I do not know of any description that it would have pleased them better to hear," added Whitman. "Both very clerical-looking—thin—wanting in body: men of truly proper style, God help 'em!" But the Duyckincks had a correct, bowing acquaintance with literature: they represented culture, tradition, a knowledge of English grammar; and for a good while they were not the least appreciative of Melville's critics. If, when they published their Cyclopedia of American Literature, they gave fourteen pages to Longfellow and only three and a half to Melville, they were but reflecting the judgment of gentlemanly men for the next generation. More than thirty years later, Mr. Barrett Wendell and Mr. George Woodberry had advanced no further on the road to appreciation.

6

Melville's brother, Gansevoort, had procured an advance from Murray on the English edition of Typee; and his new fame and financial success must have made Melville look forward to literature as the source of a permanent livelihood. In that "maturer and larger interior development" that was now taking place in Melville, pride of career supplanted pride of race: it was himself, his own nature, his experiences, his thoughts, that mattered, and not the size of his grandfather's breeches or the length of that other lineage which perhaps joined him with bonnie Jeanie Melville in the Scots ballad. His racial inheritance had but added to his humiliation; by his own exertions and skill, he had achieved his first triumph. He is now a proper child of the Revolution; he knows, like Napoleon, that men make families quite as much as families make men—and there is no ancestor so powerful as one's earlier selves.

Melville promptly followed Typee with a sequel of his adventures in the South Seas called Omoo, which signifies rover. In the meanwhile, Gansevoort, who had been the mainstay of the family while Melville was growing up in Albany, had found nothing in the bleak streets and grimy housefronts of London to lessen his own depression; and he died. The early struggle, which had left such a bitter taste with Herman, had even more fatally taken the heart out of Gansevoort. From the last of his letters home one has the feeling that he resigned from life, rather than that he was suffering from any physical malady. "Selfishly speaking," he declared, "I have never valued life very much." The fibre loosened in Gansevoort; the grip relaxed; he passed out. There is no sign in Omoo that Gansevoort's death was a very profound event for Melville; and yet one suspects that his sadness and hopelessness came in later years to mingle with Melville's pain.

Omoo is a description of Melville's life from the day he escaped the Typees to his signing up for another whaling voyage off the coast of Japan: its contents I have already used in telling about his life during that period. The narrative itself is done in the direct, vigorous, rapid style of

Typee: if anything, there is more humour in it, and Melville gave himself greater liberties in using the material and embroidering it. Omoo is perhaps the most underrated of Melville's books. While it solidified the reputation he had gained in Typee, the first book has held first place, because of the unique people and customs Melville dealt with there; whereas Omoo, which is a more raffish tale, and in some respects superior in literary quality, has been treated as if it were but the rinsings of the heady Typeean jug. This is far from being true. The relatively unromantic, if outlandish, quality of these later adventures, with the exception of the mutiny of the Julia's crew, made him rely more heavily upon his own skill: and although the main incidents are probably accurate, all the characters are focussed with a slight distortion, through Melville's sense of the comic: Dr. Long Ghost's adventures and peccadillos are filled out a little, and the venial doctor of Papeetee was treated in such a fashion that the actual character uttered a cry of belligerent protest when the book came to his attention.

Melville's skill at character-drawing, of which his description of Mehevi and Kory-Kory gave promise in Typee, became in Omoo more firm. Here is a scene in which two minor characters, a land-lubber, Rope Yarn, and an "affable-looking scamp"—Flash Jack—appear only for a minute.

"Flash Jack crosses the forecastle, tin can in hand, and seats himself beside the land-lubber.

" 'Hard fare this, Ropey,' he begins; 'hard enough, too, for them that's knowed better and lived in Lun'nun. I say now, Ropey, s'posing you were back to Holborn this morning, what would you have for breakfast, eh?'

" 'Have for breakfast!' cried Ropey, in a rapture. 'Don't speak of it!'

" 'What ails the fellow?' here growled an old sea-bear, turning around savagely.

" 'Oh, nothing, nothing,' said Jack; and then, leaning

over to Rope Yarn, he bade him go on, but speak lower.

" 'Well, then,' said he, in a smugged tone, his eyes lighting up like two lanterns, 'well, then, I'd go to Mother Mill's that makes the great muffins: I'd go there, you know, and cock my foot on the 'ob and call for a noggin o' somethink to begin with.'

" 'And what then, Ropey?'

" 'What then, Flashy,' continued the poor victim, unconsciously warming up to his theme; 'why then, I'd draw my chair up and call for Betty, the gal wot tends to the customers. Betty, my dear, says I, you looks charmin' this mornin'; give me a nice rasher of bacon and h'eggs, Betty, my love; and I wants a pint of h'ale, and three nice hot muffins and butter—and a slice of Cheshire; and Betty, I wants—'

" 'A shark steak and be hanged to you!' roared Black Dan with an oath."

This quotation serves not merely to show how immediately and vividly Melville can put before us a forecastle ragging. The passage is interesting for another reason. Despite his admiration for Melville, Robert Louis Stevenson gave rise to one of the parrot judgments about Melville's work when he said: "At his christening some influential fairy must have been neglected. 'He shall be able to see, he shall be able to tell, he shall be able to charm,' said the fairy godmothers; 'but he shall not be able to *hear*,' exclaimed the last." In this passage Stevenson was reproaching Melville for his inadequate rendering of the Marquesan speech, a matter over which there is small cause for wonder, since Melville's four months among the Typees were followed by four years before he committed the names and words to paper; but the actual fact is just the reverse of Stevenson's dictum: Melville had a curiously accurate ear; and the little passage just quoted proves it. Here, from an American writer, is perhaps the first clue to the existence of modern cockney. One will not discover that speech in the pages of Thomas Hood's

Punch; one will not discover it in Pickwick Papers or Oliver Twist; what one finds there, as Mr. Bernard Shaw has pointed out, is an earlier urban dialect. In Omoo, on the contrary, Melville gives us the modern forms: the *ink* ending for *ing* and the dropped and added aitches. He was almost equally felicitous in rendering the difficult Belfast brogue: his transliteration of *haul* into *harl* is a test of it; and only an accurate ear will thus catch the living tongue. Unlike Ruskin, Melville was not a painter with words, but a musician; and in his maturity, his great passages have a musical structure of their own. In a phrase like "a soft seething foamy lull" he uses the sound of lull, rather than its sense, to convey his meaning; and among the modern poets it is natural to find him turning, later in life, to Shelley and to James Thomson.

Omoo was a rambling book: it had in a formal sense neither beginning nor end; but it had something of the bright immediacy of a sketchbook filled with graphic notes that might be worked into a finished picture. There were no clouds over Melville when he wrote Omoo; even its ugly parts were saturated with sunlight; beachcombing left Melville a little brighter for being scoured by the sand. Smollett had taught him all he needed to write this kind of work, Smollett and Defoe. Omoo had the sharpness, the force, the exaggeration of character which the eighteenth century had in its satiric artists; and every episode was carried off with a dry discretion. With the habit of long verbal practice, Melville watched his listeners: he never overloaded Omoo: he knew where to skip and where to elaborate: he is a writer who knows that one wants everything in a travel book except the tedium and fatigue of actuality. Throughout the narrative, one always feels that Melville has more up his sleeve: one is prepared to believe that he has a hundred Omoos in his bosom: perhaps he had, and at all events it required talent to make us believe so. More and more, his speech cleansed itself of affectations: the direct, vigorous

lingo of the sea, with all its Elizabethan locutions, was doubtless a sound influence in this part of his development: of the
young man who wrote the sublime gibberish in the Lansingburgh newspaper, there is scarcely a trace left. One measures such growth in feet, not in inches: in seven years Melville had not merely renewed his physical body completely:
he had acquired an equally complete literary shape.

In every sense of the word, Omoo is a companion volume
to Typee. It is not merely that the milieu is still these wild,
wooded, mountainous, sun-drenched islands, with their attractive brown inhabitants: it is not simply that as soon as
Melville steps aboard a boat, the deck begins to climb and
fall under one's feet and the smell of pitch and hemp rises to
one's nostrils: it is not merely that this South Sea Prospero,
as Robert Buchanan called him, is a weaver of spells, as full
of happy mischief as a Polynesian maid and as seductive as
a tropical night. In Typee and Omoo, Melville had that
superb aplomb—formed by an athleticism, an inner poise,
a dexterity of hand, a sharpness of eye—which we call
Greek because for a little while the Attic peoples experienced
it as a community; the attitude which Whitman valued as
the sign and seal of the new American. Melville is appreciative; he is humorous; but he is neither a professional
funny man nor a syrupy preserver of glamour. His aplomb
never deserts him. He is always in command. That trait
is the key to his early literary success; it explains the effort-
less accuracy of his descriptions. Such poise, such aplomb,
such confidence, rest on the nicest sort of spiritual and
physiological interplay: blood and muscle form a part of it
as well as mental serenity. We have seen this balance in
our own day, embodied in a young man who flew to Europe
alone. The gesture surrounding this act was the same precious essence that Typee and Omoo give us in the form of
art. I have called this quality youth; but it is what the
Athenians called virtue; and as soon as we depart from it we
are hoary with sin, and there is no health in us.

CHAPTER FOUR: AZZAGEDDI

In 1847 Herman Melville was twenty-eight years old. Omoo had been finished at the end of the previous year; and, in the excitement of finding himself established as an author and recognized as a man of promise, he was casting about for a theme that would more fully evoke his own proper powers. So far he had been living on his material: it was time for his material to get a living from him. He found the theme in Mardi, the vast allegorical romance of Mardi; but before he settled down to it, the friendship or the affection between him and Judge Shaw's daughter, Elizabeth, deepened, and in August, 1847, they were married.

One can only dimly speculate upon what manner of girl Elizabeth Shaw was. There is no reason to think that Melville drew her portrait in Pierre, and the "wife" of the stories he wrote in the fifties is always a conventional feminine foil. The letter she wrote to her mother during the first week of her marriage was dutiful, girlish, commonplace; and ten years later her letters were equally inexpressive and jejune. Her freshness or her amiable temper or her capacity for devotion may have attracted Herman; but more likely, he loved her because he loved her; and there is no need or possibility of explaining that. Certainly, there was no intellectual parity between them, as there was between Hawthorne and his linguistic blue-stocking, Sophia—and Elizabeth had none of his ranting high spirits.

Melville probably worshipped Elizabeth at first, and idolized her beyond all reason; for he loved romantically, and romantic courtship is a heightened and extravagant season even for men of less imagination and hot impulse than Melville. He who wishes to keep that original and etherealized image of his lady should run away from her: when he breaks it, he will feel, Melville later declared, like Pluto snatching his Proserpine, and once the image is broken every fragment will be a reproach. It is the romanticized Circe, and not her victim, who under the spell of marriage turns into an animal, not a swine, of course, but a pea-fowl, grey-feathered and not gorgeous, or a hen, clucking over her chicks and moving only within the limits of the farmyard, or a dove, cooing a little plaintively, unable to awaken the proud strut of the eager, following male, who has wooed once too often.

After an arduous honeymoon, by stage-coach and rail through the mountains of New Hampshire and Vermont, on up through Montreal, and back by Lake Champlain and the Champlain Canal, a rough, jouncing, crowded, distracted sort of journey, and a brief sojourn with Herman's mother at Lansingburgh, they settled down at 103 Fourth Avenue, New York, in company with Melville's brother Allan and a swarm of sisters. Elizabeth Melville has left us a picture of that household and her husband's daily routine; one cannot do better than put it in her own words:

"We breakfast at 8 o'clock, then Herman goes to walk and I fly up to put his room to rights, so that he can sit down to his desk immediately on his return. Then I bid him good-bye, with many charges to be an industrious boy and not upset the inkstand and then flourish the duster, make the bed, etc., in my own room. Then I go downstairs and read the papers a little while, and after that I am ready to sit down to my work—whatever it may be—darning stockings—making or mending for myself or Herman—at all events, I haven't seen a day yet, without *some* sewing or other to do. If I have letters to write, as is the case today, I usually do that first—but whatever I am about I do not much more than get thoroughly engaged in it, than ding-

dong goes the bell for luncheon. This is half-past 12 o'clock
—by this time we must expect callers, and so must be
dressed immediately after lunch. Then Herman insists upon
taking a walk of an hour's length at least. So unless I can
have rain or snow for an excuse, I usually sally out and
make a pedestrian tour a mile or two down Broadway. By
the time I come home it is two o'clock and after, and then I
must make myself look as bewitchingly as possible to meet
Herman at dinner. . . . At four we dine, and after dinner
is over, Herman and I come up to our room and enjoy a
cosy chat for an hour or so—or he reads me some of the
chapters he has been writing in the day. Then he goes down
town for a walk, looks at the papers in the reading room,
etc., and returns about half past seven or eight. Then my
work or book is laid aside, and as he does not use his eyes
but very little by candlelight, I either read to him, or take a
hand at whist for his amusement, or he listens to our reading
or conversation as best pleases him. For we all collect in the
parlour in the evening, and one of us reads aloud for the
benefit of the whole. Then we retire very early—at 10
o'clock we all disperse."

Admirable Elizabeth! In your direct, simple way you
have told us everything we need to know. You are busy and
happy: you have adapted yourself, with the aid of such
extra space as was once enjoyed by all families of moderate
means, to the clan of sisters and brothers and cousins and
aunts that make up the provincial family of the old kind:
you make it possible for Herman to economize all his energies, and go ahead, with gentle resolution, at his work.
What a beautifully divided day it is: Herman working
behind closed doors, and you yourself, very cheerful and
attentive and industrious, cocking your ear occasionally
for sounds of restlessness. Then the little breaks: the so-
ciability and—do you not perhaps overestimate a lover's
capacity for conversation?—the hour or two of cosy chat.
Already Herman's eyes must be saved, and you are there

to save them. True: he has devoted sisters, too; and they are very nice in their way, all such a jolly, helpful, numerous family. People are a little more punctilious here than they are in New England; that is part of the European air which New York somehow preserves; the men bow lower, make prettier compliments, and get drunk more often. When you go to a dance without Herman, you are treated as one of the sisters, and by virtue of your supposed maidenhood, you are quite a belle again. Herman doesn't like dances and parties overmuch: the late hours and the late suppers take the edge off his writing next morning: he finds it hard to begin and is a little cross and irritable: but what difference does that make? You would give up all these frivolities for such a shapely, manly, courteous, thoughtful man: if he will stay by, the world may gaily pass.

You are not alone, Elizabeth Melville: Mrs. Darwin feels the same way, too; so, with less satisfaction and complaisance, does Jane Carlyle; so, presently, does Sophia Tolstoy. But such helpfulness and affectionate sacrifice cannot last forever. Children will come; you and your fine, high-spirited boy will see less and less of each other: you will interrupt his deepest intimacy with concern for the baby's bottle. You will wonder, when you are alone, whether you have any right to thrust these burdens on his shoulders: you will feel that the world is a little cruel, and your being joined to this lover who is so strange and remote, this affectionate man who is also so exacting, is uneasy bewilderment. . . . I do not understand you, Elizabeth Melville? Reflect again carefully: do not be afraid of your feelings: some of them are still visible in the fading ink of old letters; and some of them are in your heart, because you are a human being. If you do not resent sharing Herman so much with his family, you are a greater angel than you should be.

"How much," wrote Melville in Pierre, "that goes to make up the deliciousness of a wife already lies in the sister." Do you sometimes feel, Elizabeth, that Herman has only added another sister to the family; that Lizzie is now but a step away from Kate and Helen and Augusta? It is not that he loves them too tenderly, but that he worships you too much, or, in alternate fits, is far too indifferent and puts you at a sisterly distance from him. Do you feel that he will never get near enough to you, will never appreciate the you that is, although he may be disappointed because of the you that is not? He accepts you, of course, accepts you tenderly: you darn his stockings and sew new tapes in his drawers when he breaks them: you put up patiently with the languors and irritabilities that follow an intense morning at the desk, and at times, you have the power to erase them and make his eyes shine with triumph instead.

But this Herman is not the jovial boy who once played with Fayaway: he has his turns of high spirits, but his humours are a little obscure and beyond you, and his face shades a little with disappointment when he notes that your plain, literal mind does not follow his sallies. He is growing beyond you: in the very act of writing Mardi, Elizabeth ceases to exist: the book is haunted by a phantom called Yillah: a Yillah who will never mend socks or replace broken tapes. Some day he will learn, perhaps, that women, like whales, are objects of natural history; and when he is weary with his wandering and his quests, he will not despise your tired arms: one of the best and tenderest of his poems, The Return of the Sire de Nesle, will be addressed to you. But before that happens, you have both a long hard journey before you. Courage! The burden of writing these books will not fall upon his shoulders alone.

2

The spring of 1848 was full of turbulence all over the world. In Paris the red flag was raised, and in a froth of oratory men dreamed and fought at the barricades and died. Germany seemed on the verge of a republic, and the frag-

ments of Italy made convulsive movements; with these and
many other events fomenting, chaos and disorder and perhaps some glorious new society, based on universal suf-
frage and national workshops and the commune, seemed
about to be instituted. One looks back with a tolerant smile
to those days, days when a formula seemed as powerful as a
siege gun, when the ballot seemed by itself a guarantee of
order and justice in human affairs. The effect of the French
uprising was the pastry cook's Empire of Napoleon III;
the final result of the German revolution was the brutal,
semi-feudal industrialism of Germany after 1870. "I should
not be surprised," said Melville's Redburn, "if there were
more words than things in the world"; and in 1848 there
was surely far more Peace, Progress, Political Perfection,
Liberty, Fraternity, Equality, in the mouths and minds of
men, than there was in political society.

The contrasts and absurdities in all our institutions made
1848 a great year for satirical observation, so long as the
observer could remain far enough away from humanity to
laugh at its errors rather than weep, as Alexander Herzen
did, over its sins, and over the dark collapse of hope and
ambition that followed. Melville, fortunately, lived in America: its own 1848, namely, the Civil War, was just thirteen
years away; and the book which began in 1847 as an adventurous idyll of the South Seas, poetically conceived with
a remote allegorical quest running through it, came to an
end as a savage parody of the whole economy of Western
Civilization, and its lofty Christian professions.

Just as Melville was finishing Mardi, this eventful spring,
Elizabeth Melville conceived: and the summer months that
followed were devoted to final preparations for the book and
the baby. Augusta worked hard to copy Melville's manuscript for the press; and with even greater zeal she conned
the genealogical tables for a name for the infant—having
settled in her mind that it would be a boy. Her zeal was

justified. When in February, 1849, Herman Melville became a father, Augusta's name for the child prevailed: it
was Malcolm.

If Mardi throws any light upon Melville's personal relations at all, I think one must acknowledge that the light is a
happy one. The true test of a writer's feelings is not what
he says: it is the way in which he says it. Mr. Chesterton
once happily pointed out that in Byron's most melancholy
lines the spontaneous gallop and thud of Byron's metre
betrays his sanguine feelings; and I think one can say much
the same thing of Mardi. There are large sections of Mardi
that are written with a sort of sleepy ease; the words flow
so languorously from Melville's pen that he floats along
with them and lets them carry him where they will; the
rhythm is not always subtle; the voice lacks modulation and
change of tempo: it lulls one like the even murmur of the
ocean at low tide on a beach. When lovers are conversing on
a summer's afternoon, it does not occur to them that any
one could call such heavenly intimacy tedious: what they
would like to prolong for eternity one who did not share
their mood would not tolerate for five minutes. And it is so
in Mardi. Melville is so happy that he does not notice one
cannot always share the emotion with him.

Whether the beginning of Mardi was set up in type
before the end was reached one cannot surely tell: Melville
made this happen to Pierre, and explained what a handicap
this method of production was to the writer, since it did not
allow him to work over the earlier parts and create a unity.
If the slowness of hand-setting and the customs of the market made Melville actually do this, it would explain a certain
inconsequentialness in Mardi as due to external circumstances, and not to Melville's inability to master his material
and criticize his workmanship. But certainly pressure and
speed seem absent from Mardi: a soft tropical breeze is all
that carries the story on, and more than once this drops to a
dead calm. Financial difficulties were not yet pressing in

Melville's domicile when he began Mardi: no baby demanded care: no breach had opened between the writer and his audience: Elizabeth's approaching confinement doubtless renewed some of the tender, pre-nuptial feeling: these are all fairly objective facts; and if one doubt them, the repeated, even cadences of Mardi, as of a sleeping bosom, slowly heaving and falling, have the value of corroborative testimony.

3

Mardi has been forgotten while lesser books have flourished. Let us see how much we have missed. It is not a perfect book; but it has something in it that defies death; and that something is the presence of Melville himself, now arriving at maturity, a traveller who has gone to the ends of the earth, and has not left his head smugly at home—a vehement, clear-witted, copious, steady-eyed, jocose, untamable man. The poise and completeness of Typee is gone: much as we prize youth, the cost of continuing that balance, without a fresh integration, is arrested development; and Melville went on. Mardi has all the promise of imperfection.

The story begins on the plane of fact. We are off! The courses and topsails are set, and the Arcturion is sailing dead before an equatorial breeze in search of the whale. Overwhelmed by the monotony, the teller of the story escapes at night in a whaleboat, in the company of a faithful, taciturn sailor of the old Norse breed, Jarl. The sun shines; the bonetas and sharks swim around the boat; the devil-fish undulate repulsively in the deeper waters below; or at night the phosphorescence spreads across the surface, and the hand dropped over the side ripples through fluent silver; they sail on and on, making for distant islands, tormented by the lack of water and the unyielding sun, and worse still, by a dead calm, when the grey firmament of sky collapses into the grey firmament of water. When at long last they encounter a sail, it turns out to be an apparently deserted brigantine: they board it and find themselves, after creepy suspicions, in the company of a South Sea Islander and his wife, the sole survivors of a Christian crew.

We are still on the plane of physical adventure: Annatoo is an amusing termagant, and when Samoa, her husband, amputates his own arm by the most primitive surgery and cautery, Melville might still be merely describing curious South Sea customs, as in Omoo. In a little space all this changes. The brigantine is lost, and the shipwrecked sailors, again in a whaleboat, come upon a South Sea priest, with Seven Sons, who is carrying a white maiden with golden hair and blue eyes, Yillah, to another island. The hero rescues Yillah from the priest, and kills him to make good his escape. With Yillah's advent, the atmosphere changes: a perfumed mist of unreality creeps over the sea from Mardi itself.

Yillah's mind is a spider-web of myth, in which the butterfly of her spirit has been caught: she has dim recollections of being born in Amma and spirited away, as a child, to Oroolia, the Island of Delights, somewhere in the paradisial archipelago of the Polynesians. The waters of Oroolia turned her olive skin to white and tinged her hair with gold: she was transformed into the blossom of a vine, and hung there in a trance, until the blossom was snapped from its stem and borne away on the ocean, drifting to the island of Amma, where it was taken over by the priest. The whaleboat floats on; the sea-fowls fly above it; the fish dart and ripple and flash in the water: Yillah's own dreams of her past fade into the sweet vision that had haunted the hero's earliest thoughts. As love draws near, her divinity languishes: "Love sometimes induced me to prop my failing divinity, though it was I myself who had undermined it." The Yillah of dream dwarfs into the Yillah of reality.

At last the voyagers reach the coast of Mardi, and, in the guise of the Sun-God, Taji, the hero announces himself to an assemblage of Mardian chiefs. His ruse is accepted; and for a brief while Taji finds himself in Eden.

The wide blue lagoon, the froth of breakers at the reef, the milk-white smoke curling up from the volcanoes of Mardi: the nights of starry entrancement, day dawning with Yillah, breaking along the waking face, peeping out from her languid lids, then shining in longer glances, till, like the sun, up comes the soul. All beauty and beatitude Taji finds in Mardi. With Yillah for company, he retires to a wooded islet, fringed with palm trees, watered by brooks. Near by, in Odo, the kingdom of Media, is a harder world, where helots toil at brutal tasks; but for a time Taji is happy with his Yillah. It all ends. One day Taji finds her arbour vacant; she does not return; the world becomes sour and empty; and Taji resolves to rove through Mardi in search of Yillah.

With the disappearance of Yillah, the break from the actual becomes complete: Yillah is a phantom, and Taji follows Yillah, in the company of Media, the king, Mohi or Braidbeard, the historian, Babbalanja, the philosopher, and Yoomy, the poet, through all the kingdoms and principalities of Mardi. Where has Yillah flown, and where is the peace that she gave?

4

Had Melville closed Mardi at this point the book would, I think, have been hailed with delight as another, a purer, Typee: he need only have searched a little farther and finally recaptured Yillah, wiping out the last trace of ethereality and converting her into a less primitive Fayaway—the stolen daughter of a highly respectable missionary, perhaps—to have delighted his contemporaries with the sweet concoction. This was the Melville they knew and could understand. The language of Typee had become freer and in a limited sense more poetical: but that only accentuated the banquet of sunrises and sunsets and starry nights and palm groves and maidens more luscious than Ingres' odalisques, mixed with an occasional bite of tart adventure or terror—

almonds or olives—a banquet of unalloyed deliciousness after the tame domestic lamplight and the corseted and petticoated heroines of Victorian fiction, the Janes, the Doras, and even for that matter the Beckys who were coming into fashion. The exotic has its glamour, and somehow, those distant Polynesian maidens of Melville were a little nearer, a little more thinkable in the flesh, than the Annabel Lees of Poe, however near Adair and Oroolia might be to Aiden.

But Melville had grown. He started from the South Seas in order to have familiar ground to spring from; he had no intention of merely amusing his public with a less literal Omoo. Mardi is the world, and Yillah is not a maiden but the spiritual life, who was brought to Mardi and given a home there, but treacherously treated by the fates: the priests took charge of her and sought to sacrifice her for their own purposes. Taji slew the priest, and though the quest of Yillah is as tormenting as the possession of her is peaceful and replete with happiness, still, he would slay the priest again, if necessary, to bring her back. Once Melville sets out on this quest, the South Seas of the Acushnet and the Julia and Kory-Kory and Dr. Long Ghost vanish: these tropical isles are a counterpart of the Western world, and in a thousand wild metaphors and noble tropes, all the triumphs and follies of our civilization parade again before the mind, clearer because of the disguise, more immediate because they are so distant. Evil has entered Melville's paradise; evil, that "chronic malady of the universe" which, "checked in one place, breaks forth in another," and the knowledge of good and evil is the beginning of his own sad wisdom.

Now witness Melville as he becomes conscious of life and history and the recesses of his own spirit. Not for nothing were those brooding hours on the maintop; not for nothing those lonely walks through the crowds of Broadway, smiles, sunshades, shop-fronts, dashing rigs, or, returning in the evening from the reading-room, with the stale smell of wine coming up from the wine-cellars, the prostitutes already ogling in front of the blue and red witches' bowls in the apothecaries' shops; not for nothing was it that he had exchanged calls with urbane acquaintances of the family and succumbed to the customs of Pimminee, where the Tapparians, in lieu of brains, carry a drop or two of attar of roses in the corner of their craniums, and are the victims of two incurable maladies, stone in the heart and ossification of the head—with all their fripperies, fopperies, finesses. But I am beginning to anticipate Taji's Mardian discoveries. Let us retrace our steps and survey this Mardi with Melville.

The isles of Mardi are easily recognized: Dominora, where King Bello lives, is Great Britain: Vivenza is the United States: all the historic states and empires are reduced, by translation into Mardian terms, to something like their proper human proportions. Swift had used this method once; and Melville employed it with little less effect, particularly when he worked out the parallels carefully and retained the South Sea atmosphere. In the guise of king, poet, philosopher, Melville became a philosophic commentator, retelling the story of Europe and Christianity and faith and doubt and religion and science, exploring time, delivering himself through his dreams, disclosing, in Babbalanja's demonic inner man, Azzageddi, his own ultimate perceptions. It is almost impossible to convey the vastness, the variety, the genuine wealth of these pictures. I will only bring a sample or two of his ore to the surface; the whole book is veined with it.

Time and Eternity come before Melville. "And that which long endures must long have remained in the germ. And duration is not of the future but of the past; and eternity is eternal; because it has been; and though a strong new monument be builded today, it only is lasting because its blocks are as old as the sun. It is not the Pyramids that are ancient, but the eternal granite of which they are made; which had been equally ancient though yet in the quarry. For to make an eternity, we must build with eternities; whence the vanity of the cry for anything alike durable and new, and the folly of the reproach—your granite hath come from the old-fashioned hills." His copious mind swarms to the idea; he throws fuel on it from a hundred sources. "No fine firm fabric ever yet grew like a gourd. Nero's House of Gold was not raised in a day; nor the Mexican House of the Sun; nor the Alhambra, nor the Escurial; nor Titus' Amphitheatre; nor the Illinois Mounds; nor Diana's great columns at Ephesus; nor Pompey's proud Pillar; nor the Parthenon; nor the Altar of Belus; nor Stonehenge; nor Solomon's Temple; nor Tadmore's Towers; nor Susa's bastions, nor Persepolis and its pediments."

So he goes, sentence by sentence, till he has heaped into this fiery furnace of death-defying things the grottos of Elephanta and the Giants' Causeway and the Grampian Hills and a score of other examples. And at last: "If time was when this great quarry of Assyrias and Rome was not extent; then, time must have been when the whole material universe lived in its Dark Ages; yea, when the ineffable Silence, proceeding from its unimaginable remoteness, espied it as an isle of the sea. And herein is no derogation. For the immeasurable altitude is not heightened by the arches of Mahomet's heavens; and were all space a vacuum, yet it would be a fulness, for to Himself his own Universe is He. Thus deeper and deeper into Time's endless tunnel does the winged soul, like a night-hawk, wend her wild way, and finds eternities before and behind; and her last limit is her everlasting beginning."

When Melville's French critics called Mardi Rabelaisian, and when the English critics mentioned Sir Thomas Browne, one group was thinking of these solemn, cadenced sentences, piling up phrases swollen with sound like the great stops of an organ; while the other referred to these prodigious catalogues and collocations. In Mardi Melville keeps ideas in the air like a juggler's balls; the images pass and repass, making in those agile hands a single pattern. Satire is only one of the moods of Mardi: poetic reverie, as in the chapter on Dreams, and philosophic reflection, thread their ways in and out these scattered islands of sense. Far more deeply and authentically than the author of Eureka, Melville had anticipations of the drift of modern science and philosophy. He accepts the notion of evolution, which Chambers had popularized, saying, "Let us be content with the theology in the grass and the flower, in seed-time and harvest." And Babbalanja says: "I live while consciousness is not mine, while to all appearances I am a clod. And may not this same state of being, though but alternate with me, be continually that of many dumb, passive objects we so carelessly regard. Trust me, there are more things alive than those that crawl, or fly, or swim. Think you, my lord, there is no sensation in being a tree? feeling the sap in one's boughs, the breeze in one's foliage? Think you it is nothing to be a world? one of a herd, bison-like, wending its way across boundless meadows of ether? In the sight of a fowl, that sees not our souls, what are our own tokens of animation? That we move, make a noise, have organs, pulses, and are compounded of fluids and solids. And all these are in this Mardi as a unit."

After much exploration and much disappointment and much wine and witty conversation to pass the time between, the travellers come finally to Serenia, where the dictates of Alma—Christ—are embodied in the polity. Here they find their quest come to an end, or rather, it has lost all reason, "not because what we sought is found; but that I now possess all which may be had of what I sought in Mardi." Babbalanja tarries there, to grow wiser; he counsels Media to return to Odo and transplant to it the amaranths and myrtles of Serenia, letting no man weep that he may laugh, and no man toil too hard that the king may be idle: "Abdicate thy throne but still retain thy sceptre. None need a king, but many need a ruler." As for Taji, he will never find Yillah: he may search further on the still unexplored islands; but when all is seen he must "return, and find thy Yillah here."

On the travellers sail. Their canoe is followed by the three avenging brothers who have lurked in their wake all through the adventure, bent upon taking Taji's life; whilst the three messengers of Hautia, the enchantress queen, with the iris, the venus-car, and a flower white as alabaster, with forked and crimson stamens, trembling like flame, bade the voyagers follow them to Hautia's bower. They follow, three pilot-fish in advance, three ravenous sharks astern. In some wild way, Hautia, queen of the senses, has made a captive of Yillah, and into some one of her black-eyed maids the blue-eyed one has been transformed. But Taji could not find Yillah: Hautia claims him, with wine and flowers and love: she offers him all the treasures of the world, Health, Wealth, Long Life, and the Last Hope of Man, if he will take her hands and dive with her into the crystal grotto: she will make it easy to forget Yillah: he will lose his past, and learn to love the living, not the dead. In vain she pleads. "Better to me, oh Hautia, all the bitterness of my buried dead, than all the sweets of life thou canst bestow; even were it eternal."

All is over: the adventurers must go back to Serenia; they must deliver Taji from Hautia, and save him from the avenging sons of the priest, sin, conscience, remorse. Taji will not go. " 'And why put back? Is a life of dying worth living o'er again? Let *me*, then, be the unreturning wanderer. The helm! By Oro, I will steel my fate. Mardi, farewell!'

" 'Nay, Taji, commit not the last, last crime!' cried Yoomy.

" 'He's seized the helm! Eternity is in his eye! Yoomy, for our lives we must now swim.' . . .

"Now I am my own soul's emperor; and my first act is

abdication. Hail, realm of shades! and turning my prow into the racing tide, which seized me like a hand omnipotent, I darted through.

"Churned in foam, that outer ocean lashed the clouds; and straight in my wake, headlong dashed a shallop, three fixed spectres leaning o'er its prow; three arrows poising.

"And thus, pursuers and pursued flew on, over an endless sea."

5

Mardi is strong enough as a satire and a criticism of life to stand a frank admission of its weaknesses; and I shall not try to conceal them. The book starts about to be one thing; it presently becomes another; and before Mardi is entirely explored it becomes a third: the adventure, the strange scenes and personages, the philosophic reflection, the satire, all accrete together rather than form a single intermingled whole. Taji, who begins as the hero and narrator, takes a smaller and smaller part in the actual dialogue; presently the first person becomes the third, and Taji emerges at the end out of the shadow of silence. The reader who expected another Omoo was disappointed once the first quarter of the story was over; the reader who might have welcomed the dialogues, the political moralizings, the epigrams, was put off a little by the original sea-yarn.

This is not all. The satire at its best achieves its end by a delicate parody of actuality, as in the scene where Melville takes off a session of the United States Congress; but sometimes Melville's invention flags, and he repeats actual history, with altered names, instead of distorting, magnifying, transposing. Verbally, his touch is almost as uncertain: at times he drops into obvious metres, only to rise into passages of prose that have far greater claim to be set off as verse than any of Yoomy's stanzas. The verses interspersed in these pages are worthy of the poet laureate that Yoomy is supposed to be; and that is the best one can say about them. When Taji sits down with the five-and-twenty kings, the invocation to wine is about at the level of Peacock's drinking songs: and the poorest of Yoomy's songs are poetry only by typographic courtesy. These are all faults; and not little ones; but what means infinitely more is the fact that a brave, vigorous spirit presides over Mardi, appraising all the evil and injustice and superstition and ugliness in the world—as they masquerade under the guise of religion and patriotism and economic prudence and political necessity. In Mardi, one begins to feel Melville's range, and his depth.

In this satiric fantasy, Melville had not the sure touch he later achieved in Moby-Dick: but for all that, his thoughts exploded in a succession of great rockets and Roman candles and flag-bombs; and the spectacle was a dazzling and beautiful one. Such wit, such humour, such starry intelligence, such wide knowledge, such resolute diving, were not known in American literature before; and they are rare enough in any literature. Much though we value Melville's great American contemporaries, he had something to give in Mardi that is beyond their reach: we will search Emerson in vain for anything like the Antiquarian's catalogue; we will run through Hawthorne's notebooks without finding anything like the description of authorship in the chapter on Lombardo. The Literary World said that the public would discover in the author of Mardi a capital essayist, at least, in addition to the fascinating novelist and painter of sea-life, and find that the author had "original powers of high order"—and the praise was accurate and just.

Mardi performed a more important work for its author than it did for its immediate readers: it disclosed to him the nature of his own demon—that deeper other half whom Babbalanja called Azzageddi. Melville's thoughts at this period paralleled each other in somewhat unrelated layers. There was a Babbalanja who reflected the ideas of his own time and country, who was a thoughtful Christian, a loyal republican, a solid provincial, who met adversity with a jest or a wry smile, who drank brandy with Mr. Duyckinck, and paid his respects with genteel punctuality to all the Gansevoorts and Melvilles and Shaws. This Melville never entirely disappeared. The pious man who wanted to return to Serenia made a pilgrimage to the Holy Land: and when the Civil War came, Melville accepted without question the doctrine of a single, indivisible nation, as an unshakable postulate. In this aspect of Melville there was something correct and limited, characteristics whose chief advantage was that they kept him within speaking distance of his contemporaries. In Mardi, however, Melville discovered a deeper self: the unconscious Melville was not a man of his time, and he often had intuitions which undermined or destroyed his more commonplace convictions. This deeper Melville did not altogether supplant the man of convention: they do not represent several and successive phases of growth: but, as Melville suggested in Moby-Dick, they represented aspects of a cycle which one goes through again and again, never reaching a terminus, because there is in a proper sense no terminus, no ultimate point of rest, or resolution.

Now it is Melville as Azzageddi, the demon who captures and speaks from within the man, who interests us. The pious Christian is troubled by the problems of physical immortality; but Azzageddi says, thinking how even the sublimest thoughts fade and are lost, "If the fogs of some few years can make soul linked to matter naught, how can the unhoused spirit hope to live when mildewed in the damps of death." The sociable townsman continues to correspond with Mr. Duyckinck and respect his judgment; but Azzageddi says: "All round me, my fellow-men are new grafting their vines and dwelling in flourishing arbors; while I am forever pruning mine, till it becomes but a stump. Yet in this pruning I will persist; I will not add, I will diminish; I will trim myself down to the standard of what is unchangeably true. Day by day I drop off my redundancies; ere long I shall have stripped my ribs; when I die, they will but bury my spine. I may have come to the Penultimate . . . but where is the Ultimate?"

From Azzageddi's mouth the deepest perceptions of Melville's spirit came forth first, in the form of jests and demonic laughter. Azzageddi was free in the only unqualified sense of freedom: he was irresponsible. Nothing will daunt him, no opposition to his conscious habits, statements, prejudices, conventions will prevent him from declaring himself. He was Melville, shorn of everything that might make him circumspect and limited, a skeleton facing the world with its ultimate grin. Azzageddi brought Melville to his supreme triumph in Moby-Dick, and plunged him into temporary disaster in Pierre; for he worked out of the bottomless parts of Melville's unconscious, and when he was given free line, he might haul up anything out of those depths—a chest of gold or a white whale or a green corpse. His appearance in Mardi was the first sign of Melville's maturity; and the attempt of the world to rebuff and castigate and repress Azzageddi was excellent proof that Melville had found within himself something worth the saying. Mardi was Melville's spiritual Omoo. It gave him the courage to be an intellectual rover, and to scorn the easy domesticities in which thought reposes, and snores.

"There are those who falter in the common tongue, because they think in another; and these are accounted stutterers and stammerers," wrote Melville in Mardi. Melville was plainly aware of the fact that he was now acquiring a new language, not a new set of weaknesses: his inward eye was now keeping pace in its growth with his outward one: he was at last achieving that genuine bi-focal vision wherein "matter" and "spirit" united to give depth and perspective to the world which only through joint effort do they effectually behold. Already, he had eternity in his eye. The easy triumph was no longer for him. Clay crumbled, marble chipped, wood rotted, granite eroded: all the common materials out of which monuments and civilizations are made

lie under the doom of a fatal metamorphosis: Melville sought
a truth, no matter how infinitely small in quantity and precious, which, like radium, would undergo time and change
and emanate energy without losing perceptibly its bulk or
its quality. It was useless to tell him that there were no ultimate truths; that itself was perhaps the ultimate truth which
he sought. If Mardi were not ready for this search, he would
go it alone—and be the unreturning one. No grey shroud
of ocean, with threat of storm and sleet, would keep him
from setting out for that ultimate destination.

6

"Had I not written and published Mardi," wrote Melville
to Mr. Evert Duyckinck in 1849, "in all likelihood I would
not be as wise as I am now, or may be. For that thing was
stabbed *at* (I do not say *through*) and therefore I am the
wiser for it."

The truth is that Mardi got a mixed reception; whereas
except for the missionaries and the unco guid his first two
books had been hailed and acclaimed with a heartiness that
is rarely accorded to a new author with no well-defined connections. Mardi was praised in the Revue des Deux Mondes,
and damned as a rubbishing parody in Blackwood's; the
Democratic Review said that it compared to Typee and
Omoo as a cartoon of Raphael to a seven-by-nine sketch of
a sylvan lake; but the Dublin University Magazine found
it one of the saddest, most melancholy, most deplorable and
humiliating perversions of genius of a high order in the
English language. So it went, hot and cold, huzzas and
hisses.

A book that could evoke such different responses must
either be a highly original book or a many-sided one; and
Mardi has, it seems to me, both qualities. It was, there is
reason to believe, the wealth, the profusion, the diversity of
ideas in Mardi that brought down on Melville the irritation
of contemporary critics: instead of retiring into after-

dinner lethargy with Melville's smoking, calabash-drinking philosopher and king and poet, they were stirred into unaccustomed mental activity. They resented that: they resented above all the fact that Melville played with ideas. One could not be sure whether he was fooling with the ideas or fooling with the audience; besides, respectable ideas should not be played with: there is a time and a place for everything. In the South Seas one expects to fondle brown maidens: in a library, one locks the door on maidens and wrestles with ideas. Their lips were whetted for another Fayaway: she evaporated into Yillah: and Yillah vanished, leaving only a gritty taste in the mouth, criticism, criticism of Christianity, politics, morality, things that gentlemen prefer to take, if at all, in medical capsules, not as food.

Am I wrong in thinking that Mardi has been damned for its virtues? The idea is all the more plausible because for more than a generation, during which Melville's work almost disappeared from critical notice, Melville was reprobated, when he was noticed at all, for becoming interested in abstruse philosophy and for writing extravagantly. The burden of this criticism was that a writer of South Sea romances had better leave Plato and Spinoza alone, and get his opinion of the universe from professional purveyors, or rather, not be troubled by such foreign interests. This attempt to keep Melville in his place was absurd enough in itself; but it led to further stupidities, far more deplorable in character. "As early as 1848," wrote an historian of American literature in 1903, "the quasi-speculative romance entitled Mardi gave premonition of aberration and of the eventual frustration of a promising career." This criticism is nonsense, and libellous nonsense at that: the aberration it refers to did not exist in Melville but in the historian himself. At the very outset of his career, Melville found himself confronting a similar opaqueness, blank as a wall, in his own contemporaries. One remembers Macaulay's withering condescension over Plato and the scholastic philosophers; and one realizes that any view of life which did not immediately sanction the pragmatism of the nineteenth century was bound to seem an aberration for those who regarded the local values of the time as ultimates. Melville's "aberration" was his great intellectual distinction: none of his contemporaries had such a broad base in the fundamental activities of the time, and yet rose so loftily above them. He did not rebel against his milieu; like Thoreau, he reached outside of it, and grew beyond it, taking out of the very environment from which he escaped the necessary materials for his own development.

The scene is now set: the struggle in which Melville is to participate is defined. It is a struggle between a plastic, conventional self, moulded in the fashion of his fellow citizens and fellow writers, and a hard, defiant, adamantine self that springs out of his deepest consciousness of life, and is ready to assault, not merely human conventions, but the high gods themselves. In a conflict between his career and his family duties, between pot-boiling and his maturest literary aims, this drama externalizes itself: it is present in the man, and it is present in his outward relationships. Let us make no mistake about it: Melville was not a writer of romances: it was a mere accident of history that turned the world's attention to him through the charm and tropical radiance of the South Sea adventures. Herman Melville was a thinker, in the sense that Dante was a thinker, who clothed his thoughts in poetic vision. That thought and vision was one of the most important things the century produced. All honour, then, to the few critics who appreciated Mardi when it appeared: for Melville had a greater work in store; and it was out of the freedom and intellectual audacity acquired in writing Mardi, out of the discovery of his Azzageddi, that he achieved the strength to attack it.

WE RETURN to Herman Melville's daily life. In January, 1849, Mrs. Melville went up to Boston to live with her mother and await her confinement. At the end of January the last proof-sheets of Mardi were corrected; in the middle of February Malcolm was born. With the coming of the baby, Melville must have felt a certain tightening of responsibility. One knows very little about the economic conditions under which Melville lived during the first years of his marriage, or to what extent Allan may have carried a good part of the burden of the household. But early in 1849 Melville must have begun to write Redburn, which was a potboiler; and before Redburn was printed he wrote, with greater strength and fuller powers, having probably recovered by that time from the strain of writing Mardi, the masterful account of navy life in White-Jacket.

We now have a chance to watch Melville at work under every disadvantage: the distraction of a household with a young baby, the necessity to make a living, and to do this promptly, the handicap of having to produce something on the level of his audience. If there are flaws in the man, they should come out under these conditions. If he has no sense of reality, he will not know how to meet them; if anything has lurked under the surface of his life, it will rise, like dead fish in poisoned water.

2

In Redburn, Melville went back to his youth and traced his feelings about life and his experiences up to his eighteenth year. The book is autobiography, with only the faintest disguises: Bleecker Street becomes Greenwich Street, and the other changes are of similar order. Following Mr. Weaver, I have relied upon Melville's account of himself in Redburn in giving a picture of his life in the earlier chapters; for it tallies with all the other independently known facts.

For the first time in Melville's writings, the note of personal disappointment and bitterness appeared. He had, it is true, said in Mardi that the highest happiness known to Mardians was the absence of sorrow, and he had said also, as if to explain his hilarity, that woe is more merry than mirth and only shallow sorrows brought tears. But these observations were not peculiar or original; and they were biographical only in the sense that all a man's thoughts are autobiographical—whether they arise out of his experience or his reading or a passing mood conditioned by the state of his digestion. In Redburn, Melville discloses to us a disappointed boy, who had hopes of education, cultivation, gentility, and who resented the fate that tore these things from his grasp and made him fight for a living in a fighting world. "Claret for boys, port for men," he exclaimed in White-Jacket, is a good rule for travel: Mrs. Glendinning uses the same phrase in another application in Pierre: the words took hold of Melville, and one suspects that in his youth he had had an overdose of port, and had participated in experiences that required a stronger stomach.

Now, for the first time, Melville is conscious of the black maggot within him, deposited as a mere egg in his youth, and growing day by day, nourished by his later disappointments and sorrows and frustrations. Things have begun to go badly: he thinks back without difficulty to times when they were even worse. The physical misery of those early years, the patched clothes, the bad food, the rough treatment of the sailors, the feeling of homelessness, the consciousness of being an Ishmael—all these experiences tallied point by point with the world outside, its cruelty, its misery, its sordidness and vice. These events and sights poisoned life for Melville: he had not realized it at the time, he had certainly not realized it while browsing through his father's books in Lansingburgh, or tramping to school through the wide valleys of the Berkshires or brooding over the calm Pacific seas—but the poison had been slowly working in his bones. Life was not kind. All its hints of kindness, its proffers, its affected politenesses were shams. He had married a divine creature—and she was nearest him when she mended his stockings. The books that he wrote fared best when they revealed least of the author and his deepest thoughts. He wanted something central and solid in life, a house, a family, a sense of continuity and security for his future work—and the baby was an expense, the future was a blank, and instead of being able to plan another Mardi, he must hastily improvise a salable article. "It is not with a hollow purse as with a hollow balloon—for a hollow purse makes the poet *sink*—witness 'Mardi.' "

"When a poor devil writes with duns all around him, and looking over the back of his chair, and perching on his pen, and dancing in his inkstand—like the Devils about St. Anthony—what can you expect of that poor devil? What but a beggarly Redburn?" So Melville wrote to Mr. Duyckinck in December, 1849. Those were the words of a harassed man. Redburn, recalling the cruel memories of his youth, was also the first bitter cry of his maturity.

We must not, however, take Melville's disappointment at its face value. On its level, Redburn is a sound, well-written book. Mr. John Masefield has singled it out among Melville's books, after Moby-Dick; Mr. Van Wyck Brooks has seconded his judgment: with this praise in mind, one cannot dismiss Redburn as contemptuously as Melville himself did. At his lowest stage of strength and confidence, he could not write anything that did not have his signature on every page. The marks of haste in Redburn are in its simplicity and its reliance upon memory: the reflective and critical passages, which are so copious in Melville's other books, scarcely appear in Redburn. He wrote about a boy's consciousness of the world, with a boy's amazement at its cruelty and hard-heartedness, even as he recalled a boy's confusion when he was placed in the midst of a strange institution like a gambling-house, something outside book, memory or dream. The captain of the ship will not chat with Redburn: Redburn thinks him no gentleman! Redburn is summarily booted out of a Liverpool club when he intrudes: these English, thinks Redburn, have no manners!

These reflections are just and true; but they are true and just by the criterion of a boy's world, which has not yet learned the pragmatic justification of lies, cheats, hypocrisies, and hard-heartedness. "Unless ye be as little children, ye shall not enter the Kingdom of Heaven." The kingdom of heaven is this naïve world, where lies are lies, even if they save one's face; where cruelty is cruelty, even if it be the custom of the club. To treat human beings as human beings, and not as counters, tools, conveniences, is one of the ultimate efforts of morality; but half the practices of society are, from this point of view, definitely immoral. In Redburn, Melville found himself treated, not with respect to his character and needs and spiritual wants: he found himself treated like any other pauper: put to work and told to keep out of sight. He never forgot that lesson; for, in more subtle and various ways, society kept on dinning it into him. If, when he was a sailor-boy, he was not supposed to converse freely with the captain, after he had written Typee he was not supposed to hold conversations with Plato or Sir Thomas Browne. But he was a man! Society denied it; a sailor, yes, a South Sea adventurer, yes, that too: but a boy, a sailor, a South Sea adventurer always, not a brooding, pondering, philosophic, imaginative man, whose further developments lay in seas unvisited by whalers or Captain Cooks.

"We have had vast developments of parts of men," wrote Melville in Mardi, in words that anticipated Thoreau and Whitman, and show his kinship with them, "not of any wholes. Before a full-developed man, Mardi would fall down and worship." It was the consciousness of being clipped, deformed, degraded, that made Melville bitter: circumstances had done this to him as a boy, and now, with duns standing over him, it was doing the same trick in his manhood. Better be a full Polynesian, as large as a native can grow, than be the deformed creature who accommodates himself to success in business or letters.

But Redburn is not primarily a book written about a grievance: it is a narrative of a boy's trip to sea, an honest narrative, with none of the mildewed rainbows and lily-livered romanticism that usually characterize such efforts. As so often happens with mere decent veracity, Redburn, too, was denounced by one of its contemporary critics as "outrageously improbable," and though the brutality, vice, and misery it pictured were certainly outrageous, there was nothing at all improbable about it. The book, for all its boyish directness, has the wry humour of the grown man, reflecting on his callowness, and the characters it presents are surprisingly realized—surprisingly because one doubts if Melville spent much pains on them. When one compares Redburn to a much more elaborate work, like Two Years Before the Mast, one discovers at once where Melville's specific talents lay. While Dana wrote directly and straightforwardly, he was not a creator of character, and he had no gift of selection: in order to realize the sea, he scatters tackle, blocks, mainsails, booms, compasses, bulwarks, bulkheads on every page of the narrative: one is perpetually stumbling over some recondite nautical term which Dana had mastered, and, like a true landsman, hastened to exhibit. Two Years Before the Mast sounds like a Bluejacket's Manual.

Now, Melville, when he wrote Redburn, had seen far more of the sea than Dana had; and since it was impossible to work a sailing-ship without naming every article of its gear and tackle, he knew the names and uses of these things quite as well as Dana did. But in Melville's work the lingo enters incidentally; and one encounters, not the physical ship of the shipwright, but the ship in action, the ship that is part of the sailor's consciousness—in brief, the living ship as contrasted with an abstract compendium of names and relationships. The same is true of the characters. Dana describes his shipmates accurately enough: Melville embodies them. The difference is the difference between a commonplace photograph and a significant portrait. One does not forget Harry or Jackson or Captain Riga or the Negro cook: they live as authentically, within their narrow compass, as Colonel Newcome or Samuel Weller. That is art; and even in his minor passages, Melville was an artist.

Redburn, in sum, showed only a portion of Melville; but he had no reason to be ashamed of it, except for the reason that it fell short of the higher standard he had now set himself, and the maturer art he was now capable of creating. By 1850 twice as many copies of Redburn as of Mardi had been sold, a difference accounted for partly by the difference in bulk and price, but even more, I think, by the preferences of Melville's public. He had accomplished what he set out to do: he had faced his immediate situation and improved it. That Melville was forced to write such a potboiler was bad luck, and nothing to be proud of: but that he met the situation squarely was a mark of his resolution and balance. As long as Melville could fall back upon his adventurous past, he had something to support him, something that was viable in the marketplace. It was only when he had exhausted his accumulated capital, and was forced to mine his ore and smelt it and cast it, all under pressure of financial necessity, that he drew too heavily on his resources. But we must not read back into these earlier years his later difficulties. Redburn was a victory.

3

On the heels of Redburn came White-Jacket, or, the World in a Man-of-War. White-Jacket was the sort of book that Melville could hardly have attempted until he was sure of his capacities as a writer. Although there is more than one adventurous passage in White-Jacket, it is full of sober description and realistic criticism; and it depends for its interest on Melville's own strength of character, his shrewd, quick insight, and his easy, seamanlike way of taking the world, rather than on the glamour of his adventures.

The young writer casts about for interesting materials; the experienced writer knows that no materials are uninteresting if they are capable of being absorbed in the blood, and pumped through all the organs and chambers of a man's being: the more command a writer has of his own resources, the more confident is he of his ability to turn any experience to account. White-Jacket shows, I think, a greater art and control over the material than any of Melville's earlier books: in Typee the art is gracefully unconscious: in White-Jacket it is deliberate. Melville's personal distinction and his own peculiar adventures were subsumed under the jacket itself: he announced the theme in the first chapter, recurred to it from time to time, when he sought to waterproof the jacket, when he rounded the Horn in it, when he tried to dispose of it at auction, and finally when he was blinded by it and lost his hold on the yard-arm. The white jacket gave the narrative a unity without introducing the extraneous mechanism of a plot: it also symbolized his position as a white sheep in the black flock of a man-of-war. Omoo was more fitful and inconsecutive for lack of such a thread; Mardi did not open, like White-Jacket, on the theme with which it closed. Like Redburn, White-Jacket was written under pressure; but by now Melville knew his business. At thirty he had mastery: he could take the dull routine of the man-of-war and make every part of it live, from the maintop to the hold: he could take a hundred dispersed facts and weave them into a solid pattern.

White-Jacket is a great portrait gallery. From the Commodore to the rascally Master-at-arms, from Jack Chase of the maintop to Mad Jack, the sea-going lieutenant, who, like Jermin, knew his business so well he commanded Melville's deep respect, from Mr. Pert the Midshipman to Surgeon Cuticle—Melville typified, and yet individualized, every character. The Neversink is an old-fashioned frigate of the line, now long out of date, and it is all warships, down to the latest airplane carrier. Mad Jack is an actual person; and he is all the officers who exercise command by knowledge and capacity, none the less liked for being a strict disciplinarian. Surgeon Cuticle is a man; and he is all professional men who become specialized by their skill into a brief-case or a textbook or an operating knife. Melville, who had found that the world was something of a man-of-war discovered also that a man-of-war's crew was a pretty good representation of the world. "Wrecked on a desert, a man of war's crew could quickly found an Alexandria by themselves, and fill it with all the things which go to make up a capital." Melville conveyed this feeling of richness and varied capacity: every face was accentuated slightly in caricature, except Jack Chase's for Jack stood out among the officers and crew as the real captain, the one complete, full-bodied man among them all, robust, bearded, Jovian, ready in war or love or seamanship, singing Dibdin's ballads or reciting Camoëns' Lusiad with equal gusto. Jack Chase would have pleased Whitman: indeed, they had the same large, sympathetic, readily dramatized personalities.

In White-Jacket, Melville's power of invention appears only a few times; but when it does, it is magnificent. The chapters on the Surgeon of the Fleet and his operation show Melville's satire at its acutest: the picture would do honour to the Hogarth Melville loved. One sees Cuticle, the eminent man of science and surgery, languishing for three years in a man-of-war without a single major operation. Fate at last hands Cuticle a poor wretch who has broken his leg; and Cuticle cannot ease the itch to amputate. The consultation with the other surgeons is handled with cruel fidelity: they are all against the operation; but Cuticle, with great presence, browbeats the junior surgeon into an equivocation which his superior pounces upon as a sufficient sanction for the operation. The grizzly preparation and performance is told with the grizzliest humour; Melville went through every detail of the butchery with a terrible levity, and an eye for the vanity, the professional hypocrisy, the routine which, rather than humanity and understanding, so often decide the issues of life and death. The operation was a triumph for science and Mr. Surgeon Cuticle: incidentally, it happened to be the death of the poor man who was brought needlessly to the operating-table.

The satire is perfect; and it is perfect because, at the broadest extreme of caricature, it does not lose sight of the pathetic reality underneath. Melville did not waste breath dissecting the obvious impostors and charlatans; for all but the simple can escape them. It is the man in command, the man we admire, respect, put all our confidence in, that Melville so skilfully opened up. No one has done a better job of it: Cuticle and his operation must be put alongside the best passages in Molière. If operations cannot now be performed in the Navy without the consent of the principal party, Melville's account of their professional abuse is perhaps responsible, in part, for the improvement.

Nor was this scene merely a lucky hit by Melville; the scene between the two sailmakers, sewing up the corpse, is equally strong and equally endowed with imaginative life. In his earlier books, Melville had defined his limits: they ranged between utmost fantasy and grossest matter of fact: he could grub with Caliban or fly with Ariel, but when he flew, his course was still a little erratic, and when he remained on the ground, he was tied a little too close to actuality. In White-Jacket his powers did not widen; but they gained firmness and control. He could fly groundwise, giving the commonplace the benefits of his imagination, carrying the double theme, the theme of life itself and naval experience, under the same figure; and when he cut loose, he did not need to throw overboard the ballast of good sense before he could reach the upper air. The prose of White-Jacket is an advance on all his previous writing; it has a richness of texture, a variety of rhythm, a decisiveness of phrase that his earlier work had only promised and that Mardi itself had not quite fulfilled.

White-Jacket is a portrait gallery: but it is more than that: it is one of the best all-round characterizations and criticisms of a powerful human institution that the century produced. Melville dealt with the effect of regimentation, with the relation of superior to underling, with the accidents and mischances and the ordinary routine of a man-of-war's life, in such a fashion that he included other institutions as well: the human truths and relationships would remain, though all the navies of the world were scrapped next week. The malevolence of the Articles of War, the essential degradation of the whole military process, the hectoring, the arrogance of station (the quarter-deck face!), the military necessity of converting all the variable human potentialities into mechanized patterns—that is, human defectives —are here once and for all coolly observed and demonstrated: White-Jacket forms a sort of illustrated supplement to Blake's keen and devastating epigrams on war. The fact that flogging was abolished in the Navy as a result of an agitation in Congress that followed directly upon White-Jacket's publication, is a tribute to the moving truth of what Melville wrote: his words on the sham republicanism of a country that fostered an autocratic navy were a little too sharply aimed for even the military racketeers to dodge.

Had Melville's picture been that of a mere propagandist, I doubt if it would have taken such immediate effect: on the contrary, it was that of a genuine critic, who portrayed the whole truth in such a fashion as to make evasion of the unpleasant parts of it almost impossible. He overreached his antagonists by knowing more about their business than they themselves did: as when he used the example of the British admiral, Collingwood, to show that capable officers could govern the rowdiest crew without the lash. Apart from Moby-Dick, White-Jacket is, I think, Melville's fullest achievement: and it is the best reasoned and seasoned of all his factual narratives. The charm of youth was gone, perhaps, but the manly grasp of maturity had succeeded it— the manly grasp and the steady, unfaltering eye.

Melville's appetite for facts, his voracious reading, his wide range of experience, his philosophic brooding, at last had an imagination capable of assimilating all these materials and using them to further its own ends. Now was the time for a great leap, a leap which would gather all these powers together and focus them on an object of epic dimensions, a Typee, a Mardi, a Redburn, a White-Jacket, all in one. Melville gathered himself for the leap; but before he could make it, he was forced to attend to more mundane affairs; and in October, 1849, he went over to England to arrange in person for the English publication of Redburn and White-Jacket.

For a few months, we have the rare good luck to follow Melville day by day, almost hour by hour. When, on October 11, 1849, he stepped aboard the Southampton, a regular London liner, on a raw noon, leaving behind his brother Allan and Mr. Duyckinck, who had come to the docks, he began to keep a journal of his voyage. This journal, a later one kept during his trip to the Near East, and a small sheaf of letters, constitute with his books almost the only firsthand material for Melville's biography. Let us take advantage of this good fortune. The literal, unadorned journal, made up hastily day by day, is the least impeachable sort of testimony, unless the writer has an eye on posterity. One need harbour no such suspicions about Melville's simple record.

4

(*Enter Herman Melville, in a green overcoat, with polite manners, and a wary reticence underneath his appearance of rank conviviality. He is just past thirty, and at times his grave demeanour and abstracted look might pass him for forty; but there are other moments when the fringe of brown beard seems only a mask, and one detects beneath the thoughtful brow of the author and the anxious brow of the husband and father an irrepressible boy. One wants a name for this combination of outdoor strength and bookishness, this Bohemianism and gentlehood, this mixture of the bronzed god himself and the plaster cast, and, for lack of an epithet, one will have to call it Melvillian.*)

What a queer business, this getting away. Yesterday one said a passionate farewell to every one in the morning; but the winds were unfavourable, and in the evening one was back again at home, feeling almost as if one had accomplished the tour of Europe; the final farewell was made a little stale by repetition; one felt relief when the ship was at last under way. For almost the first time, one travels as a passenger, travels alone, in a room as big as one's own room at home. It is good to be at sea again: one feels it more keenly among the land-lubbers, who make anguished noises at the first choppy water beyond the Narrows. In the morning, one is up early for the sunrise, and, since the captain is friendly, one has the run of the ship. Fine to be up in the rigging again! When a man is overboard one knows how to act promptly: one raises a cry, drops overboard the tackle-fall of the quarter boat, and when he fails to reach it, drops over the side oneself to swing it toward him. Poor fellow: he sees it and does not grasp it: he drowns with a demented smile on his face, when he might have saved himself. The passengers say later he was insane. . . . To work a boat, to know how to keep it pointed on its course, or to throw out a life-line, this sort of knowledge gives one back one's old confidence. There's no gammon about the ocean; it knocks the false bottom right off a pretender's keel.

The passengers prove better than one had dared hope: there is Adler, a German philologist, who will talk to one till midnight about fixed fate, free will, and foreknowledge absolute: his philosophy is Coleridgian, a sort of friendly bridge between Kant and Hegel and Schelling and Schlegel and one's own less conscious metaphysics, one's hitherto dim doubts and intuitions. There is also a genteel sociable youth named McCurdy, whose father is a New York merchant, and there is a cousin of Bayard Taylor, the pedestrian traveller, all good fellows over a bowl of punch. Taylor has a notion of going through the Near East: down the Danube from Vienna to Constantinople—Athens, Beyrut, Jerusalem, Cairo, Alexandria. That would be something neither Polynesia nor the Hudson Valley could give: marvellous, if it were not for the strain on one's purse. Four hundred dollars at least. Already, too—one isn't a week away from them—Lizzy and Barney the baby begin to tug at one. No: one isn't free any more. One is going to England to get a little ready cash from Bentley or Murray or Moxon on White-Jacket: one can't dissipate that in travel. One is tied: there is no getting away from that. One wants to travel far, perhaps; but not with the same old lust and confidence: all paths lead home again. Where's Lizzie now? Where dat old man? The nice little beggar: those were the first connected words he uttered.

Ah, well: the vacant days, the rough days, the dozy sunlit days: they all relieve the tension a little. Five years ago one scarcely knew that Hegel existed: now one is on one's way to England—an author! One of the ladies is reading a book by H. M.; she keeps on raising her eyes to take one in, as if comparing the real man with the self-portrait. People say: Are you *the* Mr. Melville—the man who lived among the cannibals? A fine way to go down to posterity. . . . What a slack lot of sheep a company of passengers is; one's sympathies are all with the forecastle. There is the buxom Irish lady who sings, the gushy Miss Wilbur who is so obviously marriageable and who talks of winning souls to Christ, the Frenchmen with the bleak, sea-sick faces. When one goes aloft to muse a little, they stand around and gape, as if one were a performer in Barnum's museum. Already we are three weeks from home. How quickly time flies when one day is like another. Dear Lizzie: dear little Barney: where dat old man!

With a fresh wind and a clear sky and land near, the passengers suddenly re-galvanize into life: faces appear that had been below decks most of the sail. The food tastes better; one plays shuffleboard gaily, not dutifully; one reads Pickwick Papers and wonders about the England that lies somewhere between one's father's journals, one's own grim memories of Liverpool, and the warm, roast-beef, veal-pie, ale-drinking, punch-sipping, toddy-smacking England of Dickens. At last the cliffs of Portland, where the Portland stone comes from, bleak, melancholy; then the run along the Isle of Wight, past the Needles, with the ploughed fields neatly marked off, and the lower shore of Hampshire with its low cliffs on the other side. Oh, to get ashore, to feel dry land, to quit this endless, tedious tacking: to rush ashore at Portsmouth and let the ship find London by itself! No: it can't be done: out in the Channel and up to Dover now: one is restless and impatient. Up in the morning in the dark at four, and into the cold cutter, which heads for Deal, not Dover, to make a landing. Well: England at last! Ten years ago, thirteen to be exact, a poor boy, half orphan, teased and tormented by foul-mouthed sailors, young, hopeful, innocent, a mere ship's monkey—now, Herman Melville, traveller, novelist, romancer, author of Peedee and Hullabaloo and Pog-Dog: the conquering hero, with debts and

duns at his back and a potboiler in his carpet-bag. Triumph
—and how raw the wind is at dawn!

Through the dark, narrow streets of Deal, the keen air
faintly reeking with the first kitchen-coals, then out into the
country on foot for a day's walk to Canterbury with Taylor
and Adler. A castle and a Roman fortification before one
is two hours ashore! Deal: the square mound of the Roman
castra: somehow, these things mean more than a hillful of
arrow-heads: the men who built them worried about God and
Eternity: a thousand years does not separate one from
them. Canterbury is even better: the nave, the cloisters, the
queer fine thoughts one finds on some of the tombs. Yes: this
is a little nearer the England of one's dreams. Dinner at the
Falstaff Inn, and in the evening a provincial theatre, with
a stage that might have been peopled by Dickens, every
actor more of a character than the character portrayed:
an ineffably funny business all round.

Next day, by train in a third-class open carriage to London: cold to one's marrow: cold and ravenous. When one
arrives at London Bridge one can think of nothing but a
chop-house. While the chops and the porter and the treacle
pudding are digesting, one realizes that this is England,
old England, the dark, slightly grimy eating-stalls, the red-
cheeked, pert, coarse, kindly stupid waitress, the silent men
eating methodically, piling their forks up like a hod with
food, the lawyers' clerks, shabby, rusty, genteel, the countrymen with leather leggings and purple veins on their
cheeks, the bagmen, voluble and expansive for Englishmen,
just one remove from the country pedlar, a faint odour of
musty paper and soot over one kind of Londoner, or of
ploughed fields and manure over the other: in short, England, London—a society like that at Albany, bedded deep in
dust, must, precedent, and vast augmentations of gold. One
is in it and out of it. The crowd on the Strand stares at one's
green overcoat: some one had ominously warned one on the
steamer that it would set one down for a crude American.

Colour is already a little old-fashioned in this drab, utilitarian England: this is the City of Dis: black coats, black hats, have survival value in a sulphur-and-brimstone world: the damned need protective colouration. One sinks down at last before a small fire in a tall, draughty room in Craven Street, just off the Strand. One's journal has been a blank these last three days, and one must catch up with it. Travelling takes the ink out of one's pen as well as the cash out of one's purse.

But time is limited and one must quickly set to work. Murray is out of town; so is Bentley, the publisher; but Bentley will come up from Brighton to suit one's convenience. In the meanwhile, one can drop in for Julien's Promenade Concert at Drury Lane, see the pictures at the National Gallery, prowl through Chancery Lane, or go down into Cheapside to witness the surviving pomp and gilded fustian of the Lord Mayor's show, exploring the Guildhall the next day, in the company of an affable functionary in the finance department whom one picks up, by chance, in the street, to witness a bit of infernal charity, worthy of Dis itself: a horde of beggars pours into the tawny-warm twilight of the hall, with all its flags and banners and fine timbering, to pick and grab at the remains of hams, fowls, pastries, left over from the high-and-mightinesses of the previous day. A comical sight at first; but on slight reflection, not comical: no, not comical. Thank heaven, civilization has not gone quite that far in America.

The world that holds Lord Mayor's shows—and the starvation and misery behind the show—also holds a bus-ride, on a mellow autumn Sunday, through Piccadilly, by Hyde Park and Kensington Gardens, and then on, past red cottages and little taverns and open commons, through Hammersmith, Chiswick, Kew, and across the Thames to Richmond Hill, where, at the crest, overlooking a long stretch of parkland, one can see the distant castle of Windsor in the mist beyond, with the Thames itself flashing occasionally like a fish's back in the sun, in the valley between. After that, one is ready for the sober crimson of Hampton Court—the Van Dycks and the Titians and the Rembrandts: this is what one means by a cultivated life. Must one be harried, must one struggle over vain things, must one know so much temporal bitterness, hardship, evil, in order to live? Not the Marquesans: not the Olympians of England: they both live as the lilies, planting themselves in a nourishing soil, drinking in the sun, growing, forming pollen and fertilizing and becoming fertilized, flowering and seeding. That is life, not the struggling, the harrying, the deprivation. But tomorrow one must leave Rembrandt and Hampton Court far behind: one must dicker for good terms and a fat advance with Bentley.

The greyness of London comes over one: the glacial greyness of St. Paul's: the brown greyness of Bloomsbury: the smeary greyness of the Strand: the dank blue greyness of the Temple. The choir chanting in St. Paul's leaves one feeling wan and unhappy. What is Lizzie doing? Where dat old man? If only they were here, or better, if one could be with them for a little while, and come back to the quiet inwardness of one's days, warmed, refreshed, revivified. One could absorb so much more, if one were settled and secure.

How near one feels to these English, these people who like good solid food and ale and port, who have a manly straightness in their dealings, merchants whose signature makes paper valuable, poets who have created in words poems that atone for all the pictures that remain unpainted and all the music that remains unsung in the English soul: hearty, robust, gay, ready to turn a farce in Beaumont and Fletcher or in a market Punch and Judy show, but grave, serious, at bottom very deep: no one, not Dante, had struck more ruthlessly at the sinister meanings of life than Shakespeare, no one had been more relentless and sardonic than Swift or Hogarth—and yet with what tenderness, what warm love of life, in Swift's letters to Stella or Hogarth's portrait of the Shrimp-girl, as fresh as a newly opened wild-flower. A country of sound men, buxom girls, beautiful tidy fields, snug inns—and terrible revealers of life's immense blackness. How intense the candle in those brave hands: how sullen and eventful the grave shadows that swarm around it!

But that other England—one was very distant from it. The England of wealth and station and reputation and family in the county sense, with its arctic Oh? and its hard, oysterlike rudeness, a stupid England, but influential in everything, governing its very enemies by choosing the issues over which they would fight. The England that had kicked an innocent youth out of a Liverpool club and would doubtless do the same, with less provocation, to a distinguished American author whose reputation was growing in France and Germany: the England of hard-faced men who rolled the wheels of progress over usury and penury as twin rails: the England that had impressed seamen, struck down its continental rivals, enclosed the commons, introduced an inhuman system of industry, and defended privilege and empty title as the very cornerstones of Civil Order —in short, the England of snobs and flunkeys and a complacent, servile, self-righteous middle class—New York, to be sure, without a hinterland that was still free and unclaimed.

How trivial this other England essentially is. What a stupid lot at Murray's party, and what a bore old Lockhart was, with his ghastly, grinning, mincing way: such a moth-eaten lion! Oh, conventionalism, what a ninny thou art! How completely one felt out of it, how superior one felt to these superiorities. Perhaps there was such a thing as real aristocracy: one wonders if the Scotch Melvilles would show it, or whether one might get a taste of the real thing at the Duke of Rutland's own seat: but these fishy eyes, these stupid faces, this intellectual torpor, do not reassure one.

Blackwood's had printed a long ponderous review of Redburn: that was a comical black mark against the reigning
Tory intellect, wasting good white paper on a book one
knows oneself to be trash, which one wrote to buy tobacco
with. In a society where the mask, the reputation, the hall-
mark count for so much, how little any one is concerned
with the substance beneath! One is a well-known author: a
success: ergo, Blackwood's takes Redburn seriously, not
fathoming how little it is worth serious criticism.

One meets the publishers one by one, Bentley, who did
Mardi, Murray, who published Typee and Omoo, Mr. Long-
mans, Mr. Chapman, Mr. Bohn, Mr. Moxon, who was
Charles Lamb's crony; and when one can't make the deal
one had hoped for, one goes down the line; but the answer
is always the same: the copyright is unsatisfactory, the
work may be pirated in America; and they cannot risk two
hundred pounds on the rights for the first thousand copies.
The prospects are not too pleasant; but if the matter could
be settled at once one wouldn't have the excuse and the
opportunity to visit the Dulwich Gallery, remote from London, but full of splendid treasures; one couldn't sit with the
Greenwich pensioners at Greenwich; one couldn't spend a
Sunday morning, a little too conspicuous for comfort, at
the services in St. Bridget's; nor could one discuss metaphysics with Dr. Adler at the Edinburgh Castle, dark-
walled and like a beefsteak in colour, where the ale was so
mellow and the waiters so polite. One absorbs a city by food
and drink, as well as by sight and conversation: the Mitre—
Johnson's tavern—and the Cock and the Rainbow—Tenny-
son's haunts: the little French hotel in Soho where one has
morning coffee and a jelly omelette, or, to know the worst
about life in London, a cup of brackish coffee, a dirty roll,
an unappetizing piece of bacon, on a dank, foggy morning
in a cheap eating-house: such depression of taste, sight,
sound, feeling adds a new circle to life's possible hells.

There are bright spots that serve for perpetual contrast:

hours spent over the bookstalls in Great Green Street and Lincoln's Inn, picking out folios of Ben Jonson, Beaumont and Fletcher, Thomas Browne, coming, with a sudden recognition of kinship, upon De Quincey's dreams of an Opium Eater, with passages so much like one's best feats in Mardi; or a sumptuous dinner with Mr. Bates at East Sheen, nine miles from Richmond, where one meets Lord Ashburton's nephew, and Baron This and Baroness That and Mr. Peabody the Boston merchant, a warm old soul: where the glasses and the silver are brilliant and the conversation ripples in reflection of it, or at least seems to, as one intricate piece of French cookery gives place to another, as white wine, champagne, hock, claret, port, and Madeira follow in grand procession: Taji dined no better among the five-and-twenty kings.

Yes: but then the melancholy of a day when one has spoken no more than "Good morning" to the slavey: when a frightful nightmare fills with a turbid residue the commonplaces of the diurnal routine: when one feels lonely and apart in the haunts that thrilled one most: when one sits at night in a damp chamber, thinking back to poor Gansevoort, who, two years before, three, was sitting in such a chamber, in the midst of such a silence, withdrawn, homesick, alone. What deep thoughts one seems on the brink of in that silence and solitude: no wonder the Greeks made silence the vestibule of the mysteries. But the weariness of this inward communion, too—oh, solitude, where are thy charms! One's desires are fulfilled indeed: but always wryly, never in the right proportion. . . .

While one waits around doggedly, hoping for more favourable offers, one had better seize the opportunity and make a flying trip to France: one never knows if one is coming this way again; and besides, if one does that story of the revolutionary beggar, Potter, one ought to be able to follow him on his French mission. Very well: by steamer to Boulogne, then by rail to Paris. A lodging-house on the Rue

de Bussy, then a room at Mme. Capelle's on the Left Bank.
This is civilization: the Rue de Rivoli: the Place de la Con-
corde: the Tuileries: the Sorbonne: these things have the
imprint of logic and law. Chaos and old time are somehow
set at naught. The Louvre makes the National Gallery itself
seem a little provincial: Notre Dame, under repair, is still
a noble mass: there is a vivacity, an eagerness, an upright
peasant homeliness in the housewives in felt shoes, in the
rosy-cheeked market-women, that makes one feel a little
nearer home. Courtesy takes the place of servility here, innate courtesy; a market-woman may have it as well as a
duchess. The Hôtel de Cluny, on the site of the old Roman
bath, is just such a house as one would like to live in, venerable, spacious, solid; and the bookstalls by the Palais Royal,
with their Latin translations and their Voltaire and their
Fénelon, give one a sense of a nation bred to thought and
expression, not merely sharp and acquisitive, like the
Yankees, although, obviously, they do not let the sous go by.
And yet—well, the devilish nonsense of this passport business: the tapeworm of an ancient bureaucracy. What a
disappointment to stand on line, once, twice, to get admission to Rachel in Phèdre, and be turned away. Rachel acting
at the Palais Royal: Victor Cousin lecturing at the Sorbonne
—and somehow, one remains out of it, unable to get sight of,
much less to understand, these things. For consolation one
has *eau de vie* and a metaphysical talk with the ubiquitous
Dr. Adler.

One is a little downcast: but what did one expect? The
truth is, one's heart is not altogether in it: one wants Lizzie
and Barney, now, far more than one wants Rachel, Cousin,
and the triumphs of culture generally. Still: one will make
one last try: by train to Brussels, that venerable but obviously stodgy place, Paris minor, and then over into Germany for a little trip up the Rhine to Cologne, an anti-
quated, gable-ended town, with the crane still aloft in the
unfinished tower of the Cathedral, full of associations that

go back as far as Charlemagne. How concentrated history becomes in Europe: here Rubens was born and Marie de Médicis died: much lore and history to interest a pondering man. Down the Rhine itself at night, between black cliffs and crags, from Cologne to Coblentz. Metternich was born near this great fortress, Ehrenbreitstein, but, more significant symbol than this, the finest Rhenish wine-grapes are grown right under its guns. Does not that stand for life itself? Our rarest triumphs and ecstasies are touched with the shadow of ancient death. At dusk one finds oneself standing in the place where the two rivers meet: opposite towers the fortress: some four thousand miles away are Lizzie and America. Tomorrow, the last lap begins: definitely one is homeward bound.

London itself seems halfway home, when one returns to the old chamber overlooking the Thames. Back in London with a few presents, a pair of gloves and shoes from Paris for Lizzie, a medallion one bought from an old woman near the Arc de Triomphe, and a breast-pin one bought in Cologne from a rascally shopwoman who cheated one, cheated—and by a woman—and not even a pretty woman! If only one could splurge a little on presents. No: one must be sensible: a trencher and breadknife, as used of old at commons in New College: fine thing. One for Mrs. Shaw, too. At last Mr. Bentley has come around to one's terms; it was worth waiting for. Two hundred pounds sterling on a note of hand for six months, on White-Jacket. If only Lizzie and the Little One were here—thank heaven for good letters from Lizzie—one might settle down to a little enjoyment. The Duke of Rutland has sent one a courteous invitation to visit Belvoir Castle in January. Alas! that is three weeks ahead. Can one put another three weeks between one and home? If one does not go, one will miss a royal opportunity to see the aristocracy under the best possible conditions: not merely an interesting experience in itself, but—a prudent author mustn't forget it—so much good

material to be hoarded up for another book. If one passes
this up, Allan, shrewd fellow, will set one down for a ninny.

Ah! if only one could get over the three weeks: if the two
images at home would only down for that space of time.
Another cigar: one must weigh it over carefully. No: no:
the visit to Leicester would be very agreeable—at least very
valuable—but the three weeks couldn't be borne. It is bad
enough to have to go back in a thirty-day boat to save
money, instead of dashing in on a twelve- or fifteen-day
packet steamer. That's settled: one goes. Yes: one goes.
Now one can enjoy a bright day, and an hour at the National Gallery looking at Rembrandt's Jew and the saints
of Taddeo Gaddi and Guido's Murder of the Innocents.
One is going home. Things brighten. Davidson has promised
to discount Bentley's note at the banker's; one even begins
to enjoy old Bentley: he is a fine, frank, off-handed old gentleman, opening up gradually, like all Englishmen, but as
solid as oak once he is sure of you and of his own feelings.
One begins to like these English: they are not all masked
and corseted in iron. There is Alfred Crowquill, for example, Punch's funny man, whom one meets at Bentley's—a
good fellow, free and easy, and no damned nonsense. The
Benchers at the Temple Bar are men after one's own heart:
a Paradise of Bachelors, this! Well, one sails a week hence.
Ironically, one leaves for the old home just as one is beginning to feel settled in the new one! One breakfasts for the
last time at the old place; one says good-bye to Bentley;
one has one's last dinner at Morley's; one's first and last
glimpse of the Reform Club, a last good-bye to the somehow
pleasantly dingy room in Craven Street. Waterloo Station
—Portsmouth—and one steps, with Captain Fletcher,
aboard the Independence, a small, ancient-looking wooden
ship. In less than twenty-four hours we are past Land's End.

Nothing happens between December 26, when one sets
sail, and January 30, when one gets sight of a pilot boat:
nothing can possibly happen outside that would compete

with the memories, the stimuli, the anticipations, the impetuous dreams, the regrets at visits forgotten and experiences omitted, the whole inner tumult of this four months away from home. Or rather, what happens most importantly now, comes by way of books: De Quincey, Rousseau's Confessions, Ben Jonson, Thomas Browne, The Castle of Otranto, Lamb's Essays, Hudibras, Marlowe, Anastasius, Vathek, Goethe's autobiography. The vessel is again one's cloister: but instead of a long, unconscious growth it contains a vivid and conscious development: every day one is aware of new shoots, ideas, emotions, feelings, insights, sprouting out of one: why, before one had reached twenty-five one hardly had any growth one could point to at all. And now. . . . If one could not write books one would burst. One is big with a book; it kicks at the walls of the womb; it wakes one in the night with its anticipatory motions.

The low-lying hills of Staten Island at last. The clack and clamour of Whitehall, Broadway. Lizzie. Barney no longer says, "Where dat old man?" He has a dozen other things to talk about. Lizzie is busy with the household, her mother, her mother-in-law, Sam, Father, Uncle Peter, Allan, the sisters: she chatters on about all of them, and about what baby did last week. She will never quite realize, perhaps, what one has been through, how deep one's longing is, how strong one's need for escape is, too. She loves one, yes, but not with that gnawing intensity; she will never appreciate how lonely one has been. Before a fortnight is over one wonders why one had ever been so feverishly anxious to come back. Lizzie would have waited another three weeks: an invitation from the Duke of Rutland is irretrievable. No matter: spring is coming, and one must get down to work, and be midwife to one's own progeny. What earthly shape will this embryo take on?

(*Exit Herman Melville, pondering his future.*)

TITAN

CHAPTER SIX: RED CLOVER

IT WAS time for Melville to begin work again. In February, 1850, he owed his publisher, Harper's, more than seven hundred dollars in advances not covered by royalties. He did what he could to reduce the scale of his living. In the spring, he left New York and went up to Broadhall with his family —the old homestead that his Grand-Uncle Thomas had sold when he emigrated to Ohio, had now been converted into an inn: his grandfather's old desk was still mildewing in the barn, and Melville brought it to light, cleaned it up for his own use, and sat down to it.

The Berkshires were "home" for Melville quite as much as Albany or New York; perhaps more so, for he had a feeling for the open country and its ways. By October he had found a near-by farmstead, with a house that had been an inn during the eighteenth century, an apple orchard on the south side, broad hay fields to the north, and pasture rising in back of the house to the west, which ended in a wood lot on the summit of the hill. The countryside was well cultivated. Maple trees lined the highroad on each side, the willows dropped lazily over the banks of the Housatonic, and, on the poorer upland soils, where the amaranth grew, the white threads of birch trees stood out against the dark pattern of the woods. Pittsfield, a village with metropolitan pretensions, the capital of the Berkshires and the resort of palpable celebrities, was only two miles or so away by a road that led down the valley and across the river, past a sawmill, and through the parklike streets of the village itself.

Judge Shaw advanced Melville funds on a friendly sort of mortgage to purchase Arrowhead; and Melville doubtless intended by modest and spasmodic farming, with a vegetable garden, hay fields, a wood lot, a cow, and a horse, to eke out the narrow income derived from his books. For a man in prime health there was nothing injudicious in this arrangement: winter leaves a considerable amount of free time from farm work, and, with only a few hundred dollars in ready cash every year, Melville might have made a pretty good go of it. But there were handicaps. He had a wife and child to support; other children came presently, four in all; and Elizabeth Melville was a duffer as a housekeeper: try as she would, she could not cook without strain nor manage a servant; and her chief equipment for facing the work and the winter was an admirable set of party dresses and slippers. Melville's picked-up knowledge of cookery must have been called upon for service during the first weeks they were definitely on their own; and presently Mrs. Maria Melville and his sisters came to join the household, in order to teach Elizabeth the rudiments of the household arts. It was a humiliating experience for Elizabeth; but there was no help for it: to the end of her days she did not like housekeeping; the art of "managing" was apparently not in her. The many hands in Arrowhead doubtless made light work; they also made inroads upon the larder, and what the Melvilles gained in service they lost in supplies. The house itself was commodious in rooms, but cramped in space, since it did not so much exist in its own right, as it did as a sort of annex to the chimney, a vast brick structure, with a circumference of forty-eight feet at the base; the chimney was ample enough, but it swallowed wood on a winter day as a whale swallows little fishes: and the rooms that were left were none too large.

On any realistic canvas, this new move, with all its unexpected burdens, was a dubious one. But in 1850 Melville was at the top of his energies: the impetus from Typee and

Omoo had not been lost: the reception in England had probably added to his confidence: and when he looked around him, the American scene itself reinforced his courage and his convictions, and gave him new strength.

2

In the spring of 1850, Nathaniel Hawthorne's Scarlet Letter appeared, and Melville presently awoke to find that Hawthorne, whose books he had hitherto kept away from, despite the praise of them he had heard, was a kindred spirit. "A man of deep and noble nature has taken hold of me in this seclusion," he exclaimed; "his wild, witch-voice rings through me; or, in softer cadences, I seem to hear it in the songs of the hillside birds that sing in the larch trees at my window." This discovery must have added to Melville's refreshing sense of welcome on coming back to America. Melville had perhaps begun to doubt whether he could find an audience among his fellow countrymen; and here, at last, was one man capable of understanding every part of him. America and its promise were not a fraud: Hawthorne seemed a deeper writer than any one who had gained the public's ear in England as a novelist, or, for that matter, as a Victorian poet. When, this summer, Melville came upon the Mosses from an Old Manse, which had been published some years before, he realized he had lost much by his aloofness from the Salem magician. He hastened to repair his neglect; for he gave to the Literary World presently one of the best appreciations of Hawthorne, and incidentally one of the keenest expositions of the situation of the creative writer in America, that Hawthorne was in his own lifetime to get.

The "soft ravishments of the man spun me round about in a web of dreams," Melville announced. In Hawthorne, humour and love were developed in that high form called genius, and "no such man can exist without also possessing, as the indispensable complement of these, a great, deep intellect, which drops down into the universe like a plummet."

Hawthorne, without all of Rembrandt's warmth, had this great quality of Rembrandt: there were blacks in the midst of his sunlight, as Melville had found there were blacks in the world. The blackness fixed and fascinated Melville: it brought Hawthorne to the level of Shakespeare, not in language and performance, perhaps, but in insight: "those occasional flashings-forth of the intuitive truth in him; those short, quick probings at the very axis of reality," the dark things Shakespeare announced through his dark characters, Hamlet, Timon, Lear, Iago, "these qualities, in spite of Hawthorne's quiet temperateness, so different from Shakespeare's popularizing noise and show of broad farce and blood-besmeared tragedy," brought him on the same level. Melville had re-discovered Shakespeare only two years before: and that discovery, reserved happily for maturity, had contributed decisively to his own rapid burgeoning: "Dolt and ass that I am," he had exclaimed then, "I have lived more than twenty-nine years, and until a few days ago, never made close acquaintance with the divine William. Ah, he's full of sermons-on-the-mount, and gentle, ay, almost as Jesus. I take such men to be inspired. I fancy this Mons. Shakespeare in heaven ranks with Gabriel, Raphael, and Michael. And if another Messiah ever comes he will be in Shakespeare's person." . . . "I would to God," he wrote shortly after, "Shakespeare had lived later and promenaded in Broadway. Not that I might have had the pleasure of leaving my card for him at the Astor, or made merry with him over a bowl of the fine Duyckinck punch; but that the marble which all men wore on their souls in the Elizabethan day, might not have intercepted Shakespeare's fine articulateness. Now I hold it a verity that even Shakespeare was not a frank man to the uttermost. And, indeed, [who] in this intolerant universe is, or can be? But the Declaration of Independence makes a difference."

Shakespeare had prepared the way for Hawthorne in

Melville's mind. If what one could not quite get from the Shakespeare of the printed page one might get directly from the shy man himself, what great good fortune to find a similar person, alive and abroad in one's own century! And if the Declaration of Independence did make a difference, if the American had cut loose in more ways than one, and could face life with a little less show and pretence and caste-spirit than Europe had known, why, then one might really get to the bottom of the matter with Hawthorne. That possibility piqued Melville. He risked much in utterance himself; and he hoped that Hawthorne would venture much in return. When they at last became friends, he contrived a hundred different ways of assaulting Hawthorne's reserve: he staggered up mountains, uncovered mounds of debris, jumped gaily off into innumerable abysses, all to excite Hawthorne to some equivalent disclosure. He did not know at the outset of his enthusiasm for Hawthorne that nothing would ever shake that mountainous reserve, that no leaps and sorties of his would stimulate Hawthorne to put one foot before the other. But Hawthorne caused Melville to hope for much; and that hope mingled with the plan of Moby-Dick, while he was writing it.

What a difference there was between Hawthorne and the graceful Washington Irving or the scholarly Longfellow, the men who had heretofore stood before the world as the highest representatives of American letters, urbane, elegant, sedulously following foreign models, and avoiding all topics but smooth ones! Better to fail at times with such originality as Hawthorne's than to succeed in the easy, bland, gentlemanly way—knowing one's powers, because they are so small, and keeping within them, because nothing beckons one to stir beyond.

Here, thought Melville, was a fellow spirit at last! Melville had partly realized before that other men were working below the surface of things in America; but the transcendentalists had put him off a little by rallying around

them the people who thought they were lifting themselves
above material things by taking cold water rubs, on prin-
ciple, or by being dreadfully concerned over the items of
their diet or the cut of their clothes: whereas Melville felt
that champagne and oysters were the proper nourishment
for the body, if one could get them, and he believed that
one was less devoted to the material life when one accepted
its daily routine than when one attempted to substitute plain
living for high thinking, and lost true simplicity, by making
its attainment such a complicated matter. Even Hawthorne
at first seemed to lack something. Hawthorne was wonder-
fully subtle, Melville wrote to Mr. Duyckinck, and his
deeper meanings are worthy of a Brahmin. Still, there was
something lacking—a good deal lacking to the plump spher-
icality of the man. What was that? He doesn't patronize
the butcher—he needs roast beef, done rare.

Hawthorne became Melville's sole connection with the
transcendentalists, and it never developed into a very deep
union. Melville had listened to a lecture of Emerson's a
year before and defended Emerson from Mr. Duyckinck's
censure: he respected this Plato who spoke through his nose.
If Emerson was a fool, Melville had rather be a fool than a
wise man, and if he owed much to Sir Thomas Browne, well,
no one was his own sire: the debt was a universal one. Emerson at least dived; and Melville loved all men who dive. "Any
fish can swim near the surface; but it takes a great whale
to go downstairs five miles or more, and if he don't attain
the bottom, why, all the lead in Galena can't fashion the
plummet that will." That justified Emerson: but except as
one diver with another, Melville felt no kinship with him.
"I do not oscillate in Emerson's rainbow, but prefer to hang
myself in mine own halter than to swing in any other man's
swing." It was the blandness, the sunniness, the mildness,
the absence of curses, shadows, shipwrecks in Emerson's
philosophy that set Melville against it: Emerson was the
perpetual passenger who stayed below in bad weather, trust-

ing that the captain would take care of the ship: Melville
was the sailor who climbed aloft, and knew that the captain
was sometimes drunk and that the best of ships might go
down. *"All hands save ship!* has startled dreamers."

Hawthorne, then, was a man to be grateful for: the smell
of young beeches and hemlocks was upon him, wrote Melville; the broad prairies were in his soul; he had these
qualities because he was an American and deeply part of
the scene; but, in addition, he had an eye for the dankness
and decay and for the inscrutable malevolence of the universe: he was no sun-dial that recorded only the smiling
hours of life. If the country could nourish Hawthorne, and
if Hawthorne could produce The Scarlet Letter and the
Mosses, well, what might not Melville himself put forth?
Though Hawthorne was a genius, perhaps, like Shakespeare,
he did not appear alone. "Shakespeare cannot be regarded
as in himself the concretion of all the genius of his time;
nor as so immeasurably beyond Marlowe, Webster, Ford,
Beaumont, Jonson, that these men can be said to share none
of his power. Would it, indeed, appear so unreasonable to
suppose that this great fullness and overflowing may be,
or may be destined to be, shared by a plurality of men of
genius?"

The presence of an Emerson, a Hawthorne, gave all the
more reason for a Melville. So Melville must have felt in his
bones; and he was right. What he could not venture as a
perception—for who can see or measure his contemporaries?
—was certainly true as prophecy: in that flood of intellectual and imaginative power that I have elsewhere called the
Golden Day, Emerson, Whitman, Poe, Hawthorne, Melville,
Thoreau, were all carried along in the same current: each
reinforces and rounds out the others: and it is this corpus
of writers, rather than any single one, that forms what
Hawthorne himself called the Master Genius of America.

Melville did not suppose, when he wrote his encomium of
Hawthorne, that this same summer would bring the two men

into contact, that they would become neighbours, near enough to make occasional visits by horseback or wagon, and that, despite his premonition that "on a personal interview no great author has ever come up to the idea of his reader," he would find in Hawthorne, temporarily, that comrade and friend for whom he had been looking. There was, it is true, only half a generation between them; and this particular distance makes intimacy difficult, unless the older man is willing to treat the younger one as an assured equal. How Hawthorne himself felt about the matter it is hard to tell: Melville realized that his own boisterous democracy, which recognized the thief in the jail as the equal of General George Washington, might grate on Hawthorne a little, and that, like an English Howard in the presence of a plebeian, Hawthorne's intellectual aristocracy might shrink at this claim and this contact. But Melville had no lack of faith in his own powers; and he put forth the claim to equality with easy and assured frankness; and unless he was unusually insensitive at this point, his letter would indicate that Hawthorne accepted the relationship on Melville's terms.

On August 5, 1850, Hawthorne noted in his American Notebook that he drove from Lenox, near which he lived in a penurious red farmhouse, to Stockbridge, where he found at the house of Fields, the Boston publisher, Dr. Holmes, Mr. Duyckinck of New York, also Mr. Cornelius Matthews and Herman Melville. They ascended the Monument Mountain and the party was caught in a shower: according to tradition, it was during that summer storm, under a shoulder of rock where they had taken refuge, that these two stormy souls first overcame their reticence and shyness, and ploughed through conversation to a deeper intimacy. The New Yorkers called on Hawthorne in the forenoon, two days later, and Hawthorne treated them to a couple of bottles of Mr. Mansfield's champagne; and from that time on Melville was a familiar visitor in the Hawthorne household. The family

called him Mr. Omoo; young Julian said that he loved Mr.
Melville as well as his Mamma and Papa and Una; Melville,
who had amused the Marquesans with an improvised popgun, was not likely to fall down in intercourse with children—and he would sometimes ride over in the evening
with his great dog, and the children would ride on the dog's
back. Even Sophia Hawthorne was fascinated by Melville:
she, who adored her husband's dark, lustrous eyes, was
puzzled and a little disturbed by Melville's; and her tribute
to Melville is all the more notable when one remembers her
complete preoccupation with her husband.

"I am not quite sure," she wrote, "that I do not think him
a very great man. . . . A man with a true, warm heart, and
a soul and an intellect—with life to his finger-tips; earnest,
sincere and reverent; very tender and modest. He has very
keen perceptive power; but what astonishes me is, that his
eyes are not large and deep. He seems to me to see everything accurately; and how he can do so with his small eyes,
I cannot tell. They are not keen eyes, either, but quite un-
distinguished in any way. His nose is straight and handsome,
his mouth expressive of sensibility and emotion. He is tall
and erect, with an air free, brave and manly. When conversing, he is full of gesture and force, and loses himself
in his subject. There is no grace or polish. Once in a while
his animation gives place to a singularly quiet expression,
out of these eyes to which I have objected; an indrawn, dim
look, but which at the same time makes you feel that he is at
that moment taking deepest note of what is before him. It is
a strange, lazy glance, but with a power in it quite unique.
It does not seem to penetrate through you, but to take you
into itself."

The opportunity for real intercourse with Hawthorne, for
talk about Time and Eternity and ultimate things, smoking
a fragrant cigar, sipping brandy or cider, meant much to
Melville; far more, no doubt, than it did to Hawthorne. In
Melville's growing spiritual loneliness, he needed the affec-

tion of a sympathetic mind; and for a while he could persuade himself that, even in Hawthorne's silences, he had this. Hawthorne's example as a novelist was a stimulus: it led Melville beyond the easy shallows, where one could negligently wade, always within easy calling distance of the shore; and his philosophical conversation, or, still more, his apparently absorbed way of listening to philosophical conversation, encouraged Melville to go further and deeper along the passage he had begun to make a year before with Adler.

Each conversation opened new vistas: the night talks would often be a prelude to next morning's letters, and in those letters, particularly in those which remain from the period covered by Moby-Dick, Melville exposed the seamy depths of his own spirit. He had no reticences before Hawthorne, and above all, no false modesty. Life was becoming a long stage, with no inn in sight, and night coming, and the body cold. But with Hawthorne for a fellow passenger, Melville was content and could be happy. "I shall leave the world, I feel, with more satisfaction for having come to know you. Knowing you persuades me more than the Bible of our immortality." The hectic, desperate, ecstatic letters Melville wrote his friend during the short year and a half that brought them together in the Berkshires give one a surer insight into Melville's moods and aims than any other pages he ever wrote. Had the neighbourly relations persisted, had Hawthorne's response been wholly adequate, Melville might have weathered more buoyantly the internal tempest that set in with Moby-Dick. But Hawthorne was essentially as remote from Melville as he was from the old worthies of the Customs House at Salem or the old sea-captains he had exchanged civilities with over a mug of ale. Though one could see daylight and the blue sky from the bottom of Hawthorne's well, there was not enough of it to share with any companion. If he was touched by the homage of the younger man, he could not fully reciprocate it. He recognized Melville's moral earnestness and intellectual vigour; but I doubt if he once suspected that his extravagant friend was far nearer, by temperament and expression, to the heart of Shakespeare's genius than he himself was. In seizing upon Hawthorne as an other self, Melville more than once did homage to his own genius: his descriptions of Hawthorne's powers, Hawthorne's achievements, are nearer to his own than to Hawthorne's.

Melville's relation with Hawthorne counts as one of the tragedies of his life; and it was more than a minor one. Friendship itself must have seemed a mockery, when he found that the dearest friend and closest intellectual companion he had yet encountered was bound tight in the arctic ice, and many leagues away. But he had no sense of the distance between them until he attempted to span it: and it must have been with amazement, with incredulity, that he finally read the story of Ethan Brand, written during the prime year of their friendship, and discovered what in his heart of hearts Hawthorne felt about Melville's lofty pride and his extreme spiritual quests. Ethan Brand is a charcoal-burner, who has left his home in order to discover the Unpardonable Sin; he finally returns to his kiln and his neighbours to announce, after his long wanderings, that he has found the sin in his own breast. Brand's language is a parody of Ahab's in Moby-Dick; and what Hawthorne says about Brand he meant to apply, I have no doubt, possibly by way of warning, to Melville himself.

Ethan Brand remembered, said Hawthorne, echoing Melville's words in the scene where Ahab recalls his first pursuit of the whale, "he remembered how the night dew had fallen upon him,—how the dark forest had whispered to him,—how the stars had gleamed upon him,—a simple and loving man, watching the fire in the years gone by, and ever musing as it burned. He remembered with what tenderness, with what love and sympathy for mankind, and what pity for human guilt and woe, he had first begun to contemplate those ideas which afterwards became the inspiration of his life; with what reverence he had then looked into the heart of man, viewing it as a temple originally divine, and, however desecrated, still to be held sacred by his brother; with what awful fear he had deprecated the success of his pursuit, and prayed that the Unpardonable Sin might never be revealed to him. Then ensued that vast intellectual development, which, in its progress, disturbed the counterpoise between his mind and heart. The Idea that possessed his life had operated as a means of education; it had gone on cultivating his powers to the highest point of which they were susceptible; it had raised him from the level of an unlettered laborer to stand on a star-lit eminence, whither the philosophers of the earth, laden with the lore of universities, might vainly strive to clamber after him. So much for the intellect! But where was the heart? That, indeed, had withered,—had contracted,—had hardened,—had perished! It had ceased to partake of the universal throb. He had lost his hold of the magnetic chain of humanity. He was no longer a brother-man, opening the chambers or the dungeons of our common nature by the key of holy sympathy, which gave him a right to share in all its secrets; he was now a cold observer, looking on mankind as the subject of his experiment. . . . Thus Ethan Brand became a fiend. He began to be so from the moment his moral nature had ceased to keep the pace of improvement with his intellect."

We do not know when Melville discovered these words or felt their jagged edges in his bosom: but we can be certain that from that day forth the friendship between the two men sank like a stone in quicksand. Hawthorne had committed the unpardonable sin of friendship; he had failed to understand Melville's development, or to touch by sympathy and faith that part of Melville which was beyond his external reach. All of Melville's love recoiled, as we shall see presently, from the icy strangeness of that friendship which was no friendship, from that understanding which was almost enmity. Perhaps Ethan Brand was not Melville? Perhaps it was but a shadowy suggestion, influenced more by Ahab than by his author? Melville must have attempted this sort of reconciliation more than once: but Hawthorne's words would stick: yes, they would stick because of the touch of truth in them, and because, once Hawthorne's hand was withdrawn, the magnetic chain of humanity indeed would seem broken. This, however, was the crisis of their friendship; and Melville had no inkling of this outcome whilst he was writing Moby-Dick. There is no doubt that the presence of Hawthorne fortified him for that endeavour.

3

Some time in 1850, towards the close of summer, Herman Melville must have begun to write Moby-Dick; for the book, which is a long one, was finished in the summer of 1851. In back of the actual writing went a considerable amount of preparation; and one does not know how long before the theme of the book had begun to root itself in Melville's mind. The work itself shows that he had reached out for every book on whaling he could lay hands on, practically every book that had been written, and, in addition, he had made note of every quotation and allusion to the whale he had met in his wide miscellaneous reading. Scholarship as well as personal experience went into this writing: one of the best modern writers upon whaling, Frank Bullen, the author of the Cruise of the Cachalot, confesses he would never have gone further with his own work had he known about the wealth of information and detail that went into Moby-Dick before he set out. Did Melville consciously save the greatest of his ocean experiences for his maturity? Did he wait for Leviathan to develop in his soul? Did he begin another White-Jacket or Typee, and become conscious, in the act of writing, of this deepening of his insight, this integration of his powers, and of the vast fable that was now at his command?

One cannot even make a reasonable conjecture about the matter. All one knows are the actual conditions under which Moby-Dick was written, the reactions of the writing itself upon Melville, and its final result—the story of the White Whale.

Conceive of Melville in his new home, as he embarks upon the most extensive of his spiritual voyages. The furniture has been removed to his new house, the beds put up, the heavier articles shifted and re-shifted, and, by a month's work outdoors, the woodpile has grown and the hay been stowed into the hayloft. For the moment, all his relations are well poised: Barney is through the period of teething: Elizabeth has help in her housework and the first tension of removal is over; Mr. Duyckinck occasionally, with the most tactful sort of generosity, sends up a case of champagne in a wicker cradle or a fine bundle of cigars, or he suggests a review to be written. He even tries to nourish Melville's reputation by abetting some one who is writing about him in the papers and who wishes to publish a photograph of the famous author: here alone Melville's pride rebuffs this rudimentary effort at an art which has become a loathsome sore in our own time: he refuses his picture. "The fact is," he explains, "almost everybody is having his 'mug' engraved nowadays, so that this test of distinction is getting to be reversed; and therefore, to see one's 'mug' in a magazine is presumptive evidence that he's a nobody. . . . I respectfully decline to be *oblivionated.* . . ." But when a journeyman painter made the rounds of the neighbourhood Melville sat for him—and the portrait, which slightly resembles Allan's, remains a just punishment for his vanity.

Below the edge of Melville's horizon is this new friend, Nathaniel Hawthorne, and, as he raises his eyes from the desk in his second-story chamber and looks through the single small window that faces the north, he sees the wide valley sweeping across to successive ridges of hills, dominated by Mt. Greylock—otherwise called, from the double hump in the ridge, Saddleback. The red clover that incarnadined the summer fields is gone; or rather, its colour has mounted to the crown of the landscape; the maples are a still more glorious red. The spirits caper in the autumn air; there are glowing Byzantine days when the heavens reflect the hues of the October apples, when the sky is so ripe and ruddy it seems there must be harvest home for the angels and that Charles' Wain is heaped as high as Saddleback with autumn sheaves. The sunrises and the sunsets glow side by side in the woods, and momentarily moult in the falling leaves. Neither the Rhine nor the Moselle produces anything as heady as the landscape of the Berkshires in autumn. Now is the time to begin. When Melville writes his first words, "Call me Ishmael," he is writing out of his health and ecstasy: he himself is not an outcast, nor is his spirit drooping with the "hypos": his first touch is a black one because his canvas demands it. He is about to build up a vast pyramid of contrasts, between the whiteness of external evil and the blackness of man's inner doom; and he faces this drama with his full powers.

The apples are gathered; the autumn ploughing is done; Melville is at work. The mood of creation is upon him: he is ready not for one book but for fifty books: if Mr. Duyckinck would only send him about fifty fast-writing youths with an easy style, not averse to polishing their letters, he might set them all to work. "It is not so much the paucity, as the superabundance of material that seems to incapacitate modern authors," he had written that summer. In this autumn ferment, Melville has scarcely enough time to think about his future books separately; in lieu of using fifty youths, he must pack as much as possible into one book. Melville scarcely breaks his way through a chapter or two before he realizes that he has found his theme; and the only question is how to quarry this marble, how to get it out. "Youth," Melville said in another place, "must wholly quit, then, the quarry for a while; and not only go forth and get tools to use in the quarry, but must go and thoroughly discover architecture. Now the quarry discoverer is long before the stone-cutter; and the stone-cutter is long before the architect; and the architect is long before the temple; for the temple is the crown of the world." His apprenticeship is at last definitely over: he is at work on the temple itself—such a temple as Dante, Shakespeare, Webster, Marlowe, Browne, might each in his way have conceived and designed.

The days go by; the leaves fall; the candlelight comes early; the mice creep into the cupboard and make nests for themselves in the woodpile; the wide meadows become as bleak as a grey sea. In this most inland scene, with only the Housatonic to connect him with the watery world, Melville still dreams of the sea: his thought centres on the sea, its creatures, its boats, its fish, its men, its deeper monsters. Oh! for a dash of salt spray! he cries; and as substitute he draws upon experience and memory for the savour. The days grow cold. Snow hems in the roof and chimney of Arrowhead. Melville has a sea-feeling all the more: when he looks out of his little window on rising, he feels as if he were looking out of his port-hole in the midst of the Atlantic: his room seems a ship's cabin, and at nights, when he wakes up and hears the wind shrieking, he can almost fancy there is too much sail on the house, and he had better go up on the roof and rig in the chimney. On a winter morning he rises at eight, helps his horse to his hay and the cow to her pumpkin, stands around to take in the grateful complacency of the cow, she moves her jaws so mildly and with such sanctity; then, with his own breakfast over, he goes to his workroom and lights the fire, runs rapidly through the MS. and starts to work. At half past two a knock comes. He does not answer. Again the knock and again: till he rises from his writing, almost mechanically, and resumes the external round: feed for the horse and cow: then dinner: then he rigs up his sleigh and goes off to the village for the mail, for supplies, for a little friendly chaffer perhaps round the tavern bar. So one day follows another on the surface; but within, there is change and tumult: Melville, like Ahab, finds a creature tearing at his vitals, and that creature the thing he has created.

"How then with me, writing of this Leviathan? Unconsciously, my chirography expands into placard capitals. Give me a condor's quill! Give me Vesuvius' crater for an inkstand. Friends! hold my arms! For in the mere act of penning my thoughts of this Leviathan, they weary me, and make me faint with the outreaching comprehensiveness of sweep, as if to include the whole circle of the sciences, and all the generations of whales, and men, and mastodons, past, present, and to come, with all the revolving panoramas of empire on earth, and throughout the whole universe, not excluding its suburbs. Such, and so magnifying, is the virtue of a large and liberal theme! We expand to its bulk. To produce a mighty volume you must choose a mighty theme. No great and enduring volume can ever be written upon the flea, though many there be who have tried it."

Such intensity of effort, so many hours of writing and reading, are as exhausting as the direction of a battle: but there is no lying up in winter quarters, no delegation of responsibility: the writer does not live outside his book: the world, the familiar, homely world, becomes a weak picture, and his imagination is the body and blood of reality. Taking a book off the brain, Melville exclaims while in the midst of it, "is akin to the ticklish and dangerous business of taking an old painting off a panel: you have to scrape off the whole brain in order to get at it with due safety—and even then the painting may not be worth the trouble." Well, Moby-Dick is worth the trouble; the very writing of it becomes a powerful instrument in his own development: what absorbs so much of his time and life is not the book alone, "but the primitive elementalizing of the strange stuff, which in the act of attempting the book, has upheaved and upgushed in his soul. Two books are being writ; of which the world shall

151

only see one, and that the bungled one. The larger book, and the infinitely better, is for . . . his own private shelf. That it is whose unfathomable cravings drunk his blood; the other only demands ink."

Melville knows he must not let up on this work; he flogs himself to get his uttermost into it; the application ruins his eyesight. This small aperture and northern light are bad for his eyes: no matter: he writes with one eye closed and the other blinking. By December, in the evening, he is exhausted: he spends the aftermath of the day in a sort of physical trance: but already his mind is anticipating the developments of the next day, and he is up early, and goes back to his task.

Spring comes; but it is no spring for Melville. He will not even be bothered for dinner. Some days he sits at his desk till 4:30 without writing a word; in the spring twilight, when the catkins of the maples glow in the mild sunset and the bluebirds dart about the field like unfettered flowers, he at last comes out and creeps about like an owl. If Melville ploughs and plants, he does it mechanically; his heart is not in it; and he is not nourished by it. In the midst of his writing, his soul reaches a pitch of exaltation, as it does defiantly in a terrible gale, when the hand is firmly on the wheel, and the dangerous seas that wash the decks do not loosen the hold: the letters that he writes to Hawthorne then are prophetic, and deep, and full of proud mastery. In building up his vast symbol of the whale, he strips the universe down to his own ego; like Ahab himself, he says no to all the powers and dominions that lie beyond it. Does not Hawthorne do as much?

"There is a certain tragic phase of humanity," he writes to Hawthorne, "which, in our opinion, was never more powerfully embodied than by Hawthorne. . . . He says No in thunder; but the Devil himself cannot make him say yes. For all men who say yes, lie; and all men who say No,— why, they are in the happy condition of judicious unencumbered travellers in Europe; they cross the frontiers into Eternity, with nothing but a carpet-bag,—that is to say, the Ego. Whereas, those *yes*-gentry, they travel with heaps of baggage and damn them! they will never get through the Custom House."

But the soft milky air of June gets the better of Melville's humours: every breath of the warm earth, the spicy perfume of wild strawberries, the honeyed odour of the locust trees, the dank green fragrance of ferns, the sight of buttercups making the fields sunny even on dull days, or the daisies turning the high grass into the whitish green colour of the ocean when the waves disperse on the beach, the warm feeling of animal contentment that the sun itself pours into a man—all these things renewed his energies and revived his spirits. Melville relaxed and refreshed himself in the sunlight, building an addition to the house, and ploughing and sowing, and watching the green shoots rise. He does not doubt the reality of his black moments: for, as he tells Hawthorne, in the boundless, trackless, but still glorious wilderness of the universe, where he and Hawthorne are outposts, there are savage Indians as well as mosquitoes; still, one does not go on fighting them forever. As for the crotchety and overdoleful chimeras, "the like of you and me, and some others, forming a chain of God's outposts around the world, must be content to encounter now and then, and fight them as best we can."

Melville goes down to New York to see the first part of Moby-Dick through the press; but the oppressive, humid days in that Babylonish brick-kiln, and the long delays of the printers, disgust him; he comes back to the country, and purposes to end the book, if possible, reclining on the grass, or watching the clouds play on a summer afternoon around old Greylock, from the newly built porch he has added to the north side of the house, where the view lies. The tail of Moby-Dick is not cooked yet; though the hell-fire in which the book was broiled might not unreasonably have charred it before this. Melville's intention is sane enough, if only he had the leisure to cultivate the calm, grass-growing mood; but no: he must keep on patching and tinkering at his buildings: in July the hay waits for no author to finish his chapter: there are a hundred chores to keep him away from his book, still more from deep questions about the universe and its meaning and evil and truth and all those aspects of reality that need a Hawthorne for perfect communication. There is no help for it; he must go back to New York to finish the book in a third-story room, where there is no cow to milk, no horse to feed, no sister or wife or mother to be a little hurt or concerned by his inattentiveness or moodiness.

These last straining days in New York were not unlike, one might guess, those that Pierre experienced: the book that was begun in health and exuberance in the keen, riotous air of October in the Berkshires was finished in exacerbations and depression and desolation in the humid dog days of a dirty, unkempt city, days of unrelieved sunlight, followed by afternoon thunderstorms that leave the air even heavier than before, the pavements steaming, the waves of warm, unpleasant air, carrying slight odours of putrefaction, wafted upward into even the third story.

"In the earlier progress of the book, he had found some relief in making his regular evening walk through the greatest thoroughfares of the city; and so the utter desolation of his soul might feel itself more intensely against the bodies of the hurrying thousands. Then he began to be sensible of more fancying stormy nights than pleasant ones; for then the great thoroughfares were less thronged, and the innumerable shop-awnings flapped and beat like schooners' broad sails in a gale, and the shutters banged like lashed bulwarks; and the slates fell hurtling like displaced ship's blocks from aloft. Stemming such tempers through the deserted streets, Pierre felt a dark triumphant joy; that while others had crawled in fear to their kennels, he alone defied the storm-admiral, whose most vindictive pelting of hail-

stones—striking his iron-framed fiery furnace of a body—
melted into soft dew, and so, harmlessly trickled off him.
By-and-by, of such howling, pelting nights, he began to
bend his steps down the narrow side streets, in quest of the
more secluded and mysterious taprooms. There he would feel
a singular satisfaction, in sitting down all dripping in a
chair, ordering his half pint of ale before him, and drawing
over his cap to protect his eyes from the light, eye the varied
faces of the social castaways, who here had their haunts from
bitterest midnights. But at last he began to feel a distaste
for even these; and now nothing but the utter night-deso-
lation of the obscurest warehousing lanes would content him,
or be at all sufferable to him."

"Dollars damn me," he wrote Hawthorne, "and the malicious devil is forever grinning in upon me, holding the door
ajar. My dear Sir, a presentiment is upon me.—I shall at
last be worn out and perish, like an old nutmeg-grater,
grated to pieces by the constant attrition of the wood, that
is, the nutmeg. What I feel most moved to write, that is
banned,—it will not pay. Yet, altogether write the *other*
way I cannot. So the product is a final hash; and all my
books are botches. . . . But I was talking about the 'whale.'
As the fishermen say, 'he was in his flurry' when I left him
some three weeks ago. I'm going to take him up by his jaw,
however, before long and finish him up in some fashion or
another. What's the use of elaborating what, in its very
essence, is so short-lived as a modern book? Though I wrote
the Gospels in this century, I should die in the gutter. What
reputation H. M. has is horrible. Think of it! To go down
to posterity as the man who lived among the cannibals.
When I speak of posterity in reference to myself, I only
mean the babies who will probably be born in the moment
immediately ensuing upon my giving up the ghost. . . . I
shall go down to them in all likelihood. . . . I have come
to regard this matter of Fame as the most transparent of
all vanities. I read Solomon more and more, and every time

see deeper and deeper and unspeakable meanings in him. I did not think of Fame, a year ago, as I do now. My development has all been within a few years past. I am like one of those seeds taken out of the Egyptian pyramids which, after being three thousand years a seed, and nothing but a seed, being planted in English soil, it developed itself, grew to greenness, and then fell to mould. So I. Until I was twenty-five, I had no development at all. From my twenty-fifth year I date my life. Three weeks have scarcely passed, at any time between then and now, that I have not unfolded within myself. But I feel that I am now come to the utmost leaf of the bulb, and that shortly the flower must fall to the mould."

If it was in a mood of confidence and creative delight that he sounded his depths in Moby-Dick, it was in this other mood, chastened, almost fearful, that his stripped ego rose to the surface after this extreme plunge. He had looked into the abyss: he was dizzy, terrified, appalled. His letters to Hawthorne have this mingled sense of awe and exaltation: they are the mood of the last part of Moby-Dick. Melville's notes to Mr. Duyckinck are still jocular and robust; they might be the words of the imperturbable Stubb or the jaunty Flask: but that is because Melville gave Mr. Duyckinck only a part of himself, the polite, free-and-easy, effervescent side, meant for appreciative eating and solicitous drinking, the side he doubtless turned to his family and housemates, when weariness did not bury him from their sight—the last people who could share or understand his quest, his insight, his triumph. There is no question of wearing a mask: both sides of Melville are authentic, but the deeper part of him, which would under happier circumstances have served as ballast and made him face the waves more steadily, claimed too much of his inner space: he lost buoyancy: the water crept above the waterline: the ship rode dangerously. Now, however, we are speaking of the consequences of Melville's writing Moby-Dick. The book itself was published towards the end of 1851 by Bentley, in England, and a little later in the same year by Harper's in New York.

Whether it was an angel or a devil that Melville had struggled with this long year, he had wrestled magnificently, and the book was done. Before we go further with Melville's life, we must discuss this great fragment of it—the most important of Melville's books, and surely one of the most important books of the century.

CHAPTER SEVEN: MOBY-DICK

MOBY-DICK IS a story of the sea, and the sea is life, "whose waters of deep woe are brackish with the salt of human tears." Moby-Dick is the story of the eternal Narcissus in man, gazing into all rivers and oceans to grasp the unfathomable phantom of life—perishing in the illusive waters. Moby-Dick is a portrait of the whale and a presentation of the demonic energies in the universe that harass and frustrate and extinguish the spirit of man. We must gather our own strength together if we are to penetrate Moby-Dick: no other fable, except perhaps Dante's, demands that we open so many doors and turn so many secret keys; for, finally, Moby-Dick is a labyrinth, and that labyrinth is the universe.

Call me Ishmael, says the teller of the story. Ishmael is lured to a whaling voyage by the overwhelming idea of the great whale himself and of the forbidden seas in which he rolls his inland bulk: when Ishmael grows grim around the mouth and feels damp, drizzly November in his soul, he goes to sea. With his carpet-bag he sets out for New Bedford, and takes refuge in the shaggy comfort of Spouter Inn. His companion and bedfellow in the crowded inn is another Ishmael, a cannibal named Queequeg, who brings into the atmosphere of chowders and tarpaulins a wild odour from another continent of the soul. His harpoon, his idol, his sharp filed teeth, the human head he carries around in a bag, for sale, are for Ishmael hints of that horror in the universe which he is quick to perceive and be social with, since it is well to be on friendly terms with the inmates of the place one lodges in.

When Ishmael takes refuge from the driving sleet and mist, on a Sunday morning, in the Whalemen's Chapel, he finds reminders of luckless voyages on the memorial tablets around the hall, and Father Mapple, who had been a sailor and harpooner in his youth, delivers a sermon on Jonah! What a preacher, and what a sermon! After ascending to the pulpit by a rope ladder, hand over hand, Father Mapple drags the ladder up after him, to signify his spiritual withdrawal from all outward ties and connections; from that pulpit, shaped like a ship's bow, he expounds the fable of Jonah, seeming, as he describes Jonah's sea-storm, to be beaten by a storm himself, his deep chest heaving as with a ground-swell, his tossed arms like the warring elements at work, thunders rolling away from his swarthy brow and light leaping from his eye.

Father Mapple's words and figures belong to the Bible; but their meaning comes from that bottomless ocean of truth where Moby-Dick plies back and forth. I must quote the words: one can give no proper hint of this work, even in its smallest detail, without quoting the language through which it is expressed: and this is particularly true of Father Mapple's noble tongue.

"But oh! shipmates! on the starboard hand of every woe, there is sure delight; and higher the top of that delight than the bottom of the woe is deep. Is not the maintruck higher than the kelson is low? Delight is to him—a far, far upward, and inward delight—who against the proud gods and commodores of this earth, ever stands forth his inexorable self. Delight is to him whose strong arms yet support him, when the ship of this base treacherous world goes down beneath him. Delight is to him, who gives no quarter for the truth, and kills, burns, and destroys all sin, though he pluck it out from under the robes of Senators and Judges. Delight —top-gallant delight is to him, who acknowledges no law or lord but the Lord his God, and is only patriot to heaven. Delight is to him whom all the waves and billows of the seas

159

of the boisterous mob can never shake from this sure Keel of
the Ages. And eternal delight and deliciousness will be his,
who coming to lay him down, can say with his final breath—
O Father!—chiefly known to me by Thy rod—mortal or
immortal, here I die. I have striven to be Thine, more than
to be this world's or mine own. Yet this is nothing; I leave
eternity to Thee; for what is man that he should live out
the lifetime of his God?"

Humbly participating in Queequeg's heathenish rites,
sharing confidences with him, Ishmael pledges friendship
with the cannibal: it is the first and almost the last touch
of affection in the whole story: a compact between two strays
and outcasts! In Heaven, and presumably in Hell, there is
neither marrying nor giving in marriage; nor are there all
those little mollifications, an eloquent meal or a June garden, which belong to the middle portion of life that has long
been domesticated: once Moby-Dick gets under way, the
fable itself belongs to Heaven and Hell—all its naturalism,
all its accurate detail, are polarized between these two extremes of being, so that everything which would relieve
men's exasperation or take the edge off their lonely delight,
disappears, as the land disappears beyond the horizon's
edge. The reason for this is not obscure. In terms of Heaven
and Hell this comfortable, understandable, tolerable middle
portion of existence—that which we agree to call civilized—
is the realm of complete illusion: just as, in terms of immediate animal existence, Heaven and Hell are illusions, and
reality belongs to the realm of digestion, tropism, reflex
action, muscular movement, tactile and visual adjustments.
Melville, as we shall see, comprehended both aspects of existence: but he projected them both on the plane of eternity:
domestic life and all it implies is seen through reversed
glasses.

On the boat that takes Queequeg and Ishmael to Nantucket, Queequeg performs a daring rescue in the water.
The man he brings up is a bumpkin whom he had punished

just a little while before for mimicking him: the punishment
and the rescue are performed with the indifferent magnanimity of a soft breeze following a cold wreck of tornado.
There is the key in which the whole story is set. If we forget
it, we shall be disappointed at not finding some continued
development of these separate personalities, some further
proofs of their friendship and affection. But on the plane of
Moby-Dick friendship is a small thing, and heroism a small
one, too: the hero is not Ishmael who tells the story, nor
Queequeg, who is one of the crew, nor even Captain Ahab
who commands the Pequod, on which the two finally embark
at Nantucket: the central figure is the whale, and the whale
stands for the universe.

The mystery of Captain Ahab and the voyage lies heavy
before the sails are set or the anchor lifted. In the dawn,
when Ishmael goes aboard, he dimly sees through the mist
four or five figures running toward the ship, who completely
disappear by the time he gains the decks: the mystery is
more vexing because of a cracked old greybeard on the
wharf who mutters dreadful hints about Ahab and his voyage, not enough to detain Ishmael, but enough to make him
uncomfortable. With a last blessing of the owners, the ship
sets out on Christmas Day. The captain remains inviolate in
his cabin; and with the crew giving three heavy-hearted
cheers, the ship "blindly plunged like fate into the lone
Atlantic."

Exit the dry, tight, comfortable land: enter wind and
weather and sea and whale. We leave behind the landlord
of the Spouter Inn and Mrs. Hosea and the old owners,
with their humorous mixture of the Bible and worldly stratagem, and Charity, Captain Bildad's sister, who places a
choice copy of Watts' hymns in each seaman's berth: these
genre pictures in the manner of Teniers, with a dash of
Hogarth or Rowlandson, belong to the land and its ways,
little ways. Deliberately, Melville widens the frame of his
canvas, and alters the plan of his design: magnifying every

figure into its ideal proportions. He is about to picture this "mortally intolerable truth; that all deep earnest thinking is but the intrepid effort of the soul to keep the open independence of the sea; while the wild winds of heaven and earth conspire to cast her on the treacherous, slavish shore. . . . Better is it to perish in that howling infinite than be ingloriously dashed upon the lee, even if that were safety."

Safety we leave behind: safety and the measures of daily life. The sea is dangerous: the horizon has no bounds: and the fathom-line can never reach the bottom, once land is far astern.

2

When the whale enters, the narrative for the first time pauses; and, in the pause, one discovers that the story and the people are secondary matters, while something more wide and reaching comes into the fable. The whale is a symbol in the heart of man; it has its own existence and value there: but the whale is also a creature in natural history, and its shape, its bulk, habits, anatomical characteristics, family relations, its place in politics, economics, history, and human adventure, is a further part of that natural history. The chapter on the whale, in which the various branches are listed under a sort of bookseller's classification, into Folio, Octavo, and Duodecimo whales, is an excellent example of Melville's way of assimilating and revaluating knowledge, so that what was extraneous becomes intrinsic, and what was a fact in the history of the whale becomes an element in the myth that he is weaving.

A timid writer would have left these classifications and divisions out: how on earth is one to make interesting reading out of a bare catalogue? But Melville carries the load with Olympian levity: he invents a fresh classification, unknown to Owen or Cuvier, and then, with a final dash of apparent impatience, he leaves the system uncompleted— even as the great Cathedral of Cologne was left, "with the cranes still standing upon the top of the uncompleted

tower." This absurd, bookseller's classification, and this last
touch of impatience are not due to Melville's incompetence:
the first tells us that all systems of thought have in them
something arbitrary and human, and the zoologist's classification and system is no less so than the human foot, as the
standard of linear measurement: when one sees objects under
the figure of eternity, the scientist's divisions have the same
limitations as the bookseller's. In a century when only a few
rare-minded mathematicians were elaborating the theory
that our existing geometry was but one out of a number of
possible systems, with different sets of postulates, Melville
was slyly demonstrating that all our thought has this conventional basis. One may alter the convention, change the
point of approach, and create a different order, equally
useful, equally competent, equally true. When Melville stops
abruptly without finishing his own work, he points out to
us that knowledge of all sorts belongs to an infinite series:
there is no final stopping-place: and he who thinks his system is complete has only demonstrated his own limitations.

Although Melville plays with science, he utilizes all that
it can give him, and he never seriously departs from its find-
ings except in taking the fisherman's view that the whale is a
fish, and not, as is actually the case, an aquatic mammal. But
the whale that science investigates, the whale that is stranded
on the beach, or whose skeleton is suspended in mid-air in the
natural-history museum, is not, however thoroughly it may
be dissected and articulated and labelled, the whole whale,
even for science; for a whale, like every other creature, has
a habitat, relations with other living creatures, and certain
ways of functioning, moving, mating, finding food; and
there is a sense in which one is as near to the scientific truth
about a whale when one is fighting the creature in an open
boat, as when one is counting its vertebrae, examining its
tissues under a microscope, or comparing its skull with
other mammalian skulls. Melville gives a completer account
of the whale than the anatomists: he approaches it with a

harpoon as well as a dissecting-knife: he observes its characteristic reaction to stimuli as well as the organs by means of which these reactions are effected. On the other hand, the physical pursuit of the whale is only a part of the story: the more one learns about such a creature, the more widely do its relations ramify, not merely in its own world, but in man's: and the higher the significance of the hunt itself. These passages about the whale and the methods of whaling, about its dignity and adventure, these comments upon the science of cetology—all these things are not uncouth interruptions in the narrative: they are profoundly part of it: the stream widens here, as the Hudson widens at Tappan Zee, without losing its flow and purpose. From now on the universal, symbolic aspect of the story, and its direct, scientific, practical aspect move in and out like the threads of a complicated pattern: one modifies the other, and is by turns figure and background. The physical expanse of the book, its deliberateness of movement, its slow undulations, are necessary, like the long swells and the wide expanse of the ocean itself, to give a feeling of immensity, immensity and power.

3

Who are the men summoned together for this voyage? The chief mate, Starbuck, is a Quaker by descent, a "long earnest man, and though born on an icy coast, seemed well adapted to endure hot latitudes, his flesh being hard as a twice-baked biscuit." Starbuck is conscientious, prudent, inclined to respect outward portents and inward presentiments: above all, the memory of his young Cape wife and child bent the welded iron in his soul. Stubb, the second mate, is a different man: "A happy-go-lucky; neither craven nor valiant, taking perils as they came with an indifferent air; and while engaged in the most imminent crisis of the chase, toiling away, calm and collected as a journeyman joiner engaged by the year." Beneath these two stands little Flask, the third mate, a native of Tisbury, in Marthas Vineyard.

In his poor opinion, the whale was but a species of magnified mouse or at least water-rat. If Starbuck is the prudent imaginative man, and Stubb is the competent sensible matter-of-fact man, Flask is the happy ignorant man, inclined to be waggish in the matter of whales.

Only slightly lower in rank than the mates stand the savage harpooners: Queequeg, and Tashtego, a Gayhead Indian from the Vineyard, and Daggoo, a gigantic, coal-black negro savage, with a lion-like tread, moving about the deck in all the pomp of his six feet five in his socks. "A white man standing before him seemed a white flag come to beg truce of a fortress." As for the crew itself, they were not merely islanders, usually; they were Isolatoes, each man living on a separate continent of his own. Above them all towers Captain Ahab. The first time he appears on deck, a foreboding shiver runs over Ishmael. "Reality outran apprehension. . . . He looked like a man cut away from the stake, when the fire has overrunningly wasted all the limbs without consuming them, or taking away one particle from their compacted aged robustness." One of Ahab's legs has been snapped off by a whale: he stands on a stump made of whale ivory, with a crucifixion in his face, in all the nameless regal overbearing dignity of some mighty woe. "A Khan of the plank and a king of the sea and a great Lord of Leviathans was Ahab." In his presence, his mates shrivel and crumple up, like a paper in a fire. Compared with Ahab's titanic pride, their decent professional self-respect is nothing. There is madness in that pride, the madness of a tormented soul.

What goads Ahab? What goads him is the memory of his encounter with that white whale, Moby-Dick, who, in malice or play or accidental defence, had bitten off Ahab's leg and left him humiliated and crippled, for long months of days and weeks, stretched in one hammock, his torn body and gashed soul bleeding into one another, and so interfusing, making him mad. . . . "Ever since that almost fatal encounter, Ahab had cherished a wild vindictiveness against the whale, all the more fell for that in his frantic morbidness he at last came to identify with him not only all his bodily woes but all his intellectual and spiritual exasperations. The White Whale swam before him as the monomaniac incarnation of all the malicious agencies which some deep men feel eating in them, till they are left living on with half a heart and half a lung. That intangible malignity which has been from the beginning; to whose dominion even the modern Christians ascribe one-half of the worlds; which the ancient Ophites of the East reverence in their statue devil; —Ahab did not fall down and worship it like them; but deliriously transferring its idea to the abhorred white whale, he pitted himself, all mutilated, against it. All that most maddens and torments; all that stirs up the lees of things; all truth with malice in it; all that cracks the sinews and cakes the brain; all the subtle demonism of life and thought; all evil, to crazy Ahab, were visibly personified, and made practically assailable in Moby-Dick. He piled up on the whale's white hump the sum of all the general rage and hate felt by his whole race from Adam down; and then, as if his chest had been a mortar, he burst his hot heart's shell upon it."

Ahab assembles his crew, and after working them up with a reminder of their common duties, to sing out, to lower away, to get a dead whale or a stove boat, he nails a goldpiece to the main mast and in a high, raised voice exclaims: "Who ever of ye raises me a white-headed whale with a wrinkled brow and a crooked jaw . . . shall have this gold ounce." Daggoo recognizes Moby-Dick. Ahab, surprised, confesses his past humiliation and announces his purpose. "This is what we have shipped for, men! to chase the white whale on both sides of the land, and over all sides of the earth, till he spouts black blood and rolls fin out!" The crew is seized with Captain Ahab's wild purpose. Starbuck alone, prudent, thoughtful, pious, remonstrates with his captain. " 'Vengeance on a dumb brute!' cries Starbuck, 'that simply smote thee from blindest instinct! Madness! To be enraged with a dumb thing, Captain Ahab, seems blasphemous.' " And Ahab answers:

"All visible objects, man, are but as pasteboard masks. But in each event—in the living act, the undoubted deed— there, some unknown but still reasoning thing puts forth the mouldings of its features from behind the unreasoning mask. If man will strike, strike through the mask! How can the prisoner reach outside except by thrusting through the wall? To me, the white whale is that wall, shoved near to me. Sometimes I think there's naught beyond. But 'tis enough. He tasks me; he heaps me; I see in him outrageous strength, with an inscrutable malice sinewing it. That inscrutable thing is what I chiefly hate; and be the white whale agent, or be the white whale principal, I will wreak that hate upon him. Talk not to me of blasphemy, man: I'd strike the sun if it insulted me. For could the sun do that, then could I the other; since there is ever a sort of fair play herein, jealously presiding over all creations. But not my master, man, is even that fair play. Who's over me? Truth hath no confines."

Ahab pledges his crew; they drink and swear death to Moby-Dick. Ahab withdraws to his cabin, to contemplate his own madness, maddened: there he defies the great gods themselves, mere cricket players and pugilists. "I will not say as schoolboys do to their bullies—Take some one of your size: don't pommel *me!* No, ye've knocked me down, and I am up again, but ye have run and hidden. Come forth from behind your cotton bags! . . . Ahab's compliments to ye; come and see if ye can swerve me." The crew, lightened by drink, burst into revelry: they jig and frolic and dream about girls. Ishmael's shouts go up with the rest: his oath had been welded to theirs; a wild mystical feeling is in him:

'Ahab's quenchless feud seems his. With greedy ears he learns the story of the monster against whom he and his shipmates have taken the oath of Ahab's revenge.

4

And now comes Moby-Dick. In all the sperm whale fishery there is no whale more prodigious in magnitude or malignity. All whales are dangerous to hunt with harpoon and spear in a whale-boat; but Moby-Dick multiplies the vicissitudes of the chase: he turns on his pursuers, and again and again escapes them, with an apparently immortal destiny, however accurately the harpoons may have been planted in his side, and however strong the line that makes him fast. A wrinkled forehead, a high white hump, and a streaked and marbled body add to his formidable size: as sperm whales are more dangerous than Right or Greenland whales, so Moby-Dick is more terrifying than the usual sperm whale. The rumours about Moby-Dick raise to enormous dimensions what was already great enough in actuality; but the very whiteness of the whale adds something more.

While white, says Melville, has a hundred fine mythological allusions, conveying some special virtue or perfection to the elephant of Siam or the Imperial charger; while the white wampum of the red man was the deepest pledge of honour, and the most august of religions had made of it a symbol of divine spotlessness and power—for all these accumulated associations with whatever is sweet, and honourable, and sublime, there yet lurks an elusive something in the innermost idea of this hue which strikes more of a panic to the soul than that redness which affrights in blood. The whiteness of the white shark, the whiteness of the white squall in southern seas, the terror of white breakers when a ship is skirting the coast—all these things gain an element of bleak terror from their cold hue. White is the terrible, elemental truth: all warmer hues and colours are but laid on from without: nature paints like a harlot, and beneath these happy colours is the ghastly white uniformity of the charnel-house. "Pondering all this, the palsied universe lies before us like a leper; and like wilful travellers in Lapland, who refuse to wear coloured or colouring glasses upon their eyes, so the wretched infidel gazes himself blind at the monumental white shroud that wraps all the prospect around him. And of all these things, the Albino whale was the symbol. Wonder ye then at the fiery hunt?"

5

Night and day Ahab's mind broods over Moby-Dick. In his cabin he pores over his charts, endeavouring to follow the seasonal tracks of Moby-Dick from one probable feeding-ground to another; but, as he knows his crew have common daily appetites, and the permanent constitution of the manufactured man is sordidness, although he may occasionally be fired into knight-errantry, on the first raising of a whale, the Pequod goes in pursuit.

In his virgin encounter with the whale, under the "prudent" Starbuck, Ishmael finds himself in a swamped boat, riding through the night in the hope of being picked up in the morning; and on top of the long vigil, the little whaleboat, lost in the mist, is run down by the Pequod, and all the cold, drenched hands take to the water for their lives. It is all in a day's work. When terror and anguish become unbearable, what seems most momentous becomes part of a general joke. This humour of desperation colours and effervesces through all the bitter potions that the tale itself offers: it does not remove the bitterness, but, as sweet and bitter may mingle in the same draught, it offers a countertaste: and it keeps the most frenzied blackness from having the unrelieved and inhuman quality of a maniac's delirium. The men who face death and danger most constantly, the sailor, the miner, the soldier, the lonely pioneer, develop this shrug and grin at the very moment of encountering death—and in the whale fishery, these moments are plentiful. Little

Pip, the negro, pops out of his boat in fright, and is left behind in the heat of the chase, and, though finally rescued, is turned into a blank idiot: Tashtego, ladling out the fragrant sperm from the dead whale's head, falls into it, the entire mass drops into the sea, and the Indian is rescued only by a feat of almost obstetrical skill: any hour, one may drop from a lookout station or get tangled in the whale-line itself, as the whale races with it, and perish in the coils. But what of it? "All men live enveloped in whale-lines. All are born with halters round their necks; but it is only in the swift, subtle turns of death that mortals realize the silent, subtle, ever-present perils of life. And if you be a philosopher, though seated in the whale-boat, you would not at heart feel one whit more of terror than though seated before your evening fire with a poker and not a harpoon by your side."

As the pursuit of the whale goes on, as the Pequod encounters the sperm whale and the right whale, and kills them, fastens them to its side, and dismantles their corpses, getting sperm oil from one and whalebone from the other, as they watch the spout of the whale from the distance, or see, at midnight, an apparition of a spout, perhaps a portent, perhaps jetting from the head of Moby-Dick himself: as they sample the whale as food, as they render down its blubber into oil, as they watch the sharks thrust their slithering upturned mouths at the carcass, as they squeeze the lumps of cold, solidified fat back into liquid; as all the events and preparations take place, the whale finally emerges as a complete body. What the whale is to the whaleman and what he is to the artist; what he is to the naturalist and what he is to the merchant; and what he is in the chase— and in the museum—and in human history—all these things come forth. There is not one method of knowledge: every manifestation in human experience contributes to the reality of the whale itself. No one lives to himself, or comprehends himself, except by establishing relationships with that which is outside himself: man gives to the whale something that the creature is incapable of giving back: his own needs, his own desires, his own understanding. Melville no more forgets the aesthetics of whaling than he forgets the economics. He is a free spirit: he explores everything, embraces everything, reports on everything. We must not confuse Moby-Dick with the monomaniac captain who belongs to the fable: the book itself has a hundred sides, and is the precise opposite of that narrow quest. For immediate action, people forget many of these relations: the artist or the scientist is just as narrow in his interests as Flask, just as single-minded in his pursuit as Ahab. But Melville is neither Flask nor Ahab nor artist nor scientist: he philosophizes out of a completer experience and a more coherent consciousness than any of these partial figures. The whale is no phantom symbol; and this stage is no pasteboard stage. If this is not the universe, the full universe, that Melville embodies under these symbols, no one in our time has had inkling of a fuller one. Moby-Dick is an imaginative synthesis; and every aspect of reality belongs to it, one plane modifying the other and creating the modelled whole.

6

The ship sails on: she meets other ships and the crews mingle in a conversation or "gam." But Ahab restlessly drives on towards his ultimate goal: to each captain his first question is—"Hast seen the White Whale?"

Passing through the straits of Sunda, which divide Sumatra from Java, the Pequod spies great semi-circles of whale-jets sparkling on the horizon: she spreads sails after the Grand Armada; and presently, the boats are in the midst of it: among sires and cows and calves, the big and the little, spouting, playing, plunging, frantically mobbing the whale-boat, a tumult of power and virile energy on the outskirts of the Armada, but safe within the circle, calm and bliss, dalliance and delight, calves milking their mothers, and amorous bulls warm-bloodedly a-wenching. The boats, luckily, get out of this jam and tumult without damage; but while they set their pennoned poles on many, only one of the drugged whales is captured. This is but one of a score of scenes in Moby-Dick that remain in the memory like a personal experience: one exclaims with Ishmael: I was one of that crew, I pulled in that boat, I floundered around in those waters. A thousand things happen in life with less vividness and impact than they make in these printed pages: the Straits of Sunda are nearer than the neighbouring street.

Shortly after this encounter, the chase grows hotter: the Pequod meets the Samuel Enderby of London, and the Samuel Enderby has met Moby-Dick. Captain Ahab cannot contain himself: his gam with the English captain ends abruptly, and, with the blood pounding in his veins, he springs back to the ship—so precipitately that his ivory leg is shattered and the carpenter must fit him with a new one. The indignity increases Ahab's impatient pride: "Here I am," he exclaims, "proud as a Greek god, and yet standing debtor to this blockhead for a bone to stand on! Cursed be that mortal inter-debtedness which will not do away with ledgers. I would be free as air; and I'm down in the whole world's books." Ahab causes a new harpoon head to be forged: he mans his own boat with the mysterious figures that had crept on the Pequod in the twilight of the morning they left Nantucket, Orientals, led by a Parsee, Fedallah. But at every move, Ahab stumbles on some new obstruction, or delay; and his words become more frenzied, while the effort of his will leaves a white scar of terror wherever his lightnings momentarily strike. When the Bachelor, homeward bound, full of oil, seeks to detain the Pequod for a friendly parley, Ahab leaves it behind with a curse.

Against the under-chorus of Stubb's common sense and Starbuck's prudent humanity, Ahab's shrieks mount more wildly: he even throws the quadrant overboard, to steer by compass, fathom-line, and dead reckoning. In the last extremity of pursuit, in utter arrogance of purpose, he thrusts aside the quadrant as the foolish toy and baby's plaything of haughty admirals and commodores and captains: in the final issue of life and death, science is impotent: it can but tell where the ship is on the planet, but not where one drop of water or one grain of sand will be tomorrow noon. Now the Pequod must ride out a typhoon; and in the midst of the electric storm, three corposants, tapers of white flame, appear on the three lightning-rods of the masts. For Ahab, his purpose is only beating nearer its goal: instead of bowing to the blind forces around him, the storm, the sea, the lightning, the whale, his resolution is more deeply fortified. Note his words: there are none more sudden and final with meaning in the whole book.

"Oh! thou clear spirit of clear fire, whom on these seas I as Persian once did worship, till in the sacramental act so burned by thee, that to this hour I bear the scar; I now know thee, thou clear spirit, and I now know that thy right worship is defiance. To neither love nor reverence will thou be kind; and e'en for hate thou canst but kill; and all are killed. No fearless fool now fronts thee. I own thy speechless, placeless power; but to the last gasp of my earthquake life will dispute its unconditional, unintegral mastery in me. In the midst of the personified impersonal, a personality stands here. Though but a point at best; whencesoe'er I came; wheresoe'er I go; yet while I earthly live, the queenly personality lives in me, and feels her royal rights. But war is pain, and hate is woe. Come in thy lowest form of love, and I will kneel and kiss thee; but at thy highest, come as mere supernal power; and though thou launchest navies of full-freighted worlds, there's that in here that still remains indifferent. O thou clear spirit, of the fire thou madest me, and like a true child of fire, I breathe it back to thee."

Everything conspires against Ahab's deed: the compass needle goes wrong: the log and line, hitherto seldom used, snap off when they are heaved: a man is lost overboard and the life-buoy that was sent over after him springs a leak and goes down with him; finally, another whaler, the Rachel, that has lost a boat's crew with the captain's son aboard, seeks to stay Ahab, so that the Pequod may help in the search: Ahab refuses this call of humanity. One being alone almost defeats Ahab, not Starbuck, who, rifle in hand, is tempted to kill Ahab and end his crazy pursuit, but Pip, the little Negro idiot, whose devotion rises as the isolation of Ahab grows. Ahab flees from him: his love, faith, devotion move him from his purpose as no disasters or portents have hitherto moved him. "If thou speakest thus to me much more, Ahab's purpose keels up in him," Ahab admonishes himself. The boy is black, and an outcast. The black is an idiot, and so doubly an outcast. From one as mad and isolated as himself, Ahab receives love, a love deep as his own sense of pride and power, and he is almost unmanned by it. "Spite of a million villains," says Ahab, "this makes me a bigot in the fadeless fidelity of man." But love has come too late: the chase goes on.

As Ahab nears Moby-Dick his old humanity comes back to him. He sees his own wife and child in Starbuck's eye, regrets her perpetual widowhood, and is lenient to Starbuck's own desire to return to his hearth. No: more: Ahab sees his wasted years: the desolation of their solitude: the slavery of a lonely command: the dry nourishment this isolated soul has fed upon—forty years of waste and forty years of folly since, as a lad of eighteen, on a mild sweet day, he struck his first whale, a boy-harpooner of eighteen. How is it that in spite of all this he pursues his purpose? What keeps him pushing and crowding himself all the time, recklessly making himself ready to do what in his own nature he had no desire to accomplish?

The mild day and the steel-blue sky and the smell of the wind, as if the haymakers had been mowing grass on the slopes of the Andes—this day is scarcely over before Ahab detects a whale in the wind; and at next daybreak, Ahab himself raises the hump-like snow-head—Moby-Dick. In the smoother ocean, Moby-Dick seems as mild as the day, gliding with scarcely a ripple through the water, his wrenched, hideous jaw beneath the surface. Becoming aware of the chase, he sounds—only to return with open jaws beneath the bottom of Ahab's boat, and, after playing with it as a cat with a mouse, he bites it in twain. The Pequod sails on the whale and drives him off. Ahab and his crew are rescued, Ahab with bloodshot blinded eyes, the white brine caking in his wrinkles, manly wails arising from some far inland part of his being, as desolate as sounds from out ravines.

The second day comes, and the boats lower again. Moby-Dick takes the initiative and plunges immediately towards the boats with open jaws and lashing tail, warping and manoeuvring in such a fashion that the harpoons thrust into him become tangled and the lines shortened: again the whale dives, and again he rises, this time throwing Ahab's boat topsy-turvy in the air. Ahab's ivory leg is snapped off; but again he is rescued; and a third day opens. At noon, Ahab, keeping lookout himself, and doubling on his tracks, sights the whale, making towards him in the distance. Again the calm and beauty of the day wake some old humanity in Ahab; but he is churned onward by his purpose.

"Some men die at ebb-tide; some at low water; some at the full of the flood;—I feel like a billow that's all one crested comb. I am old;—shake hands with me, man," says Ahab to his first mate.

Their hands met; their eyes fastened; but Starbuck's manly tears cannot restrain Ahab's order to lower away in pursuit, nor can the sharks that crowd around the boat and snap maliciously at the oars, nor can the hawk that tears at the red flag running on the main truck; nothing diverts him. The whale sounds; when he rises, tormented by a mass of harpoons and lines, it is as if a submerged iceberg rose suddenly to the surface, the waters flash like a heap of fountains, break in a shower of flakes, and leave the circling surface creamed like new milk round the marble trunk of the whale. Moby-Dick, churning his tail among the boats, dashes in the bows of the mate's boat: Ahab, unscathed, orders them back to the ship, while he keeps to the hunt. The whale, fagged or malicious, permits Ahab to catch up with him: Ahab darts iron and curse into his flanks; but the line snaps loose, and the whale turns upon the Pequod herself, and bears down on her, his solid white buttress of a forehead meeting and shivering the planks. The ship settles. Ahab, cut off from the ship, makes one last thrust at the whale; the line spins out and runs foul, and Ahab, stooping to unsnarl it, is caught round the neck and shot out of the boat, fulfilling the prophecy of Fedallah, who has been drowned before him. The rest of the crew turns towards the Pequod; only its masts remain above the water; and as it goes down, they are carried in the suction. As its final spar settles in the water, a red arm and hammer hover back upliftedly in the air, in the act of nailing the flag faster to the subsiding spar. A sky-hawk, pecking at the flag, intercepts the hammer with his wing; and in the death-grasp of Tashtego, the pinioned bird of heaven, with shrieks, his form folded in Ahab's flag, is dragged into the water: the boat would not sink to hell until she had carried a living part of heaven with her, and helmeted herself with it.

"Now small fowls flew screaming over the yet yawning gulf; a sullen white surf beat against its steep sides; then all collapsed, and the great shroud of the sea rolled on as it rolled five thousand years ago."

7

It is absurd and ineffectual to give a summary of Moby-Dick, or to quote, dismembered, some of its great passages. Like the paintings in the Ajanta caves, the beauty of Moby-Dick can be known only to those who will make a pilgrimage to it, and stay within its dark confines until what is darkness

has become light, and one can make out, with the help of an
occasional torch, its grand design, its complicated arabesque,
the minute significance of its parts. No feeble pencil sketch
can convey a notion of Moby-Dick's extravagant beauty;
but at the same time, without a hint of its design and its
manner of execution, all subsequent commentary must seem
flatulent and disproportionate. For three-quarters of a
century Moby-Dick has suffered at the hands of the superficial critic: it has been condemned because to one man it
seemed confused, to another it was not a novel, to a third
the characters were not "real," and to a fourth it was merely
a weird, mystical, impossible tale of dubious veracity, an
example of Bedlam literature, while to a fifth, it was just
a straightforward account of the whaling industry, marred
by a crazy captain and an adventitious plot. The final
answer to all these criticisms lies, of course, in the book
itself: but the foregoing outline will perhaps aid us a little
in defining the qualities and limits of Melville's vast epic.

Before we can take the measure of Moby-Dick we must,
however, throw aside our ordinary measuring-sticks: one
does not measure Saturn with the aid of an opera-glass and
a dressmaker's tape. The conventional critic has dismissed
Moby-Dick because it is "not a novel," or if it is a novel, its
story is marred by all sorts of extraneous material, history,
natural history, philosophy, mythological excursions, what
not. This sort of criticism would belittle Moby-Dick by
showing that it does not respect canons of a much pettier
nature than the work itself, or because its colossal bulk cannot be caught in the herring-net of the commonplace story
or romance. Even Mr. John Freeman, one of the most sympathetic interpreters of Melville, falls into this error; for,
while acknowledging the great qualities of Moby-Dick, he
refers to its "digressions and delays" as if they were in fact
digressions and delays; that is, as if the "action" in the common novelist's development of plot carried the thread of
the story.

The matter is very easily put to rights if we simply abandon these false categories altogether. Moby-Dick stands by itself as complete as the Divine Comedy or the Odyssey stands by itself. Benedetto Croce has correctly taught us that every work of art is indeed in this same position: that it is uniquely what it is, and cannot be understood except in terms of its own purpose. If, for purely practical reasons, we ignore this in dealing with the ruck of novels and stories, because their inner purpose is so insignificant, we must respect it strictly when we confront a work that does not conspicuously conform to the established canons; for, needless to say, an imaginative work of the first rank will disclose itself through its differences and its departures, by what it originates, rather than by what it is derived from or akin to. Had Melville seriously sought in Moby-Dick to rival the work of Trollope or Reade or Dickens, had he simply desired to amuse and edify the great bourgeois public that consumed its three-decker novels as it consumed its ten-course public dinners, and wanted no delay in the service, no hitch in the round of food, drink, toasts, speeches, and above all, no unaccustomed victuals on such occasions, then Moby-Dick would have been a mistake and failure. But one cannot count as a failure what was never an attempt. Moby-Dick does not belong to this comfortable bourgeois world, any more than horse-hair shirts or long fasts; it neither aids digestion nor increases the sense of warm drowsy good nature that leads finally to bed: and that is all there is to it.

The same criticism that disposes of the notion that Moby-Dick is a bad novel, by admitting freely that it is not a novel at all, equally disposes of its lack of verisimilitude. Although Melville was at first challenged on his facts, such as the ramming of the Pequod by Moby-Dick, events were just as kind to his reputation here as they were in the case of Typee: for while Moby-Dick was on the press, news came of the sinking of the whaler Ann Alexander by the ferocious attack of a whale. No one of authority has attempted to quarrel with Melville's descriptions of the life and habits of whalemen and the whale: the testimony of every observer is that Melville left very little for any one else to say about the subject. This does not, however, dispose of the charge; for those who are wisely captious of Melville here will confine themselves to saying that no such crew ever existed, no such words ever passed human mouth, and no such thoughts could enter the mind of a Nantucketer, as entered Ahab's.

Again, one is tempted to grant the objection; for it makes no difference in the value of Moby-Dick as a work of art. In the realistic convention, Moby-Dick would be a bad book: it happens that the story is projected on more than one plane, and a good part of it belongs to another, and equally valid, convention. Melville himself was aware of the difference, and early in the book he calls upon the Spirit of Equality, which has spread its royal mantle of humanity over all his kind, to defend him against all mortal critics "if, then, to the meanest mariners, and renegades, and castaways, I shall hereafter ascribe high qualities, though dark; weave round them tragic graces; if even the most mournful, perchance the most abased among them all shall at times lift himself to the exalted mounts; if I shall touch that workman's arm with some ethereal light; if I shall spread the rainbow over his disastrous set of sun." Now, the convention in which Melville cast this part of Moby-Dick was foreign to the nineteenth century; obscure people, like Beddoes, alone essayed it: to create these idealized figures called for such reserves of power that only minor poets, for the most part, unconscious of their weaknesses, attempted the task.

The objections to Melville's use of this convention would be fair enough if, like the minor poets, he failed; but, through his success, one sees that the limitations of naturalism are no closer to reality than the limitations of poetic tragedy; and, on the contrary, Melville's valiant use of this convention enabled him to present a much fuller picture of reality than the purely external suggestions of current realism would have permitted him to show. What we call realism is a method of approaching reality: an external picture of a Cowperwood or a Gantry may have as little human truth in it as a purely fanciful description of an elf: and the artist who can draw upon more than one convention is, at all events, free from the curious illusion, so common in the nineteenth century, alike in philosophy, with its pragmatism in science, with its dogmatic materialism, and in imaginative writing, with its realism, that this convention is not limited, and so far arbitrary, but the very stuff and vitals of existence. The question to settle is not: Did an Ahab ever sail from Nantucket? The question is: Do Ahab and Stubb and Starbuck and Tashtego live within the sphere where we find them? The answer is that they are tremendously alive; for they are aspects of the spirit of man. At each utterance, one feels more keenly their imaginative embodiment; so that by the time Ahab breaks into his loftiest Titanisms, one accepts his language, as one accepts his pride: they belong to the fibre and essence of the man. Ahab is a reality in relation to Moby-Dick; and when Melville projects him, he ceases to be incredible, because he is alive.

We need not concern ourselves particularly with those who look upon Moby-Dick solely as a sort of World's Almanac or Gazetteer of the Whaling Industry, unhappily marred by the highly seasoned enticements of the narrative. This criticism is, indeed, but the other side of the sort of objection I have disposed of; and it tells more about the limitations of the reader than it does about the quality of Moby-Dick. For the fact is that this book is a challenge and affront to all the habits of mind that typically prevailed in the nineteenth century, and still remain, almost unabated, among us: it comes out of a different world, and presupposes, for its acceptance, a more integrated life and consciousness than we have known or experienced, for the most part, these last three centuries. Moby-Dick is not Victorian; it is not

Elizabethan; it is, rather, prophetic of another quality of
life which Melville had experienced and had a fuller vision
of in his own time—a quality that may again come into the
world, when we seek to pass beyond the harassed specialisms
which still hold and preoccupy so many of us. To fathom
this quality of Melville's experience and imagination, we
must look a little deeper into his myth and his manner of
projecting it. What is its meaning? And first, in what
manner is that meaning conveyed to us?

8

Moby-Dick is a poetic epic. Typographically, Moby-
Dick conforms to prose, and there are long passages, whole
chapters, which are wholly in the mood of prose: but in spirit
and in actual rhythm, Moby-Dick again and again rises to
polyphonic verse which resembles passages of Webster's in
that it can either be considered as broken blank verse, or as
cadenced prose. Mr. Percy Boynton has performed the interesting experiment of transposing a paragraph in Pierre
into excellent free verse, so strong and subtle are Melville's
rhythms; and one might garner a whole book of verse from
Moby-Dick. Melville, in Moby-Dick, unconsciously respects
Poe's canon that all true poetry must be short in length,
since the mood cannot be retained, unbroken or undiminished, over lengthy passages, and if the form itself is preserved, the content nevertheless is prose. But while Poe
himself used this dictum as an excuse for writing only short
lyrics, Melville sustained the poetic mood through a long
narrative by dropping frankly into prose in the intervening
while. As a result, he was under no necessity of clipping the
emotions or of bleaching the imaginative colours of Moby-
Dick: like a flying-boat, he rises from the water to the air
and returns to the water again without losing control over
either medium. His prose is prose: hard, sinewy, compact;
and his poetry is poetry, vivid, surging, volcanic, creating
its own form in the very pattern of the emotional state itself,

soaring, towering, losing all respect for the smaller conventions of veracity, when the inner triumph itself must be announced. It is in the very rhythm of his language that Ahab's mood, and all the devious symbols of Moby-Dick are sustained and made credible: by no other method could the deeper half of the tale have been written. In these poetic passages, the phrases are intensified, stylicized, stripped of their habitual associations. If occasionally, as with Shakespeare, the thought itself is borne down by the weight of the gold that decorates it, this is only a similar proof of Melville's immense power of expression.

Both Poe and Hawthorne share some of Melville's power, and both of them, with varying success, wrought ideality and actuality into the same figure: but one has only to compare the best of their work with Moby-Dick to see wherein Melville's great distinction lies. The Scarlet Letter, The House of the Seven Gables, William Wilson, like most other works of fiction, are melodic: a single instrument is sufficient to carry the whole theme; whereas Moby-Dick is a symphony; every resource of language and thought, fantasy, description, philosophy, natural history, drama, broken rhythms, blank verse, imagery, symbol, are utilized to sustain and expand the great theme. The conception of Moby-Dick organically demands the expressive interrelation, for a single total effect, of a hundred different pieces: even in accessory matters, like the association of the Parsee, the fire-worshipper, with the death of Ahab, the fire-defier, or in the makeup of the crew, the officers white men, the harpooneers the savage races, red, black, brown, and the crew a mixed lot from the separate islands of the earth, not a stroke is introduced that has not a meaning for the myth as a whole. Although the savage harpooneers get nearest the whale, the savage universe, it is Ahab and the Parsee, the European and the Asiatic, who carry the pursuit to its ultimate end—while a single American survives to tell the tale!

Melville's instrumentation is unsurpassed in the writing

of the last century: one must go to a Beethoven or a Wagner for an exhibition of similar powers: one will not find it among the works of literature. Here are Webster's wild violin, Marlowe's cymbals, Browne's sonorous bass viol, Swift's brass, Smollett's castanets, Shelley's flute, brought together in a single orchestra, complementing each other in a grand symphony. Melville achieved a similar synthesis in thought; and that work has proved all the more credible because he achieved it in language, too. Small wonder that those who were used to elegant pianoforte solos or barrel-organ instrumentation, were deafened and surprised and repulsed.

What is the meaning of Moby-Dick? There is not one meaning; there are many; but in its simplest terms, Moby-Dick is, necessarily, a story of the sea and its ways, as the Odyssey is a story of strange adventure, and War and Peace a story of battles and domestic life. The characters are heightened and slightly distorted: Melville's quizzical comic sense is steadily at work on them, and only Ahab escapes: but they all have their recognizable counterparts in the actual world. Without any prolonged investigation one could still find a Starbuck on Nantucket or a Flask on Marthas Vineyard—indeed, as Mr. Thomas Benton's portraits properly indicate, queerer fish than they.

On this level, Moby-Dick brings together and focusses in a single picture the long line of sketches and preliminary portraits Melville had assembled in Typee, Omoo, Redburn, and White-Jacket. As a story of the sea, Moby-Dick will always have a call for those who wish to recapture the magic and terror and stress and calm delight of the sea and its ships; and not less so because it seizes on a particular kind of ship, the whaler, and a special occupation, whaling, at the moment when they were about to pass out of existence, or rather, were being transformed from a brutal but glorious battle into a methodical, slightly banal industry. Melville had the singular fortune to pronounce a valedictory on many ways of life and scenes that were becoming extinct.

He lived among the South Sea Islanders when they were still pretty much as Captain Cook found them, just before their perversion and decimation by our exotic Western civilization. He recorded life on a man-of-war half a generation before the sail gave place to steam, wood to armour-plate, and grappling-irons to long-range guns. He described life on a sailing-packet before steam had increased the speed, the safety, and the pleasant monotony of transatlantic travel: and finally, he recorded the last heroic days of whaling. Moby-Dick would have value as first-hand testimony, even if it were negligible as literature. If this were all, the book would still be important.

But Moby-Dick, admirable as it is as a narrative of maritime adventure, is far more than that: it is, fundamentally, a parable on the mystery of evil and the accidental malice of the universe. The white whale stands for the brute energies of existence, blind, fatal, overpowering, while Ahab is the spirit of man, small and feeble, but purposive, that pits its puniness against this might, and its purpose against the blank senselessness of power. The evil arises with the good: the white whale grows up among the milder whales which are caught and cut up and used: one hunts for the one— for a happy marriage, livelihood, offspring, social companionship and cheer—and suddenly heaving its white bulk out of the calm sea, one comes upon the other: illness, accident, treachery, jealousy, vengefulness, dull frustration. The South Sea savage did not know of the white whale: at least, like death, it played but a casual part in his consciousness. It is different with the European: his life is a torment of white whales: the Jobs, the Aeschyluses, the Dantes, the Shakespeares, pursue him and grapple with him, as Ahab pursues his antagonist.

All our lesser literature, all our tales of Avalon or Heaven or ultimate redemption, or, in a later day, the Future, is an evasion of the white whale: it is a quest of that boyish beginning which we call a happy ending. But the old Norse myth told that Asgard itself would be consumed at last, and the very gods would be destroyed: the white whale is the symbol of that persistent force of destruction, that meaningless force, which now figures as the outpouring of a volcano or the atmospheric disruption of a tornado or again as the mere aimless dissipation of unused energy into an unavailable void—that spectacle which so disheartened the learned Henry Adams. The whole tale of the West, in mind and action, in the philosophy and art of the Greeks, in the organization and technique of the Romans, in the precise skills and unceasing spiritual quests of the modern man, is a tale of this effort to combat the whale—to ward off his blows, to counteract his aimless thrusts, to create a purpose that will offset the empty malice of Moby-Dick. Without such a purpose, without the belief in such a purpose, life is neither bearable nor significant: unless one is polarized by these central human energies and aims, one tends to become absorbed in Moby-Dick himself, and, becoming a part of his being, can only maim, slay, butcher, like the shark or the white whale or Alexander or Napoleon. If there is no God, exclaims Dostoyevsky's hero, then we may commit murder: and in the sense that God represents the totality of human purpose and meaning the conclusion is inevitable.

It is useless to derive man's purposes from those of the external universe; he is a figure in the web of life. Except for such kindness and loyalty as the creatures man has domesticated show, there is, as far as one can now see, no concern except in man himself over the ceaseless motions and accidents that take place in nature. Love and chance, said Charles Peirce, rule the universe: but the love is man's love, and although in the very concept of chance, as both Peirce and Captain Ahab declare, there is some rough notion of fair play, of fifty-fifty, of an even break, that is small immediate consolation for the creature that may lose not the game, but his life, by an unlucky throw of the dice. Ahab has more humanity than the gods he defies: indeed, he has more power, because he is conscious of the power he wields, and applies it deliberately, whereas Moby-Dick's power only seems deliberate because it cuts across the directed aims of Ahab himself. And in one sense, Ahab achieves victory: he vanquishes in himself that which would retreat from Moby-Dick and acquiesce in his insensate energies and his brutal sway. His end is tragic: evil engulfs him. But in battling against evil, with power instead of love, Ahab himself, in A. E.'s phrase, becomes the image of the thing he hates: he has lost his humanity in the very act of vindicating it. By physical defiance, by physical combat, Ahab cannot rout and capture Moby-Dick: the odds are against him; and if his defiance is noble, his methods are ill chosen. Growth, cultivation, order, art—these are the proper means by which man displaces accident and subdues the vacant external powers in the universe: the way of growth is not to become more powerful but to become more human. Here is a hard lesson to learn: it is easier to wage war than to conquer in oneself the tendency to be partial, vindictive, and unjust: it is easier to demolish one's enemy than to pit oneself against him in an intellectual combat which will disclose one's weaknesses and provincialities. And that evil Ahab seeks to strike is the sum of one's enemies. He does not bow down to it and accept it: therein lies his heroism and virtue: but he fights it with its own weapons and therein lies his madness. All the things that Ahab despises when he is about to attack the whale, the love and loyalty of Pip, the memory of his wife and child, the sextant of science, the inner sense of calm, which makes all external struggle futile, are the very things that would redeem him and make him victorious.

Man's ultimate defence against the Universe, against evil and accident and malice, is not by any fictitious resolution of these things into an Absolute which justifies them and ultilizes them for its own ends: this is specious comfort, and Voltaire's answer to Leibniz in Candide seems to me a final one. Man's defence lies within himself, not within the nar-

row, isolated ego, which may be overwhelmed, but in that
self which we share with our fellows and which assures us
that, whatever happens to our own carcasses and hides, good
men will remain, to carry on the work, to foster and protect
the things we have recognized as excellent. To make that
self more solid, one must advance positive science, produce
formative ideas, and embody ideal forms in which all men
may, to a greater or less degree, participate: in short, one
must create a realm which is independent of the hostile
forces in the universe—and cannot be lightly shaken by their
onslaught. Melville's method, that of writing Moby-Dick,
was correct: as correct as Ahab's method, taken literally,
that of fighting Moby-Dick, was fallacious. In Moby-Dick,
Melville conquered the white whale in his own consciousness:
instead of blankness there was significance, instead of aimless energy there was purpose, and instead of random living
there was Life. The universe *is* inscrutable, unfathomable,
malicious, *so*—like the white whale and his element. Art in
the broad sense of all humanizing effort is man's answer to
this condition: for it is the means by which he circumvents
or postpones his doom, and bravely meets his tragic destiny.
Not tame and gentle bliss, but disaster, heroically encountered, is man's true happy ending.

9

Here, it seems to me, is the plainest interpretation of
Melville's fable, and the one he was partly conscious of in
the writing of it. But a great book is more a part of its
milieu than either the writer or his public knows; and there
is more in Moby-Dick than the figure of man's heroic
defiance of brute energy, and evil, and the high gods.

In another sense, the whale stands for the practical life.
Mankind needs food and light and shelter, and, with a little
daring and a little patience, it gains these things from its
environment: the whale that we cut up, dissect, analyse, melt
down, pour into casks, and distribute in cities and house-

holds is the whale of industry and science. The era of whaling which opened only in the late seventeenth century is timed with the era of modern industry; and in the very year Melville wrote Moby-Dick, 1851, industry and science were announcing their triumphs in that great cock-crow of the Crystal Palace Exhibition in London. Side by side with this purpose, which secures man's material existence, is another set of purposes which, though they sometimes take advantage of the means offered by the practical life, as Ahab takes advantage of his sordid crew and ordinary whaling to carry out his private revenge, run counter to the usual flow of our daily efforts. The white whale cannot be met and captured by the usual means; more than that: to fulfil man's own deeper purposes, the captains of the spirit must oppose the prudence of Starbuck and the common sense of Stubb. Material sustenance, home, comfort, though their pursuit occupy the greater part of the daily round of humanity, are sometimes best forgotten and set at naught: indeed, when nobler human purposes are uppermost, they must be set at naught. He who steadily seeks to preserve life and fortify it must be ready to give up his life at a moment's notice when a fellow creature is in danger: he who would provide others with daily bread must be prepared to go hungry if the wheat that would nourish him is needed for the planting. All the more does this hold in the affairs of the spirit. When the human spirit expands itself to the uttermost, to confront the white whale and hew meaning and form from the blank stone of experience, one must reverse all the practical maxims: earth's folly, as Melville says, is Heaven's wisdom, and earth's wisdom is Heaven's greatest disaster.

The crew of the vessel seek the ordinary whale: they are after comfort and contentment and a greater share of the "lay"; but the Ahabs seek danger and hardship and a lay that has no value in terms of material sustenance and magnificence. And the paradox, the hard paradox, is this: both purposes are essential: Ahab could not set out at all without the aid of Peleg and Bildad and Charity and his harpooners and sailors, and they, for their part, would never know anything except sluggish routine were they not at times stirred up to great efforts by purposes they do not easily understand or consciously accept. Yet: there is an Ahab in every man, and the meanest member of the crew can be awakened to the values that Ahab prizes: given a storm and a stove boat, and the worst rascal on shipboard may be as magnificent as Odysseus. All men live most intensely when they are moulded by such a purpose—or even, wanting that, by an enterprise that counterfeits it. Art, religion, culture in general, all those intangible triumphs of the spirit that are embodied in forms and symbols, all that spells purpose as opposed to senseless energy, and significance as opposed to routine—these efforts develop human life to its fullest, even when they work contrary to the ordinary standards of the world.

There, it seems to me, is another meaning in Ahab's struggle with Moby-Dick. He represents, not as in the first parable, an heroic power that misconceives its mission and misapplies itself: here he rather stands for human purpose in its highest expression. His pursuit is "futile" because it wrecks the boat and brings home no oil and causes material loss and extinguishes many human lives; but in another sense, it is not futile at all, but is the only significant part of the voyage, since oil is burned and ships eventually break up and men die and even the towers of proud cities crumble away as the buildings sink beneath the sand or the jungle, while all that remains, all that perpetuates the life and the struggle, are their forms and symbols, their art, their literature, their science, as they have been incorporated in the social heritage of man. That which is useful for the moment eventually becomes useless; the mummy's food and drink shrivel away or evaporate: but that which is "useless," the graven image or the tomb itself, continues to nourish the spirit of man. Life, Life purposive, Life formative, Life expressive, is more than living, as living itself is more than the finding of a livelihood. There is no triumph so petty and evanescent as that involved in capturing the ordinary whale: the nineteenth century made this triumph the end and object of all endeavour; and it put the spirit in chains of comfort and material satisfaction, which were heavier than fetters and harder to bear than the stake. By the same token, there is no struggle so permanent and so humanly satisfactory as Ahab's struggle with the white whale. In that defeat, in that succession of defeats, is the only pledge of man's ultimate victory, and the only final preventive of emptiness, boredom, and suicide. Battles are lost, as Whitman cried, in the same spirit that they are won. Some day the physical powers of man may be commensurate with his utmost spirit, and he will meet Leviathan on even terms.

10

The epic and mythic quality of Moby-Dick has been misunderstood because those who examined the book have thought of the epic in terms of Homer, and the myth itself in relation to some obvious hero of antiquity, or some modern folk-hero, a Washington, a Boone, raised to enormous dimensions. "The great mistake seems to be," as Melville said in his essay on Hawthorne, "that even with those Americans who look forward to the coming of a great literary genius among us, they somehow fancy he will come in the costume of Queen Elizabeth's day; be a writer of dramas founded upon old English history or the tales of Boccaccio. Whereas, great geniuses are parts of the times, they themselves are the times and possess a corresponding colouring."

Now, Moby-Dick was written in the best spirit of the nineteenth century, and though it escaped most of the limitations of that period, it escaped with its finest qualities intact. Heroes and gods in the old sense, as Walt Whitman plainly saw, had had their day: they fitted into a simpler scheme of life and thought, and a more credulous sort of attitude; so far from representing the ultimate triumph of the human imagination, from which the scientific mode of thought was not merely a departure but a falling off, the old myths were but the product of a juvenile fantasy. One might still use these figures, as Milton used an Arcadian image to express the corruptions of the Established Church; but they stood for a mode of consciousness and feeling remote from our modern experience. Science did not, as has been foolishly believed, destroy the myth-making power of man, or reduce all his inner strivings to bleak impotence: this has been the accidental, temporary effect of a one-sided science, serving, consciously or not, a limited number of practical activities. What the scientific spirit has actually done has been to exercise the imagination in finer ways than the autistic wish— the wish of the infant possessed of the illusion of power and domination—was able to express. Faraday's ability to conceive the lines of force in a magnetic field was quite as great a triumph as the ability to conceive fairies dancing in a ring: and, as Mr. A. N. Whitehead has shown, the poets who sympathized with this new sort of imagination, poets like Shelley, Wordsworth, Whitman, Melville, did not feel themselves robbed of their specific powers, but rather found them enlarged and refreshed.

One of the finest love-poems of the nineteenth century, Whitman's Out of the Cradle Endlessly Rocking, is expressed in such an image as Darwin or Audubon might have used, were the scientist as capable of expressing his inner feelings as of noting "external" events: the poet haunting the sea-shore and observing the mating of the birds, day after day following their life, could scarcely have existed before the nineteenth century. In the seventeenth century, such a poet would have remained in the garden and written about a literary ghost, Philomel, and not about an actual pair of birds: in Pope's time, the poet would have remained in the library and written about the birds on a lady's fan. Almost all the important works of the nineteenth century were cast in this mode and expressed this new imaginative range: they respect the fact: they are replete with observation: they project an ideal realm in and through, not over, the landscape of actuality. Notre Dame might have been written by an historian, War and Peace by a sociologist, The Idiot might have been created by a psychiatrist, and Salammbô might have been the work of an archaeologist. I do not say that these books were scientific by intention, or that they might be replaced by a work of science without grave loss; far from it. I merely point out that they are conceived in the same spirit; that they belong to a similar plane of consciousness. Much as Melville was enriched by the Elizabethan writers, there is that in Moby-Dick which separates him completely from the poets of that day—and if one wants a word to describe the element that makes the difference, one must call it briefly science.

Now, this respect for fact, as opposed to irresponsible fantasy, did not of course exist for the first time in the nineteenth century: Defoe had this habit of mind in quite as great a measure as Melville: what is important is that in the nineteenth century it was for the first time completely wedded to the imagination. It no longer means a restriction, a dried-up quality, an incompleteness; it no longer deifies the empirical and the practical at the expense of the ideal and the aesthetic: on the contrary, these qualities are now completely fused together, as an expression of life's integrated totality. The symbolism again becomes equal to the reality. Hercules no longer serves in this way: although originally he was doubtless as full of immediate relationships as whaling; and a more complex and diffuse symbol—like Kutuzov's army in War and Peace—is necessary. Had Milton sought to tell this parable of Melville's, he would probably have recast the story of Jonah and the whale, making Jonah the hero; but in doing so he could not help losing all the great imaginative parallels Melville is able to work out, through using material hitherto untouched by pre-

vious myth or history. For Ahab's hate and the pursuit of
the whale is only one part of the total symbol: the physiological character of the whale, its feeding, its mating, its
whole life, from whatever sources Melville drew the data, is
equally a part of it. Indeed, the symbol of Moby-Dick is
complete and rounded, expressive of our present relations
to the universe, only through the passages that orthodox
criticism, exercised on lesser works and more meagre tradi-
tions, regards as extraneous or unimportant!

Moby-Dick, then, is one of the first great mythologies to
be created in the modern world, created, that is, out of the
stuff of that world, its science, its exploration, its terrestrial
daring, its concentration upon power and dominion over
nature, and not out of ancient symbols, Prometheus, Endym-
ion, Orestes, or mediaeval folk-legends, like Dr. Faustus.
Moby-Dick lives imaginatively in the newly broken soil of
our own life: its symbols, unlike Blake's original but mysterious figures, are direct and explicit: if the story is bedded
in facts, the facts themselves are not lost in the further interpretation. Moby-Dick thus brings together the two dis-
severed halves of the modern world and the modern self—
its positive, practical, scientific, externalized self, bent on
conquest and knowledge, and its imaginative, ideal half,
bent on the transposition of conflict into art, and power into
humanity. This resolution is achieved in Moby-Dick itself:
it is as if a Shakespeare and a Bacon, or, to use a more
local metaphor, as if an Eakins and a Ryder, had collab-
orated on a single work of art, with a heightening of their
several powers. The best handbook on whaling is also—I
say this scrupulously—the best tragic epic of modern times
and one of the fine poetic works of all time.

That is an achievement; and it is also a promise. Whitman went as far in his best poems, particularly in the Song
of Myself; and, with quite another method, Tolstoy went as
far in War and Peace, Dostoyevsky in the Brothers Karamazov; Hardy, less perfectly, approximated it perhaps in

The Dynasts; but no one went further. It is one of the great peaks of the modern vision of life. "May God keep us," wrote Blake, "from single vision and Newton's sleep." We now perhaps see a little more clearly what Blake's enigmatic words mean. In Moby-Dick Melville achieved the deep integrity of that double vision which sees with both eyes—the scientific eye of actuality, and the illumined eye of imagination and dream.

11

I have dwelt for a little on some of the meanings of Moby-Dick; but this does not exhaust the matter. Each man will read into Moby-Dick the drama of his own experience and that of his contemporaries: Mr. D. H. Lawrence sees in the conflict a battle between the blood-consciousness of the white race and its own abstract intellect, which attempts to hunt and slay it: Mr. Percy Boynton sees in the whale all property and vested privilege, laming the spirit of man: Mr. Van Wyck Brooks has found in the white whale an image like that of Grendel in Beowulf, expressing the Northern consciousness of the hard fight against the elements; while for the disciple of Jung, the white whale is the symbol of the Unconscious, which torments man, and yet is the source of all his proudest efforts.

Each age, one may predict, will find its own symbols in Moby-Dick. Over that ocean the clouds will pass and change, and the ocean itself will mirror back those changes from its own depths. All these conscious interpretations, however, though they serve the book by approaching its deeper purpose, do not, cannot, quite penetrate the core of its reality. Moby-Dick has a meaning which cannot be derived or dissociated from the work itself. Like every great work of art, it summons up thoughts and feelings profounder than those to which it gives overt expression. It introduces one, sometimes by simple, bald means, to the depths of one's own experience. The book is not an answer, but a clue that must be carried further and worked out. The Sermon on the Mount has this quality. It does not answer all the difficult problems of morality, but it suggests a new point of view in facing them: it leads one who is sufficiently moved to follow through all the recesses of conduct which can be influenced by mildness, understanding, and love, but not otherwise. So with Moby-Dick: the book itself is greater than the fable it embodies, it foreshadows more than it actually reflects: as a work of art, Moby-Dick is part of a new integration of thought, a widening of the fringe of consciousness, a deepening of insight, through which the modern vision of life will finally be embodied.

The shadow cast by Moby-Dick throws into obscurity not merely the sand-hills, but likewise some of the mountains, of the last three centuries. Noting the extent of that shadow, one begins to suspect how high the mountain itself is, and how great its bulk, how durable its rock.

CHAPTER EIGHT: AMOR, THREATENING

MOBY-DICK WAS done. In the fall of 1851 it appeared, first in England, then, a few weeks later, in America. Melville was exhausted, exhausted and overwrought. In the prodigious orchestration of Moby-Dick, Melville had drained his energies, and, participating in Ahab's own pursuit and defiance, he had reached a point of spiritual exasperation which, like Ahab's illness after Moby-Dick had amputated him, was increased by his lowered physical tone, by his weak eyes. Books like this are written out of health and energy, but they do not leave health and energy behind. On the contrary, the aftermath of such an effort is irritation, debility, impotence.

Melville was worked up, in the writing of Moby-Dick, to the highest pitch of effort; and he was harried, no doubt, by his ever-present necessity to keep his public and add to his income. The spiritual momentum remained, but the force behind it dwindled away. With no time for recuperation, he plunged into his new work: an unwise decision. Melville was not without his weaknesses, and they rose to the surface in his new book, Pierre, or The Ambiguities. Moby-Dick had disintegrated him: by some interior electrolysis, its sanative salt was broken up into baneful chemical elements. In this disintegration, Pierre rises at times as high as Moby-Dick, and sinks lower than any of Melville's other books. It contains passages that are the finest utterances of his spirit; it also has passages that would scarcely honour Laura Jean Libbey.

What caused this break-up? What value has Pierre in the

sum of Melville's work? Neither of these questions admits of a quick and facile answer. One cannot dismiss the novel high-handedly as Melville's contemporaries did; and since the relation of the personal life of the artist to his art is still one of the major ambiguities in psychology, one cannot give a decisive or confident answer to the first question.

2

Melville's situation at the time of writing Pierre might have upset him even in a period of completer poise and more abundant health. He had written a great book: of that he could not possibly have had any doubt. Minor writers may think their rhinestones are diamonds, but rarely does a Shakespeare, a Swift, a Melville make the contrary mistake: if he speak lightly of his own work, or affect to disregard it, it is only for the reason that once he has reached the utmost depths of consciousness and realizes that vast and myriad interior which can never be fully reported, he begins to realize that diamonds, too, are only another kind of rhinestone: they are mined too cheaply.

Melville knew that Moby-Dick was bound to be his chief title to fame. In 1849 he had written to Mr. Duyckinck: "Would that a man could do something and then say It is finished—not that one thing only, but all others—that he has reached his uttermost and can never exceed it." Melville had done this: he had mined and tunnelled through every part of his experience to produce this book. "There is a sure, though secret sign in some works," he wrote in 1850, "which proves the culmination of the powers . . . that produced them," and he recognized this secret sign in Moby-Dick: his letters to Hawthorne announce it. Mid all the tribulations and vexations of his life, there was, as in the heart of the whale Armada, a quiet place of calm and inward peace; within that spot, he had no reason to doubt or be dissatisfied with his work.

Still, what a writer articulates is always, though his words stay in a private diary, an effort at communication; the very nature of language makes this inevitable. Melville was necessarily not without his curiosity as to how the world would greet this magnificent product of his maturity, the first book in which he was in full command of his powers. And what was the world's answer?

The world's answer was no doubt what was to be expected; but it was no less discouraging for this reason. The Literary World indeed treated Moby-Dick with respect, and with as much understanding as a purely bookish man, like Mr. Duyckinck, could be expected to show: though it wasted most of the first review telling about the parallel fate of the Ann Alexander, it made up for this adventitious journalism by a second article which acknowledged Moby-Dick's manifold powers and excellences. "An intellectual chowder of romance, philosophy, natural history, fine writing, good feeling, bad sayings . . . over which, in spite of all uncertainties, and in spite of the author himself, predominates his keen perceptive faculties, exhibited in vivid narration." In the light of other contemporary reviews, this was fairly handsome. The Dublin University Magazine, with steady opacity, said Moby-Dick was quite as eccentric and monstrously extravagant in many of its incidents as even Mardi, but was a valuable book because it contained an unparalleled mass of information about the whale. As for the Athenaeum, it righteously reminded Mr. Melville that he "has to thank himself only if his horrors and his heroics are flung aside by the general reader as so much trash"—criticism which reached a pinnacle in the New Monthly Magazine, which described the style of Moby-Dick as "maniacal—mad as a March hare—moving, gibbering, screaming, like an incurable Bedlamite, reckless of keeper or strait-waistcoat."

One need not go into all the forms under which the contemporary critic disclosed his insensitiveness to great prose and his servile compliance with the idola of the market; but one must note a singular fact: from Fitz-James O'Brien's

first criticism of Melville's work as a whole in 1853 down to
Mr. Vernon Parrington's commentary in 1927, Moby-Dick,
the keystone of Melville's work, has frequently been left out
of account. The book that triumphantly smothers all the
contradictory opinions about Melville—that he was a romantic, that he could only portray external scenes, that he
was a pure introvert, that he was an adventurous ne'er-do-
well, never happy or at home in a settled community, that
he was irresponsive to the life around him, that he was a
sheer realist who could only record what he had seen—the
book that makes these generalizations silly suffered something worse than antagonistic criticism: it met with complete neglect. It is only since 1914 in America that this
neglect has been even partly atoned for.

Such obtuseness, such flat stupidity, must have had a dis-
maying effect upon Melville. The writer begins to doubt
the possibility of literature in a world that so flagrantly mis-
understands or ignores its higher manifestations. Faced with
such contemporaries, the artist may retire within himself,
as Bach or Ryder or Cézanne did; but it will only be a
miracle that will keep him from taking into his retirement a
deep contempt for the people around him. That contempt is
worse than isolation; it brings isolation without hope. "I
write to please myself," exclaimed Melville in one passage in
Pierre. In that mood of wilful defiance, a man may revolt
from the good sense of his contemporaries as well as from
their deficiencies. There was nothing in the reception of
Moby-Dick that would have lessened Melville's scorn, or
helped him to fortify himself against his own weaknesses.
Quite the contrary. Like Pierre himself he was to learn "and
very bitterly learn, that though the world worship mediocrity and commonplace, yet hath it fire and sword for contemporary grandeur."

Moby-Dick was too much for them, was it? Well: it was
a mere pencilling of the ultimate blackness that was his to
paint: if one were going to tell the truth at all, one could

go much further and be much plainer. "Henceforth," proclaimed Pierre, "I will know nothing but Truth; Glad Truth or Sad Truth; I will know what *is*, and do what my deepest angel dictates." And again: "I am more frank with Pierre than the best men are with themselves. I am all unguarded and magnanimous with Pierre: therefore you see his weakness, and therefore only. In reserves, men build imposing characters; not in revelations. He who shall be wholly honest, though nobler than Ethan Allen that man shall stand in danger of the meanest mortal's scorn."

It was in some such mood of defeat, foreboding, defiant candour, that Pierre was conceived and written. Meanwhile, in November, 1851, the Hawthorne family had moved away from the Berkshires and Melville settled to his work, in the spring of 1852, on the north porch that faced Mt. Monadnock, with an intense feeling of human isolation which brought the mountain closer to him, as his only friend. The one possibility of a friendly, rapturous union of spirits was behind him: no longer could he write to Hawthorne, as he had done just a few months before: "Whence came you, Hawthorne? By what right do you drink from my flagon of life? And when I put it to my lips—lo, they are yours, and not mine. I feel that the Godhead is broken up like the bread at the Supper, and that we are the pieces. Hence this infinite fraternity of feeling." No: already that was over: dead. If the spirit burned now, it burned as ice does to the human touch. It was not altogether in irony, or in wild whimsy, that Melville dedicated his next book, Pierre, to his one solitary and steadfast companion, Mt. Monadnock.

3

There is a sense in which Pierre is an abortive complement to Moby-Dick. Moby-Dick, great fable that it is, contains a good part of human life under one figure or another; but it does not contain everything. I would claim much for it; I would claim much for Melville's work as a whole; but there is still a great segment that remained unexplored till Melville wrote Pierre, and that, to the end, he never satisfactorily penetrated or freely brooded upon.

All Melville's books about the sea have the one anomaly and defect of the sea from the central, human point of view: one-half of the race, woman, is left out of it. Melville's world, all too literally, is a man-of-war's world. Woman neither charms nor nurtures nor threatens: she neither robs man of his strength nor rouses him to heroic frenzy: she is not Circe: she is not Rosalind or Francesca or even the Wife of Bath—she simply does not exist. When the Pequod spreads sail, woman is left behind: she is the phantom of home for Ahab and Starbuck. The whales dally in Moby-Dick and beget offspring; but all the trouble, beauty, madness, delight of human love, all that vast range of experience from the mere touch of the flesh to the most enduring spiritual loyalty, all that is absent. One looks for some understanding of woman's lot and woman's life in Moby-Dick; and one looks in vain. One looks for it again in Pierre, and one is disappointed, although its ambiguities are concerned with nothing else. With experience of woman in every relationship, daughter, girl, sister, wife, mother, matron, he described her in only one aspect—that of the remote and idealized mistress of romantic courtship. Mother, sister, sweetheart, all appeared to Melville's hero in this brief and peculiar aspect.

There was, one is driven to believe, something in Herman Melville's life that caused him to dissociate woman from his account of man's deepest experience. Mr. Waldo Frank has suggested, in general social terms, that the quest of power, which has preoccupied Western man since the Renaissance, has incapacitated him as a lover and kept him from understanding woman and all her essential concerns. If that is true, Melville pushed his aberration to a logical extremity; and he, who captured to the full the poetry of the sea, became as bashful as a boy when he beheld Venus, born of its foam, rising from the waters he knew so well, the most unexpected of monsters, and the only denizen of the sea he dared neither snare nor harpoon nor otherwise dispose of, except by flight. . . .

4

The hero of Pierre is a young patrician, the heir of Saddle Meadows; he has good looks, health, an historic ancestry, and a warmly humanized environment. Handicapped in his own inheritance as a youth, Melville bestowed on Pierre not only all the things he possessed, such as the Gansevoort heritage, but all the things ill fortune had denied him.

Pierre lives with his mother, a widow; she is proud, fine, and at fifty still beautiful: he treats her beauty with the attention of a lover who resents every man that approaches her: she is "sister" and he is "brother" and there is more than familiar fondness in their touches. Pierre is on the point of open betrothal to Lucy, a simple, dewy country girl of good family. Is there to be jealousy between the mother and Lucy; must he choose between them? No: something more difficult is in store. At a village sewing-bee, where he has gone to call for his mother, a girl faints at the sight of Pierre. She seems a farmer's daughter and her fainting is mysterious; the mystery becomes oppressive when Pierre gets a secret summons from her. An interview with Isabel, the girl, topples the whole Elysium of family relationships within whose rainbow Pierre had lived. Isabel, a dark, lovely creature, brims with obscure memories of an almost unintelligible past, memories that wail through her like the sound of wind in the trees. By hint and memory and inference, she had found that Pierre's father, who had formed a union with a Frenchwoman, was her father—and this girl was the sole fruit of the union—Pierre's half-sister. Isabel offers her orphaned self to her half-brother in complete trust; and he, not doubting the relationship, although hitherto his father had seemed to him a flawless being, takes her to his bosom.

In a few hours, Pierre experiences all the perturbations that afflicted Young Goodman Brown, in Hawthorne's story, when he discovered all his respected elders, the personification of virtue and chastity, participating in a witches' sabbath. Pierre contemplates his mother, to see if there is any possible means of making her acknowledge the relationship and rescue Isabel from the mean lot that is now hers, in a family that is about to cast off its own daughter, Delly Ulver, because she has conceived a child out of wedlock. No help there! Pierre discovers a worldly front of respectability hemming him round. His mother's spiritual counsellor, the Reverend Mr. Folsgrave, gives the world's reasons for refusing to compound Delly's mistake: his mother is even more peremptorily and forbiddingly righteous. Suddenly, Pierre discovers that the kindness and charity and sweetness of the world is a poisonous mushroom, whose delicate shape is embedded in the ordure of malice, pride, cold restraint, heartlessness.

If Mrs. Glendinning acts in this fashion over Delly Ulver's plight, what sort of front would she place on Isabel's and that of Pierre's father? Would she acknowledge her husband's error: would she take to her bosom this Isabel? Even Pierre, bursting with hope, cannot hope for this: his faith is shattered: he sees the cold rectitude of his mother, and a resolution to stand against the world and its ways takes the place of his original belief that those ways are amiable and meritorious and virtuous. Pierre resolves to protect Isabel: but how? To achieve his aim, he conceives the device of living with her, in strict brotherly aloofness, under the fiction of marriage. A gallant, quixotic espousal; but not without its own deviousness and share of infirmity. Would he have been so ready to espouse Isabel, asks Melville, had she been ugly and crass instead of sombrely beautiful and delicate? Would he have been so warm in magnanimity if another kind of warmth had not lain under the surface?

Would he, one might add, have conceived this stratagem of living with Isabel as husband and wife, had he not lived with his mother as brother and sister?

Pierre does not dare to frame these questions. He is worked up to a great pitch of nobility and sacrifice: high-handedly, he throws his whole life into the scales and runs away with Isabel, taking Delly under his protection, too, and trusting to time and his own explanations to soften the action to Mrs. Glendinning and make it palatable. Lucy, to whom he has plighted marriage, he ruthlessly sets behind him; and, with a few coins in his purse, he makes his way to New York, to carve out a career as a writer. Troubles swarm about him like angry hornets, once he destroys the nest of respectability which had kept them in order. The companion of his youth, a cousin who had once been a rival for Lucy's hand, supposing Lucy to be his bride, had generously placed his town house at Pierre's disposal. Now he summarily withdraws his hospitality. The three outcasts reach New York late at night to find their quarters deserted; Pierre, hunting up his cousin, is cut dead when he confronts him: from the gutters of the city, all its noisome human refuse taints the air: Pierre returns to the town guardhouse, where he had left Delly and Isabel, to find them shrinking before the profane curses and gestures of a band of drunken prostitutes and their customers, rounded up in a raid.

This is but a foretaste of the trials that are to overwhelm Pierre and Isabel. Pierre and his house-mates presently find themselves a little flat in an old church building that has been remodelled into offices and apartments, and is occupied by broken-down lawyers, transcendentalists, vegetarians, faddists of one kind or another, each encouraging the other's special lunacy in order to have a kindly reception for his own. In the midst of this extreme poverty and disorder, Pierre, who has been a mild minor poet, a writer of aesthetic jingles which "would offend no one," probes all the terrors of his new experience and its revelations, and out of it he writes a book, not unlike Pierre, with an author for hero. The situation is impossible. Pierre has no money: his mother freezes up completely in mortification, and disowns him, keeping even that share of his estate which was meant for Pierre: the misery and ambiguity of his situation increases when Lucy, recovered from the first stupor of grief, flies for refuge to Pierre, to beg a place as humble servitor, in Pierre's already crammed and over-womaned household. Worst of all, the dark bottom of his brotherly relation with Isabel becomes faintly apparent to Pierre himself: it is reflected in the shadow of jealousy that touches her reaction to Lucy: such a feeling as Isabel might properly claim if she were married to Pierre in actuality. Pierre has outlawed himself, and missed happiness with Lucy, for a distracted passion which can have no outlet in external relationships: in aiming at purest virtue, with noble intent, he has committed a deed he cannot confront without horror. His duty towards his father's memory and towards Isabel has been the subtlest of masks for an urge that has its roots in his own instinctive nature, not solely in the teachings of charity, honesty, and justice.

Isabel herself has always been uncertainly conscious of this wild passion: but in her ignorance of the world itself, she is aware of nothing that runs contrary to the world. What had said yes to Pierre was not a mere response to his charity; it had implied more. With these fierce passages of self-revelation, Pierre finishes his own book, and his author, Vivia, finishes his! In the notion that he was walking in the highway of the loftiest morality, Pierre has only explored a blind alley, the blindest of all human alleys. Farcical disappointments mingle with tragic regrets: his publishers, on getting his masterpiece, denounce Pierre as a rascally impostor: Lucy's brother and his cousin threaten Pierre's life, treating him as a seducer and a scoundrel: his mother dies in an insane grief. In self-defence, Pierre arms himself, and, when attacked in the open by the two virtuous espousers of Lucy's honour, Pierre empties a pistol into each of them, and is taken to jail. Grief after grief, horror after horror, ensue from Pierre's original act of virtue. When Lucy learns that Isabel is Pierre's half-sister, she collapses in death. There is no issue to this passion for either Isabel or Pierre but suicide. Pierre and Isabel swallow poison together in the prison cell, and Pierre passes out, entwined in Isabel's dark hair. The fool of fate dies: his love dies with him. The scene is as freely strewn with corpses as the fifth act of an Elizabethan tragedy.

5

This story of Pierre, nard to accept in bald summary, is no less difficult to accept in detail. The plot is forced: the situations are undeveloped: the dominant colours are as crude as the lithograph advertisements of a melodrama, although there are subordinate parts which are as delicately graded as a landscape by Corot. There is no passage between the various planes of action and mood, as there is in Moby-Dick: Melville slips from prose into poetry, from realism into fantasy, from the mood of high tragedy into that of the penny dreadful.

For the moment, Melville had lost the power to fuse these discordant elements, to reject what could not be fully absorbed: he was at the mercy of his material. All that lives with a vital unity in Moby-Dick has become a corpse in Pierre: there is life in the dead members, but it does not pertain to the body as a whole. The fragments of Pierre are sometimes marvellous, as the broken leg or arm of a great piece of sculpture may be: but the whole is lost. From the moment the story opens to the fatal lines that bring it to a close, one is in an atmosphere of unreality. I do not mean that the facts are untrue to life; I mean that the work as a whole is untrue to the imagination. One accepts Ahab as a demi-god: one cannot accept Pierre as a human being,

although Pierres are plentiful, while one might dredge the
five seas without bringing up the carcass of another Ahab.

The style itself is witness to this psychal disruption, quite
as much as the fable. Pierre is quarried out of the same
quarry as Moby-Dick; but whereas there the texture is even
and firm, here it is full of flaws and intrusive granulations.
Moby-Dick, to use another figure, slides down a long run-
way before it plunges into its poetic passages: by the time
one reaches Ahab's great apostrophes, one is all prepared
for the immersion; one's imagination has reached the same
pitch of intensity and concentration, and nothing but the
most rhythmic patterns will satisfy the mood itself. The
common prose in Moby-Dick is but an interval for breath-
ing: it sustains and carries forward the movement of the
more expressive passages; and as for the words themselves,
they are the exact equivalent for the mood and purpose:
distended though the envelope may be, they never burst
outside it.

In language, Pierre is just the opposite of this: from the
first pages, it is perfervid and poetical in a mawkish way.
With the disclosure of the two lovers, Pierre and Lucy, in
the opening chapter, the style becomes a perfumed silk,
taken from an Elizabethan chamber romance: it sounds exactly like Melville's first effusion in the Lansingburgh Advertiser: " 'Truly,' thought the youth, with a still gaze of
inexpressible fondness, 'truly the skies do ope: and this
invoking angel looks down. I would return these manifold
good-mornings, Lucy, did not that presume thou hadst lived
through the night; and by heaven, thou belongst to the
regions of an infinite day!' " This is a fair sample of what
happens in Pierre whenever Melville approaches romantic
passion; his reflections were tied with the same ribbons and
furbelows, as in his description of love as "a volume bound
in rose-leaves, clasped with violets, and by the beaks of
humming-birds printed with peach juice on the leaves of
lilies." In style, Melville had suddenly lost both taste and

discretion. He opened on a note that could not be carried through. Lovers may indeed once have used such silly rhetoric, but it would take a more careful hand than Melville's to persuade us that the rest of the world adopted these affectations: when scene after scene is conducted in the same tone, the style becomes tedious, intolerable, ridiculous. It would be bad if the characters were in the Renaissance costume of Daphnis and Chloe: it is even worse in a novel that contains realistic caricatures of the slums of New York and satiric commentaries upon the bizarre habits of the transcendentalists. Occasionally, by some happy concentration of emotion, Melville either drops these flabby phrases or permits the reader to forget them, and there are passages which, when read as poetry, are almost as fine as Whitman's verses. But these intervals of good writing do not overcome the main impression; and the main impression is of hectic and overwrought language. With the powerful control he had over Moby-Dick, Melville could never have written in the style that characterizes a large part of Pierre. In Pierre he was no longer the cool rider of words, but the flayed and foaming horse, running away.

There is still another unfortunate lapse in Pierre; and that is the disproportion between stimulus and effect. When Pierre is first beheld by Isabel, then completely a stranger to him, she shrieks and faints away. Her own action was not improbable; but there is no reason why Pierre, healthy, robust, ignorant, should be so profoundly disturbed by this exhibition. The same is true of Pierre's heroic resolution to shield Isabel under the form of wedlock: it is a wild and dangerous leap out of a much less pressing difficulty. When Pierre finally comes to town, the disproportion is so broad it is grotesque, almost comical: his cousin's turning upon him and cutting him, before a group of strangers, with a frigid stare and a command to take that fellow away, does not belong to anything but the pages of crude melodrama. The turning against Pierre is not the subtle, devious series of rebukes and frigidities he would actually receive: such an affront as Melville pictures occurs only in raw dream.

In Moby-Dick, Melville carefully prepared, a hundred pages in advance, for the final effect: Mr. E. M. Forster has even suggested that the emphasis upon "delight" in Father Mapple's sermon is related to the encountering of a ship called the Delight just before the final catastrophe. In Pierre all this subtle preparation is lacking: Melville's impatience turned a genuine theme, the conflict of adolescent purity of purpose with the apologetic compromises and sordid motives of the world, into a crude melodrama. Melville was so immersed in the dilemma of his hero that he did not observe how often he failed to satisfy the demands of art, which require that the very incoherencies of life somehow hang together and be acceptable to the mind.

Finally, Pierre's emotional reaction to Isabel is entirely out of proportion to the fact that he has found a sister whose existence he had never before suspected. For a young man, filially tied to his mother, and by active courtship to Lucy, the entrance of another young woman should not have had such a volcanic effect, since, under the most ancient of social taboos, the relationship between them precludes further intimacy. Kindness and fellow feeling might easily arise there: but what Melville pictures is sudden and violent passion. "Fate," he observes, "had separated the brother and sister, till to each they seemed so not at all. Sisters shrink not from their brother's kisses. And Pierre felt that never, never would he be able to embrace Isabel with the mere brotherly embrace; while the thought of any other caress, which took hold of any domesticness, was entirely vacant from his uncontaminated soul, for it had never consciously intruded there. Therefore, forever unsistered for him by the stroke of Fate, and apparently for ever, and twice removed from the remotest possibility of that love which had drawn him to his Lucy; yet still the object of the ardentest and deepest emotions of his soul; therefore, to him, Isabel soared out of the realm of mortalness and for him became transfigured in the highest heaven of uncorrupted love."

The ambiguity that Melville finally brought his hero to confront in Pierre is that this highest heaven is not necessarily a heaven at all: such a transcendental displacement of earthly emotions and experiences is not the way of "willing, waking love": it is the mood of dream, and by continuous dissociation, it may eventually become the mood of madness. The highest heaven of love does not come with such romantic fixation upon an unapproachable deity: it comes rather with diffusion, when all men are brothers, when all women are sisters, when all children are just as dear as one's own issue. The fixation on a remote figure or symbol is in fact just the opposite of this generous suffusion of love, and of all love's corruptions it is possibly the most dangerous. In the thirteenth century, the Queen of Heaven had such a place, and her almost exclusive worship is perhaps as much a sign of the breakup of the mediaeval synthesis as any more obvious emblem of disintegration.

Man's roots are in the earth; and the effort to concentrate upon an ideal experience, that seeks no nourishment through these roots, may be quite as disastrous to spiritual growth as the failure to push upwards and to rise above the physical bed in which these roots are laid. In Pierre, Melville explored and followed such a fixation to its conclusion: disintegration and suicide. Had this been Melville's purpose in writing the book, Pierre might, in a decisive figure, have ended an epoch—the epoch of the romantic hero; for he had probed that hero's nobility and virtue and disclosed their deeper ambiguities, their conflicts, their irreconcilabilities. Pierre might have been a sort of anti-Werther. Unfortunately, this is just what it is not; for Melville identified himself with Pierre and defended his immaturity. How this came about we will inquire later; for we have not yet done justice to Pierre as a work of art.

6

What did Melville consciously set himself to do when he wrote Pierre? He sought, I think, to arrive at the same sort of psychological truth that he had achieved, in metaphysics, in Moby-Dick. His subject was, not the universe, but the ego; and again, not the obvious ego of the superficial novelist, but those implicated and related layers of self which reach from the outer appearances of physique and carriage down to the recesses of the unconscious personality. "The novel will find the way to our interiors, one day," he wrote in Pierre, "and will not always be a novel of costume merely." Melville, to use his own words, had dropped his angle into the well of his childhood, to find out what fish might be there: before Mardi, he had sought for fish in the outer world, where swim the golden perch and pickerel: but now he had learned to dredge his unconscious, and to draw out of it, not the white whale, but motives, desires, hopes for which there had been no exit in his actual life. Men had been afraid to face the cold white malignity of the universe; they were even more reluctant to face their own unkempt, bewrayed selves. Even Shakespeare, deep as he was, had had reserves: Melville would set an example.

Melville was not concerned to portray "real life," for the unconscious is not for most people part of this reality: in a later book he gave an explanation of his own literary method. He describes readers after his own heart who read a novel as they might sit down to a play, with much the same expectation and feeling. "They look that fancy shall evoke scenes different from those of the same old crowd round the Custom House counter, and the same old dishes on the boarding house table, with characters unlike those of the same old acquaintances they meet in the same old way every day in the same old street. And as, in real life, the proprieties will not allow people to set out themselves with that unreserve permitted to the stage, so in books of fiction, they look not only for more entertainment, but, at bottom, for more reality, than real life itself can show. Thus, though they want novelty, they want nature, too; but nature unfettered, exhilarated, in effect transformed. In this way of thinking, the people in a fiction, like the people in a play, must dress as nobody exactly dresses, talk as nobody exactly talks, act as nobody exactly acts. It is with fiction as with religion: it should present another world, and yet one to which we feel the tie." For this conception of literary method, there is much to be said, and had Pierre carried it out with plausibility and consistency it might have made an even more important contribution to the art of the novel than George Meredith and Henry James were to make. If Melville met failure here, it was not because he had chosen a poor method, but because he lacked adeptness in using it.

As concerns his psychological purpose, however, Pierre for all its weaknesses will stand comparison with the pioneer works of its period. Pierre is one of the first novels in which the self is treated as anything but a unit, whose parts consist of the same material, with the grain, as it were, running the same way. Pierre's double relation towards his father's image and towards his mother's actual presence, his mixed attitudes towards Lucy and Isabel, the conflict between his latent interests and his actions and rationalizations, all these things are presented with remarkable penetration: if there is slag at the entrance of this mine, there is a vein of exceptionally rich ore running through it. Pierre's identification of his mother's love with a supreme form of egotism, Pierre being the mirror in which she beholds her own proud grimace, is no less penetrating than Melville's account of the relation between Pierre and his cousin, which runs from romantic love into apathy and enmity. While the action of Pierre is full of harsh and even absurd contrasts, the psychological mood is portrayed with infinite retirement and with relentless surgical skill: Melville does not hold the pulse of his characters: he X-rays their very organs.

The supreme quality of Pierre is its candour. Like Pierre, the more Melville wrote, "and the deeper and deeper that he dived, [he] saw that everlasting elusiveness of Truth: the universal insincerity of even the greatest and purest written thoughts. Like knavish cards, the leaves of all great books were covertly packed." Melville did his best to avoid playing a foul hand: he dealt his cards as they slipped from the fingers of Fate, Chance, Necessity, Truth; and in this grave honesty of his the greatest of thinkers seemed little better than fictioneers. "Plato, Spinoza, and Goethe, and many more belong to this guild of self-impostors, with a preposterous rabble of muggletonian Scots and Yankees whose vile brogue still the more bestreaks the stripedness of their Greek or German Neoplatonic originals." Not exactly a kind criticism; but, in Melville's exacerbated state, he went even further: not merely did the "compensationists" or the "optimists" seem shallow: literature itself was a hollow business, too. The ultimate, the final truth was inexpressible, and even the mere hinting of it was inadequate: the intensest light of reason did not shed such blazonings upon the deeper truths in man as the profoundest gloom. Utter darkness is the wise man's light; silence his highest utterance. Catlike, one sees in the dark distinctly objects that are erased by blatant sunshine; indeed, one calls to one's aid senses and instincts that are dormant when one can move and see. "Not to know Gloom and Grief," said Melville, in the midst of this illumination, "is not to know aught that an heroic man should learn."

But if the gold of the transcendentalists was pewter and brass, Melville was equally honest about his own treasures. "By vast pains we mine into the pyramid; by horrible gaspings we come to the central room; with joy we espy the sarcophagus; but we lift the lid—and nobody is there!—

appallingly vacant, as vast as the soul of man." One threw away literature and philosophy, yes, language itself, only to find oneself without visible support. One eliminated not merely the debris and muck: one got rid of the miner, and the very purpose of his occupation. "In those hyperborean regions to which enthusiastic Truth and Earnestness and Independence will invariably lead a mind fitted by nature for profound and fearless thoughts all objects are seen in a dubious uncertain and refracting light. Viewed through the rarefied atmosphere, the most immemorially admitted maxims of men begin to slide and fluctuate and finally become wholly inverted. . . . But the example of many minds forever lost, like undiscoverable Arctic explorers, amid those treacherous regions, warns us entirely away from them and we learn that it is not for man to follow the trail of truth too far, since by so doing he entirely loses the directing compass of his mind, for, arrived at the Pole, to whose barrenness only it points, there, the needle indifferently respects all points of the horizon alike."

Within the heap of fragments in Pierre that mark the thrust and power of Melville's mind, there is one fragment, fallen at random in the mass, that remains embedded in the memory. It is the message of the pamphlet that comes by accident into Pierre's hand when he is making his escape to New York: in his overwrought state, the words have a peculiar significance for his own purposes; and they are remarkable enough, in their enigmatic quality, to consider by themselves. The title of the pamphlet is Chronometricals and Horologicals: in it the fictitious lecturer purports to set forth his own heretical philosophy. The moral is embroidered in a single trope: the notion that there are two kinds of time in the world, that which is established at Greenwich and kept by chronometers, and that which prevails in other longitudes, recorded by the local watches. It is a parallel of the philosophic and practical aspects of life, or rather, of ideal and working morality; and I know no better exposure of the identity, yet dualism, of thought and action, ideal and practice.

The philosophic or religious minds are always correcting their watches by Greenwich time; and, by continuous observation of the heavens, they are always trying to make Greenwich time itself more correct. They know that the compromises and conveniences of society are useful: but they also know that these things have no ultimate reason for existence, and that one's employment of them must always be modified by reference to a scale of values alongside which they are false or meaningless. Shallow people never make such a correction: they believe in "dress" or "family" or "prestige" or "success" as if these were the vestments of eternity. Melville's error, at least Pierre's error, was just the opposite of this: he did not see that watches and local time are necessary, too, that there is no truth so cruelly meaningless as to give a person Greenwich time without telling him his longitude and enabling him to make his correction: that way lies disaster, confusion, shipwreck. A belief in ideal standards and values with no *via media* is scarcely better than a superficial life with no standards or insights at all.

The passage from the universal perception to the common life is difficult to make: it is the point at which religions and philosophies perpetually flounder. Melville saw this paradox; and he was plagued and puzzled by it; he even attributes it to Plotinus Plinlimmon, the leader of the transcendentalist sect, who drinks wine he forbids to his disciples, and, following supernal ideas, seems to prize cigars and food far more; Plinlimmon, whose non-benevolent stare seems to tell Pierre that all that he does is done in vain; Plinlimmon, the very embodiment of these ambiguities. Melville tended, with Pierre, to regard horologicals as a dubious frailty instead of what it actually is—the way that Greenwich time is universalized and incorporated in local practice. Human ideals are, as Melville saw, like the points of the compass: one does not seek the north by going north-ward: one seeks to reach a humanly important part of the earth, like Pekin or Paris; and ideals are the means by which a life that more fully satisfies our human potentialities can be lived. To observe this paradox without falling into the rôle of Mr. Worldly Wiseman is the essence of an active morality. Melville confronted the paradox; but the point of it eluded him. He idealized ideals as he idealized sexual passion: he wished both to remain for him in that adolescent state in which they are pure, remote, untouchable—forgetting that life is impossible in that sterile and clarified medium. Though Melville had anatomized many human impulses and probed in many sore and hidden places, one part of the personality remained sacred to him in Pierre: the sanctum of adolescence. All the values in the book are distorted, its very purpose is deflected, by Melville's unconscious assumption that the romantic purity of adolescence, the purity that arises not through experience and fulfilment, that is, through continuous purification, but through an ignorance and stagnation within sealed vials—that this purity is central to all the other values. That chronometer was correct enough at nineteen: at thirty-three it was no longer accurate, for a single reason—it had stopped. That, we shall see, was the chief ambiguity of Melville's personal life.

Melville was not alone in parading these fundamental ambiguities. In the dissociation of society in America, the American writer was able to examine all the premises and established truths which a European ordinarily takes so much for granted that he is not aware of taking them at all; and he could separate the essence of our human institutions from their conventional overlayers. Emerson, in Uriel, gives pithy expression to the same insidious ideas one finds in Pierre: but in Melville's novel they are on every page. His mother's love for her son is self-love and her admiration for him is vanity. His father's rectitude leads to a cold marriage, where an unclerked love had shown him a little radiant and a little finer at the core. Pierre's purest love is a disguised incest; his nobility is a worldly crime—while a lack of generous impulses would have led to wealth and honour. Melville's whole life, indeed, had taught him these ambiguities: Jack Chase was the real captain of the ship, not Captain Claret: the surgeon who amputated a living man, Surgeon Cuticle, with his glass eye, his false teeth, his wig, was more dead than the flesh he carved into: the cannibals of the South Seas were civilized, and the civilization of the New York slums was lower than cannibal gluttony: the missionary of Christ inflicted servitude, and the chief goods introduced by the trader were diseases: finally, the one civilization which thoroughly disregards the precepts of Christian morality is that of the Western world, which professes it.

These paradoxes were disturbing enough; but the fundamental ones were even worse. "The uttermost ideal of moral perfection in man is wide of the mark. The demi-gods trample on trash, and Virtue and Vice are trash!" Vice might lead to virtue; virtue might beget vice: the prostitute may teach purity and the holy man blasphemy! Where is one left when Melville and Emerson are through? One is left amid a debris of institutions and habits. Nothing is safe; nothing is secure: one no longer looks for the outer label, or believes in it. If north be the direction of one's ideal, the virtuous captain may have to tack back and forth from east to west in order to reach that destination: for no chart or compass ever enabled a ship to steer blindly for its port without paying close attention to wind and weather.

Had Pierre, as an imaginative work, been a more sufficient demonstration of these ambiguities, the book would have had a high destiny. But although the ideas are clear enough, they remain a potentiality in Pierre, since the story itself lacks integrity of form. The book is a precious crystal smashed out of its natural geometrical shape. Only by a chemical analysis of its elements do we discover what its primal character might have been.

7

The failure of Pierre as a work of art gives us a certain licence to deal with it as biography, all the more because Melville identified himself with the hero, giving him the initials and the Christian name of his beloved grandfather, Peter Gansevoort, and attaching him to objects like the portrait of his father which correspond to things about whose existence there is no doubt. If, as a work of art, Pierre was whole, we should have no good reason to suspect Melville's wholeness. It is the failure of Pierre as literature that draws our attention to Melville's predicament as a man; for in this particular way, he had not erred before. The young Melville who wrote Typee is not in Pierre; instead, a much younger self is there, a self erotically immature, expressing itself in unconscious incest fantasies, and capable of extravagant rationalizations in its effort to sustain them. Pierre is not a demonstration because it is a betrayal—and the person it betrays is Melville. In Pierre, he was an Iago, driven by his own frustration to betray the Othello who had been such a valiant captain in all his previous battles.

The significant question for us is what event, or series of occurrences, caused a hiatus in Melville's emotional and sexual development; and this question cannot be lightly answered by pointing to the obvious symbols in Pierre—for a symbol describes a tendency, rather than an objective event. We know that Melville's earliest associations of sex had been with vice and sexual disease; and in a sensitive lad, this introduction to passion may place bit and bridle on his own development. We know, too, that sexual relations in the United States among respectable people in the fifties were in a starved and stunted state: Stanley Hall, a boy in this very decade, recalled that he had never witnessed the slightest passage of affection between his father and his mother. It may be that Elizabeth, patient as a wife, was timid and irresponsive as a lover: in short, there are a dozen possible circumstances occurring long after childhood, which may have contributed to Melville's regression: and the incest-attachment, so far from being the cause of this, may in Pierre only serve as its emotional equivalent. Wherever sex is mentioned in other passages in Melville's books, it is referred to in a mood of disillusion. In Clarel, for example, he says:

> May love's nice balance, finely slight,
> Take tremor from fulfilled delight?
> Can nature such a doom dispense
> As, after ardor's tender glow,
> To make the rapture more than pall
> With evil secrets in the sense,
> And guile whose bud is innocence—
> Sweet blossom of the flower of gall?

And in one of the few passages in Moby-Dick where sex is referred to, the Sicilian sailor implies that sexual joy is in swayings, touchings, cozenings, and that when one tastes it directly, satiety comes. That, I submit, is not the experience of a healthy and well-mated man, or of a mature erotic state: to long for the pre-nuptial condition, to wish for fixation in courtship, is the mark of an immature, or at least an incomplete, attachment.

When one says that Melville longed for the pre-nuptial state one does not merely imply that he found his sexual relations difficult or unsatisfactory: this earlier condition meant something more: it meant irresponsibility, freedom to roam, carelessness about health and daily bread, the opportunity to do his work without foreboding and anxiety. Sex had brought disillusion not merely because the first ardour and glow had vanished suddenly with the first physical contact: it had increased all his burdens and threatened to curtail that inner development which he had come to prize above all things—even more than the robust outer experience that had produced Typee. Sex meant marriage; marriage meant a household and a tired wife and children and debts. No wonder he retreated: no wonder his fantasy attached him to a mother who could not surrender, to a half-sister who could not bear children! The ardent impulse remained; he sought only to make it innocuous to his own spiritual life.

In view of the terrific pressure upon Melville, one can sympathize with his retreat; but one sees that, so far from aiding his spiritual development, it halted a good part of it at a critical point: for he did not carry over into his thought and his work the experiences of a husband and a father and a happy lover. He does not speak about these experiences as a mature man: he speaks as an adolescent. At this point, his self did not grow and expand; rather, it became ingrown and withdrawn; and the symbol of incest is perhaps the symbol of this shrinkage, this defeat, and the ultimate blackness of mood that resulted from it. He associated his career with the deep well of adolescent purity, instead of with the running stream of maturity, turbid perhaps, but open to the sunlight, and swift. Doing so, he blocked his own development instead of releasing it: towards later experience he said No: No: and again No. For almost a decade after this, Melville's principal characters are tired, defeated, harassed, tormented, lonely men; and to the end of his days children, the last symbol of maturity, do not, directly or indirectly, enter his imaginative life.

So closely were Melville's sexual impulses and his intellectual career bound up that I am tempted to reverse the more obvious analysis of Pierre, and to see in its sexual symbols the unconscious revelation of his dilemmas as a writer. Lucy, then, may signify the naïve writings of his youth, which promised him happiness, and Isabel, the mysterious child of a foreign mother, lost in an obscure youth, may stand for that darker consciousness in himself that goads him to all his most heroic efforts, that goads him and baffles him, leaving him balked and sterile, incapable of going further in literature, and yet unable to retreat to the older and safer relations with Lucy—the Lucy of Typee and Omoo. We must recall that in writing Moby-Dick Melville had premonitions of his own final flowering and of his sudden falling into mould; and if this prospect haunted him, the relationship with Isabel would be a perfect symbol of it, since it showed him making an effort to go on with his literary career, living under the form of marriage with Isabel, but unable, through the very nature of their relationship, to enjoy the fruits of marriage. In spite of his confidence in Moby-Dick, a doubt might still lurk: suppose Isabel were an impostor! He had given up everything for her: he had abandoned the prospects of a happy literary career, such a career as his family, Elizabeth's family, all his friends and relatives, and the reviewers and society generally would approve of—abandoned it for a mad, chivalrous espousal of his inner life. He had defied the world for this dark mysterious girl; and what she was ready to give him in return the world regarded as an abominable sin. Very well: so much the worse for virtue, if virtue meant Mrs. Glendinning's pride or Lucy's lovely shallowness. Melville was not without hopes that success might join the unsanctified household, that Lucy and Isabel might live side by side; but when the reviewers told him, upon his publishing Mardi and Moby-Dick, that he had espoused a girl of the streets and seduced a virtuous maiden, he saw that there was no way out, except to shoot them and take the consequences.

Pierre itself, then, was a blow, aimed at his family with their cold pride, and at the critics, with their low standards, their failure to see where Melville's true vocation lay, and their hearty recommendation of "virtuous" courses that promised so little. Melville anticipated defeat: Lucy dies of shock, and Pierre and Isabel make away with themselves by poison; for he saw no way to go on with his deepest self, and still continue obedient to the conventions of society and the responsibilities of a married man. His failure to mature with his actual marriage contributed, I think, to his failure to go further with his spiritual union; but how much it contributed, and by what means the injury was done, we can still only speculate. There is no doubt about the final result. The mood of Pierre, the work of art, became the mood of Herman Melville, the man, for almost a decade. Before another year was over, he recovered his grip in writing, and his art became whole and sufficient once more: but his life suffered, and his vision as a whole suffered: Pierre disclosed a lesion that never entirely healed.

CHAPTER NINE: TIMONISM

WE NOW draw near the Cape Horn of Melville's life; and I would remind the reader of Melville's own prophetic words in White-Jacket: "Sailor or landsman, there is some sort of Cape Horn for all. Boys! beware of it; prepare for it in time. Graybeards! thank God it is passed. And ye lucky livers, to whom, by some rare fatality, your Cape Horns are as placid as Lake Lemans, flatter not yourselves that good luck is judgment and discretion; for all the yolk in your eggs, you might have foundered and gone down had the Spirit of the Cape said the word."

The evidence for this part of Melville's history is incomplete and ambiguous: the testimony of his contemporaries is obscure, and what has been handed on to living people has been stated in a fragmentary way by witnesses whose limitations of knowledge and whose emotional bias vitiate their judgment, and rob their testimony of any pretence of impartiality. I do not overlook the value of family tradition in dealing with this part of Melville's life; but I prefer to use it as I shall use Melville's own expression in literature, not as recording objective events, but as indicating a certain tendency and direction. The witness of Melville's own literary works is far more objective evidence than more personal stories which can neither be substantiated nor refuted. "The data which life furnishes towards a true estimate of any being," Melville himself reminds us, "are as insufficient to that end as in geometry one side given would be to determine a triangle." During this period the nearest one can come to truth is by avoiding the grosser forms of error.

The last forty years of Melville's life have been thoroughly misinterpreted, for the reason that after Moby-Dick Melville ceased to be a popular author. This period has been referred to as the long quietus, and even such a just critic as Mr. Percy Boynton could say: "Pierre was Melville's last real and audible word, and even Pierre was an epilogue." Such a complete halt in a writer's life would indeed give reason for grave suspicions; and popular rumour has filled up this dismal gap with tales of Melville's insanity. That there is a spark of fact beneath this suffocating cloud of conjecture, I am prepared to show: but the spark was magnified into a bonfire by Melville's own contemporaries, absurdly, maliciously enlarged; and later critics have even been obtuse enough to read back into Mardi the signs of Melville's mental disruption. As a matter of fact, Melville's silence was a very audible one; and what is usually looked upon as the dark period of his intellectual quietus is in fact the bleak period of his contemporaries' neglect. One cannot call silence the reduced but steady output of short stories, novels, poems, which marked the next forty years of Melville's life.

2

Let us separate the romantic overlay of rumour from the actual facts, and see what is left of the silence and the mystery. The first tangible bit of testimony as to Herman Melville's condition in the year that followed the publication of Pierre is a note that Elizabeth Melville left in her annotation of his papers: "We all felt anxious about the strain on his health in the spring of 1853." By now the direct cause of this strain should be fairly plain: Melville had exhausted himself in writing Moby-Dick, and without waiting to recuperate, he had embarked upon another long work: the effort of writing two such books in two successive years was a terrific one. In Pierre, Melville has left more than one picture of his condition. Pierre, writing of his own hero-author, Vivia, says: "Cast the eye in there on Vivia; tell

me why those four limbs should be clapt in a dismal jail,—
day out, day in—week out, week in—month out, month in—
and himself a voluntary jailer! Is this the end of philosophy? This the larger and spiritual life? This your boasted
empyrean? Is it for this man should grow wise, and leave
off his most excellent and calumniated folly?"

When one pushes the organism so hard, all its latent
weaknesses tend to come out. Presently, the long and terrible exposure he had suffered rounding the Horn on his
return from the South Seas, came back to exact its physical
penalty. As early as 1849, Melville alluded to that experience and its aftermath; and in 1855 he suffered a severe
attack of rheumatism, and in June an attack of sciatica.
Dr. Oliver Wendell Holmes attended him, and it is a pity
that he did not leave a record of the case: one could have
spared a few autocratic conversations for this precious evidence. These attacks continued to undermine Melville: in
1858, he was laid up with a severe attack of "crick in the
back" at his mother's home in Gansevoort. It is difficult, of
course, to draw a line between the physical and the psychical
aspects of an organism; but the tangible evidence of a drain
on Melville's strength is sufficient to justify us in calling
these disabilities primarily physical ones. His perfect health
deserted him. He was to know pain, confinement, lassitude;
and instead of tanned cheeks and hard muscles, pallor and
debility.

In any appraisal of his condition and his fate, this new
element of physical weakness must play a part; for Melville, like Whitman, wrote out of his health, and just as the
paralysis of Whitman, after the Civil War, resulted in the
diminishment of his writing, and a certain curtailment of his
creative effort, without any sign of mental decay, so Melville was deprived of his immense physical buoyancy and
power. That power had counted for much in his own work.
"Real strength," he wrote in Moby-Dick, "never impairs
beauty or harmony, but often bestows it; and in everything

imposingly beautiful, strength has much to do with magic.
. . . As devout Eckermann lifted the linen sheet away from
the naked corpse of Goethe, he was overwhelmed by the massive chest of the man, that seemed a Roman triumphal arch.
When Angelo paints even God the Father in human form,
mark what robustness is there. And whatever they may re-
veal of the divine love in the Son, the soft, curled, hermaph-
roditical Italian pictures, in which his idea has been most
successfully embodied; these pictures, so destitute are they
of all brawniness, hint nothing of any power, but the mere
negative feminine ones of submission and endurance. . . ."
Melville did not easily submit and endure; but without
health he was a shorn giant. His shortened breath would not
sustain the long periods of Moby-Dick, nor would his frame
suffer that "downright infatuation, and no less [which is]
both unavoidable and indispensable in any great deep book,
or even any wholly unsuccessful attempt at a great deep
book."

Such an explanation is sound as far as it goes; but one
must not ignore the psychological accompaniments of this
debility, or all the spiritual obstacles that burked Melville
and made him doubly anxious, strained, desperate. Chief
among the external obstacles was the chorus of disapproval
that had greeted Moby-Dick and grew louder and more universal with Pierre. One London paper denounced it as an
"unhealthy, mystic romance," the Literary World called it
"an eccentricity of the imagination," and Fitz-James
O'Brien, writing in Putnam's Monthly in February, 1853,
fresh from a bout with Pierre, described it in the following
terms: "Thought staggers through each page like one
poisoned. Language is drunken and reeling. . . . Let Mr.
Melville stay his step in time. He totters on the edge of a
precipice, over which all his hard-earned fame may tumble
with such another weight as Pierre attached to it."

The worst of it was that the critics were not altogether
wrong in their judgment of Pierre alone: what was at fault

was their failure to see that the author of Moby-Dick could not be scolded like a child who had mixed up his declensions: he was entitled to the critic's most patient, sympathetic understanding. To pretend that such a mistake might forfeit Melville's whole claim to recognition showed that neither O'Brien nor any one else at the time realized what a strong claim Melville had, or what a profound mark he had made on the literature of the world. I have looked in vain through the collected works and biographies of Emerson, Whitman, Thoreau, Lowell, Holmes, and even Conway and Sanborn, to see if these writers recognized a fellow in Melville, as Emerson had so generously done with Whitman: but except for a brief note on Omoo by Whitman, written in his Brooklyn Eagle days, and a comment in a chance letter by Lowell—exaggerated praise followed by complete indifference to Melville's worth—there is no sign that the contemporaries he might have respected even knew of his existence.

Melville stood alone, alone in a desert. "Who shall tell all the thoughts and feelings of Pierre in that desolate and shivering room, when at last the idea obtruded, that the wiser and profounder he should grow, the more and more he lessened his chances for bread; that could he now hurl his deep book out of the window, and fall on some shallow nothing of a novel, composable in a month at longest, then could he reasonably hope for appreciation and cash. But the devouring profundities now opened upon him, consuming all his vigor; would he, he could not now be entertainingly and profitably shallow in some pellucid and merry romance." This conviction, borne in on him perhaps while writing Moby-Dick, now haunted him when Pierre met its disastrous reception. "The brightest success," he says again in Pierre, "now seemed intolerable to him, since he so plainly saw, that the brightest success could not be the sole offspring of Merit, but of Merit for the one-thousandth part, and nine-hundred and ninety-nine combining and dovetailing accidents for the rest. . . . So beforehand he felt the unrevealable sting of receiving either plaudits or censures, equally unsought for, and equally loathed ere given. So, beforehand, he felt the pyramidical scorn of the genuine loftiness for the whole infinitesimal company of critics. . . . In that lonely little closet of his, Pierre foretasted all that this world hath either of praise or dispraise; and thus fore-tasting both goblets, anticipatingly hurled them both in its teeth. All panegyric, all denunciation, all criticism of any sort would come too late for Pierre."

Needless to say, Melville's pyramidical scorn did not dis-arm the critics, nor did it, one suspects, counteract the effect of the salt that they poured, with such fine antiseptic inten-tions, into his wounds. He was greeted with the embarrassed shamefulness which sometimes appears upon the faces of sophisticated people when a fresh young girl confesses impulses or desires that her elders are forever discreetly hiding. Melville had revealed too much. His contemporaries, with a feeling of guilty repression, denied that any one had the right to take off his clothes, and they equally denied that such harassed, crippled souls could be found beneath the shapely costumes provided by society. Nervous, these re-spectable people will be on the watch for any similar per-formance; more than that, they will read back into Melville's earlier books the same dangerous, unhealthy innocence and exposure.

One and all, the critics agreed with an English writer whose diatribe on the American psychological writers was reprinted, somewhat pointedly, in the Literary World for August 28, 1852. "It is a melancholy sign for the prospects of a rising American literature that some of its most hopeful professors should have, in recent works of fiction, been evi-dently laying themselves out for that species of subtle psychological romance, first introduced to the reading world by such authors as Balzac and Sand. . . . To pass from Scott and Dickens to Sand and Balzac is like giving up the smiling landscape glowing in its freshness and beauty, for the loathly atmosphere, the wretched sights and smells of a dissecting room, or abandoning the busy street or the pleasant social circle for charnels and catacombs. And yet this is what Young America seems bent upon. Instead of sketching the really representative men of their country— instead of conveying to us on this side of the Atlantic a true idea of American society—society in the great seaboard city or in the far west settlement—instead of presenting us with stories racy of the soil and instinct with its vigorous and aggressive theories, the misguided party in question selects some half dozen morbid phases of mind, brings before us some three or four intellectual cripples or moral monsters . . . and instead of laying before us a wholesome story of natural character and motive, he lets us into the secret turns and tidings of unhealthy and abnormal mental power and promptings."

No one saw even dimly then that these psychological novels and short stories, William Wilson, The House of the Seven Gables, The Scarlet Letter, Pierre, were signs of the broken American psyche, alienated by its removal from the solid tissue of Europe, and seeking, by further analysis, to establish a more primitive and elementary state, from which a new integration, more satisfactory and complete, could emerge. These relentless psychologists were far more deeply immersed in the American scene than any of the writers who succeeded them in the next generation, however closely Bret Harte and Howells and Mark Twain met the English prescription for natural character and robust health. If anything could have infuriated Melville, it must have been the suggestion that he could write in another fashion than he had done: "In tremendous extremes," he said in Pierre, "human souls are like drowning men: well enough they know they are in peril; well enough they know the causes of that peril; nevertheless, the sea is the sea and these drowning men do drown."

Baffled by his dilemmas, rebuffed by his contemporaries,

harassed by financial anxiety, curbed by ill health, kept
from the solace of reading by poor eyesight, made doubly
desperate by the cold mysteries he had explored—what was
there to sustain Herman Melville and bring him back to
health? The divided tenderness of a wife who was still bearing children, or the obtuse concern of a mother, a sister, or
brother—so far from relieving him, these things only quickened his exasperation and his sense of helplessness.

When harassed by external circumstances, one wants to
attack the universe: but, like Ahab, one finds that the universe will not get in one's way: so one takes revenge on the
first creature that crosses one's path. Too likely it will be
a creature one holds dear: the animus is not directed against
that one, but it strikes as if it were. An explosion: a blow:
a raised hand: an uncontrollable outburst of vituperation—
then drink, remorse, repentance, the ugly vanity of it all.
The universe is unharmed; one's own condition is unim-
proved: there is just one more blight to stand in the way
of amelioration. Whatever the outward events that mark
Melville's passage through these frantic waters, there is no
doubt of his inward state. In a word he himself coined for
Pierre, he became Timonized. In that awful solitude within,
the very touch of his fellow creatures became defilement.
"He could not bring himself to confront any face or house;
a plowed field, any sign of tillage, the rotted stump of a
long-felled pine, the slightest passing trace of man was un-
congenial and repelling to him. Likewise, in his own mind
all remembrances and imaginings, that had to do with the
common and general humanity had become, for the first
time, in the most singular manner distasteful to him. Still,
while thus loathing all that was common in the two different
worlds—that without and that within—nevertheless, even
in the most withdrawn and subtlest region of his own essential spirit, Pierre could not now find one single agreeable
twig of thought whereon to perch his weary soul."

There was Melville's own state, I believe, during and

after the writing of Pierre, in its uttermost anguish and desolation. His family became apprehensive: his friends dropped away from him, first Hawthorne, then the Duyckincks: and in his sensitive condition, small indifferences became signs of enmity, heartlessness, and alienation. In doubling this inner Cape Horn, Herman Melville may have skirted the jagged rocks of an even deeper disruption: there were moments, perhaps days and months, between 1852 and 1858 when the outcome of his physical and mental condition may well have been in doubt. But with utmost allowance for the horror and collapse of his illness, it was of limited duration, and it could not have been a continuous state, since, throughout this period, he continued to write, to write with clarity, with distinction, and without a visible touch of disorder. Not the least of his literary achievements date from these years of debilitation and infirmity.

The word insanity is far too loose to be used about Melville's mental illness, even during the limited period we are considering. At the very end of his life, Melville wrote a passage about insanity in his novel, Billy Budd, which puts the biographer's difficulty in touching this period with great point. "Who," he asks, "in the rainbow can draw the line where the violet tint ends and the orange tint begins? Distinctly, we see the difference of the colours, but where exactly does the first one visibly enter into the other? So with sanity and insanity. In pronounced cases there is no question about them. But in some cases, in various degrees supposedly less pronounced, to draw the line of demarcation few will undertake, though for a fee some professional experts will. There is nothing nameable but that some man will undertake to do for pay. In other words, there are instances where it is next to impossible to determine whether a man is sane, or beginning to be otherwise."

Melville realized from his own experience, perhaps, what few people understood until Janet and Freud re-interpreted this whole series of disorders, that the line between sanity and insanity is not a line at all but a wide gradient band. Indeed, as early as 1849, in a letter to Mr. Duyckinck written apropos the insanity of Charles Fenno Hoffman, the first editor of The Literary World, Melville had said: "This going mad of a friend or acquaintance comes straight home to every man who feels his soul in him, which but few men do. For in all of us lodges the same fuel to light the same fire. And he who has never felt, momentarily, what madness is has but a mouthful of brains. What sort of sensation permanent madness is may be very well imagined just as we imagine how we felt when we were infants, though we cannot recall it. In both conditions we are irresponsible and riot like gods without fear of fate."

3

The relationship between insanity and art has been the subject of much discussion; and it is important, in appraising Melville's life and work during this period, that we should avoid the notion that genius and insanity are one, or that the fantasies of the neurotic are the equivalent of a work of art. The difference between insanity and what we agree to call normal conduct is largely one of social utilization: given a similar set of circumstances and stimuli, the distinction between a neurotic reaction and a normal one consists largely in the success a person has in conversion. Had Napoleon, for example, merely dreamt about his conquests, magnifying them year by year as his malady grew, he would have been quite properly confined to an asylum, like so many other "emperors of the world," as soon as his patent conduct conflicted with other people's activities. The fact that his particular kind of paranoia was permitted at large was due to his ability to convert it into the forms of contemporary social life, politics and military activity, things which subjected his grandiose dreams to the shock and jar of actuality. This conversion into art signifies health and relative stability, whether the situation that causes the conversion is morbid or not. Indeed, an effectual work of art is not merely a counterpoise to psychal difficulties: it is actually an indication that the artist, during the period of his creation, has had full possession of himself. Insanity in many cases befalls those who cannot make this transposition to art, and who, through inexpertness or inarticulateness, produce therefore unusable fantasies—fantasies that do not meet the impact of reality. There is no mistaking the fantasy of the insane for the fantasy of the artist: issuing from the same headwaters, perhaps, they empty into different oceans. Had Melville remained mute during this period or had his work fallen off we might suspect the worst: his superb craftsmanship, in Bartleby, in The Encantadas, and in Benito Cereno, is, on the contrary, an objective proof—and a reassuring one. The critics and historians of literature who said that his work became "wilder and wilder and more and more turgid in each successive book" after Moby-Dick were either ignorant of his later work, or blind. Wildness and turgidity are the precise opposite of the qualities one finds in these stories and sketches, stories told with delicacy, with restraint, and with great concentration. With the rumour of his insanity in mind, these sympathetic scholars were quick to condemn Melville's work. We may confidently reverse their logic. With the achieved beauty of Melville's work before us, we can isolate and reduce the period of his mental exacerbation.

Melville's own blackness and spiritual desolation, his Timonism, recalls that of Shakespeare himself, from whose play he had taken the word. Their vision of life went through similar stages, and even in their personal affairs some of the same anomalies arise, down to the silent contempt with which Shakespeare apparently dismissed the products of his imagination, not bothering to see that they reached the world at all, still less that they did so in the exact form he had conceived them. In both men, the feeling of a shattered faith and despondency is expressed in the relationship of a young man, Hamlet or Pierre, to a proud and worldly mother; in Pierre and Hamlet, an unconscious incest-wish incapacitates the hero for marriage with the girl he has wooed; and the final result is doubt and deepest anguish, culminating in the death of all involved. Alienated from society, a furious contempt for mankind arises in these writers: Shakespeare carries this contempt into Lear and Timon of Athens, even as Melville did into The Confidence Man: the contempt is mixed with impotence and self-distrust, and the art itself is marred by an uncontrollable sense of outrage: "In Timon," as Dowden justly says, "we see one way in which a man may make his response to the injuries of life; he may turn upon the world in a fruitless and suicidal rage." Finally, when each could go no further without outward violence, he recoiled upon himself, and each in a final work expressed a reconciliation, Shakespeare in The Tempest, separating the base, in the form of Caliban, from the spiritual, in the form of Ariel, under the double mastery of a science and virtue embodied in Prospero—a resolution which, we shall come to see, is not singularly different in meaning from Melville's final work.

What caused this blackness in Shakespeare's life, what brought him to the crisis recorded in Timon, surely the worst of his plays, we can only speculate upon: but in Melville's life we are aware of tangible reasons for his frustration, with roots that reach far back into childhood, his disappointed youth, the hardships of early poverty and defeated expectations, his unfortunate experiences on his first sailing voyage, his perpetual feeling of being an Ishmael, through poverty among the gentlefolk at Albany, through intellectual superiority among his shipmates, through spiritual hardihood among his contemporaries in letters, through social isolation in his own neighbourhood, where people looked upon him as cousin german to the cannibals. Melville had witnessed this same Timonism in Jackson, and his words remind us that "there seemed more woe than wickedness

234

about the man; and his wickedness seemed to spring from his woe; and for all his hideousness, there was that in his eye at times, that was ineffably pitiable and touching; and though there were raw moments when I almost hated this Jackson, yet I have pitied no man as I have pitied him." Jackson would enter into arguments to prove that there was nothing to be believed, nothing to be loved, and nothing worth living for—and during the period of his own Timonism, out of his abysmal woe, Melville felt and wrote, at intervals, particularly in Pierre and in The Confidence Man, the same way.

Of Melville's blackness there is no doubt. That this blackness would ordinarily have led to downright insanity there is little room for doubt either. But, like Shakespeare and Goethe and many another artist, Melville found a benign and not a baneful outlet for his energies; and every evidence of Melville's work points to the restoration of his poise and health, intermittently, in the decade we are writing of, and steadily in the years that followed.

4

Returning to 1853, the year that followed Pierre, we find Melville in the midst of a series of disappointments: he was to learn the truth of Hamlet's observation: misfortunes come not singly but in battalions. Melville sought for a consular appointment in the South Seas, a place where he was fitted by experience and sympathy to perform a decent service, and perhaps, with relief from financial strain, recover a little that joy in the flesh which he had once known, and find again in his bosom the radiance of the landscape itself. Melville had no opportunity to try this remedy. In spite of Richard H. Dana's intercession, Chief Justice Shaw's efforts, and Allan's assiduous canvassing, and Hawthorne's friendly intercession, he did not get the post, nor did he get a consulship at Antwerp, which for a moment seemed possible. To make matters worse, Harper's, his publishers, lost the plates of his novels and almost all the copies of his books in a fire that gutted out their quarters. If there was something prophetic in the foundering of the whaler Ann Alexander, and the total disappearance of the old Pequod itself, as Melville was finishing Moby-Dick, there was something equally uncanny in this conflagration. The very elements played against him, as they played against Ahab. His books were put out again by Harper's, but perfunctorily: they had lost their original momentum. None of Melville's subsequent books was to meet such eager acceptance.

Another sign of Melville's weakened health and lessened energies is the fact that during 1853 his entire writing seems to have consisted only of two short stories, Cock-a-Doodle-Do and Bartleby the Scrivener, both published in magazines towards the end of the year. Melville was not at home in the narrow confines of the short story: he had scarcely time to get under way before he was back again in port. The result is that the best of his short stories are really short novels, while the lesser ones, like The Lightning Rod Man, are little more than mediocre anecdotes. I and My Chimney, The Appletree Table, The Paradise of Bachelors, The Tartarus of Maids, are more in the nature of discursive essays, "in character," than they are of tales: Melville was at his weakest in deliberately symbolic tales, like Cock-a-Doodle-Do and The Bell-Tower; indeed, the latter might be slipped into one of Hawthorne's volumes, without apology, as a minor work of his youth. When in 1852 Melville equably handed to Hawthorne the circumstances of a story he had gathered from a lawyer in New Bedford, he was so conscious of treading on the master's ground that he relinquished his own right to exploit this particular plot. But except for the original impulse, his best stories owe nothing to Hawthorne: Melville's symbolism is more delicately and carefully concealed; and his moral, like Shakespeare's, rests in the demonstration, not in the conclusion.

Bartleby the Scrivener is one of Melville's longer stories;

and it gains much by its juxtaposition of incongruous personalities. The story is told by a comfortable, pursy old
lawyer, with an office in Wall Street; the lawyer and his
copyists are hit off with a warm sense of caricature. Into
this office comes a pale, bleak creature, Bartleby, to serve as
a scrivener. He is quiet and industrious; but he refuses to
comply with the routine of the office: he will not compare
copy, even for the lawyer himself; and yet there is something
in this passive self-assertion and this methodical self-obliter-
ation which makes the lawyer humour Bartleby. With these
qualities goes a mystery; and by accident, on a Sunday at
church-time, the lawyer discovers, on attempting to enter his
office, that Bartleby not only works for him but has quietly
occupied his business premises, to eat and sleep there. In
spite of this gross irregularity, the lawyer keeps Bartleby,
only to have the little man quit work entirely. When the
lawyer demands a reason, he answers: I would prefer not to.
When the lawyer asks him to move out, he answers: I would
prefer not to. There is no getting behind his silence, his dead-
wall reveries, his blank self-possession.

The effect of this passive resistance upon the lawyer is
upsetting. "My first emotions had been those of pure melancholy and sincerest pity; but just in proportion as the for-
lornness of Bartleby grew and grew to my imagination, did
that same melancholy verge into fear, that pity into repulsion. So true it is, and so terrible, too, that up to a certain
point the thought or sight of misery enlists our best affec-
tions; but, in certain special cases, beyond that point it does
not. They err who would assert that invariably this is due to
the inherent selfishness of the human heart: it rather pro-
ceeds from a certain hopelessness of remedying excessive and
organic ill. To a sensitive being, pity is not seldom pain.
And when at last it is perceived that such pity cannot lead
to effectual succour, common sense bids the soul be rid of it.
What I saw that morning convinced me that the scrivener
was the victim of innate and incurable disorder. I might give

alms to the body; but his body did not pain him; it was his soul that suffered, and his soul I could not reach."

The lawyer moves and Bartleby remains on the original premises; but the new tenant is not so patient and he has Bartleby arrested. When Bartleby finds himself in prison, he prefers not to eat. A kind fellow, the lawyer visits him, seeking to restore his confidence and reawaken his manhood. "Nothing reproachful attaches to you being here," he assures Bartleby. "And see, it is not so sad a place as one might think. Look, there is the sky, and here is the grass." "I know where I am," he replied.

Bartleby is a good story in itself: it also affords us a glimpse of Melville's own drift of mind in this miserable year: the point of the story plainly indicates Melville's present dilemma. People would admit him to their circle and give him bread and employment only if he would abandon his inner purpose: to this his answer was—I would prefer not to. By his persistence in minding his own spiritual affairs, those who might have helped him on their own terms, like Allan or his father-in-law or his Uncle Peter, inevitably became a little impatient; for in the end, they foresaw they would be obliged to throw him off, and he would find himself in prison, not in the visible prison for restraining criminals, but in the pervasive prison of dull routine and meaningless activity. When that happened there would be no use assuring him that he lived in a kindly world of blue sky and green grass. "I know where I am!" Whether or not Melville consciously projected his own intuition of his fate, there is no doubt in my mind that, as early as 1853, he was already formulating his answer. To those kind, pragmatic friends and relatives who suggested that he go into business and make a good living, or at least write the sort of books that the public would read—it amounts to pretty much the same thing—he kept on giving one stereotyped and monotonous answer: I would prefer not to. The dead-wall reverie would end in a resolution as blank and forbidding as the wall that faced him: a bleak face, a tight wounded mouth, the little blue eyes more dim, remote, and obstinate than ever: I would prefer not to!

During the next year, Melville settled down to a steadier round of work, and one of the best of his narratives, a series of sketches called The Encantadas, or Enchanted Isles, was published during 1854 under the pseudonym Salvator R. Tarnmoor. Three other sketches followed; and finally, in July, 1854, he began to publish serially the story of Israel Potter, the Revolutionary beggar, for which he had gathered material in London five years before.

In The Encantadas Melville went back again to the ground he had ploughed so well before. He had gone ashore on the Enchanted Isles, the Galapagos, during the early part of his whaling voyage, and now, in his own sable mood —a mood reflected in the very choice of his pseudonym, Tarnmoor—the landscape of these islands corresponded to his inner state; and his description of the scene is as fine as anything in his earlier pages; if anything, there is more studious mastery. The final sketch, the story of Hunilla, who had been left in solitude on one of these islands, when her brother and her husband died, is poignant and terrible, all the more so because of the dark bestiality of the visiting crew, that Melville hints at, and then forgoes telling about, so moved is he by its inhumanity.

"One knows not," Melville reflects here, "whether nature doth not impose some secrecy upon him who has been privy to certain things. At least, it is to be doubted whether it is good to blazon such. If some books are deemed most baneful and their sale forbid, how, then, with deadlier facts, not dreams of doting men. Those whom books will hurt will not be proof against events. Events, not books, should be forbid; but in all things man sows upon the wind, which bloweth where it listeth; for ill or good men cannot know. Often ill comes from good, as good from the ill." He has returned to the ultimate moral of Pierre; and it holds good of the tales of the Enchanted Isles: out of its stark ugliness, he breathed beauty. With just as abhorrent an insight into the cruelties of life as he had in Pierre, Melville here had a firmer hand on himself: he ruefully confesses that "in nature, as in law, it may be libellous to speak some truths." Within the dark rim of the horizon, the words move, like swift white sails on grey waters. The style is again accurate, pliant, subtle, bold; but it is never hectic nor forced, nor does it smell from the mothballs of old costume chests. There is not the faintest sign that his literary powers were falling off, or his voice sinking to a whisper.

5

Israel Potter was a full-length novel, based upon a little memoir of his life, printed for the sake of gathering up a few pennies, in Providence in 1827. The fact that Melville could attempt a long work again is a sign of somewhat restored health, and though the book ranks far below Melville's best work, it differs from Redburn chiefly in that while based upon a document, it relies even more heavily upon Melville's own powers of invention. All the good things in Israel Potter come from Melville, not from Potter: the original story provided only the skeleton of events: Melville gives them a setting and a full cast of characters.

Israel Potter is a country bumpkin who is kept by his parents from marrying the girl he loves, goes on a surveying expedition into Vermont and is defrauded of his earnings, ships to sea, returns to the farm, fights gallantly at Bunker Hill, enlists in an American man-of-war, and is captured by the British and taken to England. Escaping from his guards, Israel flees into the countryside, making his way across England by devious passages, until he finally comes upon a kindly English baronet near Brentford, who gives him a job on his country estate. Rumours that he is a spy dog him, so he is compelled to change his situation and finally he achieves safety at Kew, as one of the king's gardeners. When work slacks off, Israel is again thrown on his resources, and, while hiding, he makes the acquaintance of some secret friends of America, among them, Horne Tooke, the grammarian. These friends equip him and send him on a secret mission to Dr. Franklin in Paris, where he meets Paul Jones; and eventually Israel, by another lucky chance, comes to serve on a privateer with Jones, and to participate in the fight between the Serapis and the Bonhomme Richard. The upshot of these vagrant ups and downs is a long period of toil in a London brickworks, followed by marriage and residence in London. Finally, in his old age, with his English wife dead, Israel returns with his son to his native land, only to find the landmarks of his youth gone, and a pension as a Revolutionary soldier denied him. In this state, the original Israel wrote his book; and at this point of weariness, disillusion, exhaustion, Melville left him.

Israel Potter has suffered, like all Melville's later books, from the apathy of criticism, quite as much as from its own weaknesses. Mr. Percy Boynton says of Israel Potter that "it was a perfunctory work, not as interesting as the book it was based on," and while one hesitates to differ with such an able critic, a close comparison of the book seems to me to prove exactly the opposite. Not merely does Israel Potter contain, as Mr. F. J. Mather, Jr., has remarked, one of the best accounts of a sea-fight in history; not merely is its portrait of John Paul Jones a far more illuminating study of that great shark of the seas than Cooper's picture in The Pilot; but it is one of the few works of American fiction that deal with patriotic episodes in a generous, straightforward way. Melville took a crude, bald narrative and poured life into it: he took a smudgy woodcut and made a living picture out of it, building up the background, creating incident and character where none had existed before, projecting every figure into the third dimension. The account of John Paul Jones occupies a single paragraph in the original: in Melville's novel, Jones is the largest figure in the book, and nearly runs away with the story. It is the same with Franklin. He is a colourless figure in the original: Melville, with gentle mocking penetration, puts before us the man in full length, with sly characterizations of his paunch and his purse and his methodical parsimony. Melville does so well with these characters that one wishes he had created a whole historical portrait gallery. If any one fancies that Melville's characters are merely romantic projections of his actual self, here is a clear answer.

Melville's imaginative life, it is true, flowered only when there was some soil in his own life that nourished it, and when that soil was lacking he found himself forced, again like his Elizabethan exemplar, to pick up the action and the fable in another work. As a writer, he was deprived of the fruitful contacts and adventures he had enjoyed as a common sailor: the inner life grew, but the outer life dwindled and thinned out; and so he was thrown, when he had exhausted his original adventures, upon second-hand experience. This drying up of his sources was a great handicap to him; for while books helped to form and crystallize experience, they were not substitutes for it. He transformed the bald story of Israel Potter: but, had he wholly made it his own, the central character would have been John Paul Jones, and in so far as he was dependent upon the original he was weak. Israel Potter is many removes from Melville at his best; but it would be absurd to throw it out of the Melville canon. It has some of the fine qualities of his art, the mixture of tradition and fresh experience, the purification and heightening of actuality, with a loss of realism and a gain in reality: what it chiefly lacks is centrality. It is Melville *manqué*—but still Melville. His poorest work was many degrees above mediocrity.

6

In 1856, Melville gathered together some of the short stories he had written during the previous three years, and published them as The Piazza Tales. The sketch that gives the volume its title offers us a further glimpse of Melville's life at Arrowhead.

One pictures him seated on that piazza on an August morning, with the meadow in front of him a little sear from the new-cropped hay, a haze lying over the valley of the Housatonic, and the light lavender hills billowing into Greylock's double ridge against the horizon. The landscape brings a feeling of outward serenity, unbroken by the faint happy screams of the children playing in the hayloft, or the muted hum of his wife or his sisters in the kitchen, preparing the scant and largely vegetarian meal. What a contrast with the frayed knotty feeling within! Such warm and deeply balmy days should bring peace: but no day, however balmy, can annul the anxiety and weariness of the last five years, the incessant round of writing, and, further plaguing him, instead of giving relief, the equally endless round of the farm, wood to be chopped and sawed, hay to be mowed and gathered, cows and horses to be fed, vegetables to be planted and hoed, cabbage-worms to be fought . . . oh! for a little coconut and poee-poee! Emerson had discovered that he could not tend his garden and his mind at the same time; and Melville, though at first robust, doubtless found that two careers were a little too much for a single man, exhausted, half spent. In a pinch, Melville could of course apply to Elizabeth's father or to Allan for aid; and he did: but he could not continually write out unredeemable notes for their benefit; that was all right in a matter like the mortgage, where there was security; but as a source of daily income, it was little better than outright beggary.

Melville's eyes would sweep over the valley to the hills beyond. There, ah! there perhaps lay happiness! What charming fairy might be living without relatives and grocers and publishers and promissory notes to harry her, in that little cottage on the mountainside before him? Some day he must find the road to that delectable retreat. . . . He found it, and to his sorrow and disillusion, instead of an idyllic bower, it was a weather-beaten old place, inhabited by a tired and troubled girl, who dreams of the happiness that lies in a marble palace in the distance below—Melville's own white house. No fairy maiden she: no fairy prince he: but a sad girl and a tired, dutiful husband, straining night and day for the few pennies that will shoe his children's feet, replace their tattered home-made clothes, and put bread and milk on the table. These five years, years that have enclosed his highest powers, his consummate manhood, have not left Melville with an eager taste for another fifty of the same pattern. Inevitably, he sought escape; and in his mind, escape meant the sea. Almost any slight change in atmosphere can bring the ocean back to him: the ocean, where physical sustenance, hard-tack and salt rhinoceros, was provided for one, where the hours were long and peaceful, and amid storm and rigour and dangerous courses, there brooded, within, a deep and unbreakable calm.

With a wry smile, Melville exchanges the topmast of reverie for the piazza; but tranquillity does not follow. His very pen lives only when it touches the sea; and when he gathers together these Piazza Tales, he does not bother to include most of his land-stories. He is wise: none of them has a tithe of the interest that Benito Cereno possesses. That story marked the culmination of Melville's power as a short-story writer, as Moby-Dick marked his triumph as an epic poet.

7

In Benito Cereno, published in Putnam's Monthly Magazine in 1855, Melville was again at home. It is such a tale as one might hear, with good luck, during a gam in the South Seas or at a bar in Callao; and Melville himself took it boldly from a book of voyages by Captain Amasa Delano, published in 1816.

A black, ill-kempt ship, commanded by a young Spanish captain and manned by negroes, is in distress, and calls upon Captain Amasa Delano, a bluff, frank American skipper, for aid. Delano, coming aboard with provisions and water, finds the captain almost down with a fever, and by turns confidential and queerly reserved. The Spaniard is attended by a black slave who almost smothers him with watchful endearments; and he has the air of perpetually manoeuvring, in a way that would seem sinister were his plight not so manifestly pathetic. Delano is a little troubled at heart, but he is free from intellectual suspicions. There is something wrong on the Spaniard's ship; but it is hard for Delano to put his hand on it. Don Benito is in command: but he seems helpless, and he tolerates ugly disorder even among the black boys. Promising further aid, Delano finally leaves the vessel and is about to pull for his own ship, still powerfully disturbed by the Spanish captain's pain, trouble, fever, churlishness, courtesy—does it mean some treachery? With a wild leap, the Spaniard throws himself in Delano's boat, followed by his faithful black, dagger in hand; and the black aims his dagger, not at the Americans, but at his Spanish master. When the American crew finally pulls to safety a harrowing story comes out.

I will not spoil Benito Cereno for those who have not read it by revealing its mystery; it is enough to point out that the interplay of character, the cross-motives, the suspense, the central mystery, are all admirably done: in contrast to some of Melville's more prosy sketches, there is not a feeble touch in the whole narrative. The following passage, which sets the key of the whole story, reveals Melville's undiminished ability as an artist:

"Everything was mute and calm; everything gray. The sea, though undulated into long roads of swells, seemed fixed, and was sleeked at the surface like waved lead that has cooled and set in the smelter's mould. The sky seemed a gray surtout. Flights of troubled gray fowl, kith and kin with flights of troubled gray vapors among which they were mixed, skimmed low and fitfully over the waters, as swallows over meadows before storms." As in The Encantadas, the writing itself was distinguished: it had a special office of its own to perform, and did not, as in Typee and Redburn, serve merely as carriage for the story. One can mark Melville's literary powers in the complete transformation of Delano's patent story: he adds a score of details to heighten the mystery and deepen the sinister aspect of the scene; and by sheer virtuosity he transfers the reader's sympathies to the Spanish captain, who in the original story is far more cruel, barbarous, and unprincipled than the forces he contends against. In order to effect this change, Melville deliberately omits the last half of the story, in which the Spanish captain ignobly turns upon his benefactor and seeks to deprive him of the rights of salvage. The moral of the original tale is that ingratitude, stirred by cupidity, may follow the most generous act, and that American captains had better beware of befriending too whole-heartedly a foreign vessel. In Benito Cereno the point is that noble conduct and good will, like that Don Benito felt when his whole inner impulse was to save Delano and his crew, may seem sheer guile; and, further, that there is an inscrutable evil that makes the passage of fine souls through the world an endless Calvary. "Even the best men err, in judging the conduct of one with the recesses of whose condition he is not acquainted." The world is mortified for Don Benito by the remembrance of the human treachery he has encountered: no later benefaction, no radiance of sun and sky, can make him forget it.

Man should offset the malice and evil circumstance one finds in the constitution of the universe: instead, he aggravates it. One does not need to heighten the parallels between Benito Cereno's fate and Melville's own life to catch the semblance to his own dilemma and his own bowed and wounded spirit. "Never," says one of the characters in his next book, "has it been my lot to have been wronged, though but in the smallest degree. Cheating, backbiting, superciliousness, disdain, hard-heartedness, and all that brood, I know but by report. Cold regards tossed over the sinister shoulder of a former friend, ingratitude in a beneficiary, treachery in a confidant—such things may be; but I must take somebody's word for it." The irony of that declaration is obvious: Melville had met these things, and, like a splinter of steel in the eye, they tormented him and during these harassed years the memory of them, the anticipation of them, the helpless attempt to guard against them or remove them, directed his whole life towards this single point of exacerbation. The mighty whale aroused Melville's utmost powers: there was that in man that steaded him manfully for such an encounter: but, like Timon, the spectacle of fair-weather friends and worldly sycophants, turning away from him during his moment of greatest need, unmanned him completely. Moby-Dick might slay one: but the torments of black flies and gnats made life ignoble without bringing death any nearer. Melville did not need to exaggerate these wrongs. It was their very smallness, their unassailableness, that made him desperate.

8

The Confidence Man was written in 1856, and published in the following spring, while Melville was abroad. It is by all odds the most difficult book that confronts Melville's biographer; for it is possibly a palimpsest, and beneath its obvious legend, one may read indirect revelations of Melville's own life. With Melville's actual life and predicament in mind, there are passages in The Confidence Man one cannot read without misgiving: the story of Charlemont, The Gentleman Madman, for one, and the story of the Man in Weeds, wedded to a fiendish woman, Goneril, who covers up her own lecherousness by attributing insanity to her husband. Likewise somewhat mysterious is the story of the Indian-hater, who had been injured in youth by Indians, and never lost a chance to exterminate one. It is hard to fit these incidents into the logic of the plot: and their existence becomes plausible only if one believes Melville's own torments and suspicions had, for a brief while, taken on a pathological character.

No one who approached The Confidence Man without preoccupation or bias would, I think, impute such personal and neurotic motives to the passages in question; but once the seed of suspicion is sowed, as the misanthropic one-legged man demonstrates in an early chapter, it spreads like the Canada thistle, and is almost as hard to root out. The words suspicion and confidence, that recur in these pages, increase one's suspicions and weaken one's confidence; in fact, there is no end to the pathological allusions one may discover, if one begins with the unfavourable hypothesis. Failing positive independent evidence, it would be foolish to build up a card-house of conjecture: enough to say that if Pierre partly reveals the causes of Melville condition, it is in The Confidence Man, if anywhere, that the psychologist will discover, probably, its immediate outward manifestations. The problem, though tantalizing, is not of paramount importance; for there is plenty of independent evidence to show that by 1858 Melville had regained possession of himself, and that his further life, though full of hardship and difficulty, had nothing in it that placed him outside the pale of family life and friendship and decent social intercourse—although it may have been dogged by memories and revulsions from an earlier period, and by the continuation of evil suspicions in the minds of those to whom the normal abstentions and irritations that attend productive literary effort would themselves be an evidence of eccentricity, or something worse.

9

In The Confidence Man Melville went back to the vein of satire he had opened in Mardi. He was shrewd enough, however, to curb the outward extravagance and the aesthetic vagaries of Mardi: the scene is a Mississippi steamboat, the characters are the motley company one might find on such a craft, and the story itself, so far from being incoherent, remains almost monotonously within the frame that Melville set for it in the first chapter.

At St. Louis a deaf-mute in a cream-coloured suit, with flaxen hair and a white fur hat, steps aboard the steamboat Fidele. He circulates among the crowd with a slate on which he writes: Charity thinketh no evil: suffereth long and is kind: endureth all things: believeth all things: never faileth. The passengers look upon this advertiser of St. Paul as a lunatic: that sign fills them with dubiety, although the sign outside the barber-shop, NO TRUST, seems to them an obvious and natural one.

Here in a simple image is the moral Melville confronts and elaborates in the rest of the book. This steamer, the Faithful, is the world, with all possible varieties of the human animal on board, natives and foreigners, men of business and men of pleasure, parlour men and backwoods men, farm-hunters, fame-hunters, heiress-hunters, buffalo-hunters, happiness-hunters, fine ladies in slippers and moccasined squaws, Quakers, soldiers, black, white, brown, and every religion and degree of morality. One thing mars their professions and plagues their lives: their suspicion. A wooden-legged man, apparently once a customs-officer, most suspicious of functionaries, denounces a cheery black beggar who has come among them, as an impostor: immediately, almost every man on deck turns against the poor fellow. Even a brawny Methodist minister, who first takes the black's part, becomes infected: his confidence is gone. A sad demure man in weeds of mourning makes his appearance: with great simplicity of purpose, he insinuates himself into the confidence of a merchant, and gets ten dollars from him. A little later a man in a grey coat and white tie accosts his fellow passengers for contributions to a Widow and Orphan Asylum recently founded among the Seminoles.

When rebuffed as a sharper, he asks his denouncer to be more charitable and throw off suspicion. The full title of the story is The Confidence Man: His Masquerade, and one does not go so far without suspecting that the Confidence Man is a protean character and that the mysterious appearance and disappearance of the deaf-mute, the negro beggar, the man in mourning, or the turning up of a seller of quack medicine which cures by establishing confidence, are merely his own mutations—or at least are conducted by him. By a hundred shady devices, he breaks down suspicion, makes men charitable, gives them faith in one another: but always when they are on the point of being completely disarmed, their lurking baseness or suspicion will rise to the surface. The herb-doctor's pain-dissuader is selling well until a passenger gives him the lie: "Some pains cannot be eased but by producing insensibility, and cannot be cured but by producing death." That hard truth destroys the whole baseless fabric of confidence he had built up.

Worse doubts intervene. People buy herb remedies because they think these medicines are natural, and what is natural is good. But if man is vile, what about Nature? Is the cough one attempts to cure not natural, and what of the cholera and the rattlesnake and the deadly nightshade? The Missourian, who utters this doctrine, has no more faith in humanity than he has in Nature: he is a bitter heretic, even in politics. What is abolitionism but the expression of fellow feeling of slave for slave? From Maine to Georgia the best breeds are to be bought up for any price from a livelihood to a presidency. "Machines for me!" exclaims the Missourian. So the characters pass, talking, argufying, blasting charity, killing confidence, either unconsciously or deliberately blackening the character of man, and proving the emptiness of all the sweet professions of civilization.

Two men become acquainted and hit up an intimacy over a bottle of wine. One of them, Frank Goodman, a cosmopolitan philanthropist, reeking good-will, professes to be inflamed by his friend's nobility of mind and his good opinion of his fellow men, and in a sudden burst of confidence throws himself upon his high-minded fellow: he admits he is in want of money and asks for a loan of fifty dollars. Charlie turns away in dudgeon. "Go to the Devil, sir. Beggar, impostor!" Rising quickly from his seat and taking ten half-eagles from his pocket, Frank lays them in a circle around Charlie: with the air of a magician, he summons his friend to reappear. The practical necromancy works. Ha! ha! it was all a joke, of course. Charlie had humoured him. He had played his part to the life! . . . On top of this the philanthropist has an encounter with Mark Winsome, a mystic philosopher, and his disciple, who state and practice the extreme opposite of philanthropy: his philosophy stands the test of truth: it conforms to the world and does not produce a character at odds with it! This Winsome is no visionary: far from it: "Was not Seneca a usurer? Bacon a courtier? and Swedenborg, though with one eye on the invisible, did he not keep the other on the main chance?" Winsome is the original pragmatist: a man of serviceable knowledge: the doctrines he preaches will lead neither to the mad-house nor the poor-house. When Goodman poses to his disciple a situation like that he had just tested, the disciple handles it with adroit coolness. The loan is not to be thought of: friends do not help friends. If Frank turn beggar, then Charlie for the honour of friendship will turn stranger.

The philanthropist has enough of this icy philosophy: he retreats to the barber shop, his confidence in humanity unshaken. There he arranges with the barber to take down the NO TRUST sign, promising to reimburse the man himself for any loss he may incur through his confidence. Unfortunately, Goodman leaves the shop, after signing the agreement, without paying for his own shave: and the barber, suddenly restored to his senses, tears up the contract and replaces the sign. Finally, Goodman comes to a comely old man, sitting in his berth, reading the Bible by the dim cabin light. Here is a man who has complete faith—yes, and the old man of faith equips himself with a cabin-lock, a counterfeit detector, a money-belt, a life-preserver, and an insurance policy!

It is not hard to see where all this leads, although the story itself ends abruptly. The Confidence Man, in his masquerade, represents all the sweetness and morality of the race, all that professes to see good in the heart of evil, all the benign impulses to succour the poor and heal the sick, all that would place friendliness and natural intimacy above cold circumspection, that would make every alien soul a friend, and would place the needs of man above the safety of property. This sweetness and morality had become for Melville the greatest of frauds. The people who professed it were sharpers and quacks. Nature, life, human institutions, did not encourage this fine morality: they contradicted it. The Pharisee, tightening his purse and disclaiming responsibility for his brother in distress, the old friend permitting the matter of a loan to disrupt a friendship—these things, and a score like them, shrivelled up the outward pretences of social man. Not faith and charity, but NO TRUST was the key to a prosperous and efficient life. There was nothing wrong in the profession: love, faith, and charity might make the worst of ills tolerable; but the miser clung to his money, the merchant to his reputation, the good man to his immaculateness, and he who believed in the Word of God had more faith in the insurance company and the life-preserver. No trust. Man's soul was lead. Without money or reputation, it sank.

10

I cannot leave The Confidence Man without a word about its incidental characteristics. One of the most important things about the story is that it is unfinished. Melville took leave of The Confidence Man before he had unmasked him: the meaning of the fable is left hanging in the air: the plot, which has neither up nor down, preparation nor climax, suddenly collapses—as if Melville were discouraged or a little bored by his own contrivances, or dismissed the story to his contemporaries with a gesture of contempt, hopeless that they would read it, or confident that, even if they did, they would not know the difference. The last words in the book are—"Something further may follow of this Masquerade"—as if he were waiting for some breath of popular response.

The fable of The Confidence Man is plain as far as it goes: there is nothing obscure or difficult in the symbolism; but it has the abrupt and scanty appearance of a Manx cat. In the individual sections, the writing is always competent; and sometimes far more than that: but the story moves as torpidly and sinuously as the muddy Mississippi itself, and there are repetitions of movement, as when the hypothetical Frank and Charlie go over the same ground as the original ones. Mr. Freeman's notion that the story was written for the vain purpose of exposing the hypocrisy and assertiveness of passengers on a steamboat is a little beside the point, and his notion that the characters support Dickens's worst charges in Martin Chuzzlewit is even more amusing; nor is Mr. Mather any more accurate when he speaks of The Confidence Man as "Middle Western character sketches." One might meet queer, uncouth animals on a Mississippi steamer; doubtless one did; but the queerness Melville satirized he had met in the slums of Liverpool and the drawing-rooms of New York.

When one regards The Confidence Man in its true light, not as a novel, but as a companion volume to Gulliver's Travels, its whole aspect changes: its turbid, tedious, meandering quality remains: but there are rapids of dangerous and exhilarating satire, as in the humane proposal, not yet wholly adopted, to organize the redemption of the world on strict Wall Street principles by farming out the charity and missionary work to the highest bidder, and forcing the inhabitants of Africa and Asia to pay for their own redemption and the relief of their own poverty. The Confidence Man may be considered as Melville's own masquerade; his own bitter plea for support, money, confidence. Indeed, a Mississippi steamboat whose passengers quote Zimmermann, Hume, Francis Bacon, Rabelais, Jeremiah, Jeremy Taylor, Diogenes, and Timon could scarcely be anything but Melville's own heavily laden soul, all its characters and incidents being part of that long soliloquy in which Melville struggled with a cankerous mood that threatened to remove, not merely the clothes, but the epidermis, no, the very bowels of his fellow creatures.

The passionate defiance was gone: a more savage, relentless humour took its place, a humour that stabbed and punctured with intent to kill. Melville's aim remained good: there is more than one passage like this description of a miser: "A lean old man, whose flesh seemed salted codfish, dry as combustibles; a head like one whittled by an idiot out of a knot; a flat, boney mouth, nipped between buzzard nose and chin. . . . His eyes were closed, his cheek lay upon an old white moleskin coat, rolled under his head, like a wizened apple upon a grimy snowbank."

A book with so much of Melville's ingrained thought and cast of mind cannot be dismissed as a "posthumous book," nor can it be set to one side because it lacks the human veracity of Life on the Mississippi. The book is without doubt below the level of the great eighteenth century satires; above all, it lacks the virtue of brevity; but as an indictment of humanity, The Confidence Man is far more deeply corrosive than anything in Bierce or Mark Twain. It is hard to refute Melville's black words, difficult to find an antidote for this spiritual nightshade. Melville's contemporaries did not try. They applied to the book the same medicine that worked so well in life: they agreed to forget it. Most of the sweetness and decorum of society rests on an agreement to forget. The sewer and the garbage pile and the slaughterhouse, the prison, the hospital, the slum, the asylum, the battlefield, live and flourish behind that agreement. Sometimes, though they are out of sight beyond the city's limits, their odour is carried on the wind and mingles with the air of the drawing-room. The guests shift a little uneasily in their chairs. The hostess speaks in a loud intent voice: the guests respond with vivacious eagerness: the agreement must be maintained. How that dress shimmers in the soft light! What delicious perfume that bosom exhales! Is there any pleasant sound or sight that riches cannot purchase? The hostess looks uncomfortably at the window: the guests follow her eyes uneasily: the maid closes the window, and, with a touch of finality, draws the curtains again. A long breath of relief: the agreement triumphs: the licence to forget!

Melville could not forget, and yet he could go no further with these observations and memories. He recoiled from his experience into a mournful humility. After The Confidence Man, these terrible blacks softened into greys: the wound whitened into a scar: the eyes automatically shut when the scene they beheld became too painful. When one has found the worst that can be said against the world, one must still live in it, and eventually Melville resigned himself, and lived. The crack which began to open like the gaping earth in Moby-Dick, that widened with a shiver in Pierre, became a foaming abyss in The Confidence Man. As he was on the point of falling into that abyss, Herman Melville withdrew, and the wide fissure closed—or seemed to close.

PILGRIM

CHAPTER TEN: TROUBLED FOOTSTEPS

By 1856 Herman Melville had, I think, reached the bottom of his woe, and he was on the point of resignation—resigning his career, his hope of livelihood and fame, the high place among his peers that his genius entitled him to. His short stories during this period gave hints of his gathering resolution; for he plays with his possible fate again and again, as in the story of the fiddler, Hautboy, who had been a famous prodigy in his youth, and who now, in obscurity, with genius and without fame, was happier than a king. Jimmy Rose is another story of a man who has fallen in the world and sinks into a genteel pauperism, wherein all his old graces become pathetic dodges for filling a hungry stomach. Contemplating this character, Melville became for the first time downright sentimental: one feels tears of self-pity welling into his eyes as he uttered the refrain: "Poor, poor Jimmy—God guard us all—poor Jimmy Rose!"

Melville, at least, was too proud to lift a pitiful false front. He will seek other consolations than as a defunct literary celebrity: the occasional student, like Mr. Titus Munson Coan, who finds him in the Berkshires, does not get a glimpse of the South Sea Melville he admires: instead, he must listen to Kant and Hegel and Plato and all the contemporary mysteries. But won't you tell me something about the cannibals: that was *so* interesting. Doubtless the dim Bartleby look would come into Melville's eyes: "That reminds me of the eighth book of Plato's Republic." Or perhaps, from a deeper chasm, would come Bartleby's own reply: I would prefer not to.

Melville had begun to feel, with Pierre, "what all mature men, who are Magians, sooner or later know, and more or less assuredly—that not always in our actions are we our own factors." When Melville reached this point, his youth was over; and his manhood, which had just begun, was over, too. From an experience so heavy and overwhelming as Melville's, there was no alternative but retreat, and complete submission. The Olympian had adventured, an innocent abroad in the morning; the Titan had struggled, a wise, tormented, valiant man, working and battling in the sweat and dust of noon: twilight had fallen early, and in the gloom, he could neither adventure nor struggle: "The power and dominion of the present world," as Mr. D. S. MacColl has said in describing these three dominant figures of the spirit, "is a vanity to him; the furious energy of retaliation against suffering a trivial folly, because in his vast contempt and renunciation of this and of all life, things visible or attainable, present or to come, the height and depth of any other creature dwindle to nothingness and the least is equal to the greatest." This is the mood of the Pilgrim: the mood of humility and indifference to outward things. A product of defeat and frustration, this attitude is a last attempt to circumvent it. Buddhism and Christianity represent this mood in the history of communities, racked by war, pestilence, slavery, and sheer fatigue of living and its symbol is the cloister, walled off from the distraction and struggle of the outer world. Melville sought a cloister for his spirit. Unable to batter down the indifference of his contemporaries, he endeavoured to erect within himself a fortress that would keep them at bay.

2

Elizabeth Melville noted that bad health, following too close application to work, made travel advisable in 1856: that is the outward explanation of Melville's circumstances. Melville's father-in-law again came forward with financial

aid, and in October Herman Melville set off on a journey to
Constantinople and the Holy Land. He had contemplated
such a trip in 1849; and now, from a deeper consciousness
of his spiritual dilemma, he wished perhaps to prove the advice he had given Taji in the last pages of Mardi—to return and find his Yillah in Serenia. It was characteristic of
Melville's habit of thought that he should seek for Christ's
kingdom in the territory that had known his presence, instead of plying himself with books and spiritual interme-
diaries: having come upon Moby-Dick on the adventurous
voyages of his youth, he was now, as a man of thirty-seven,
hopeful to find through another voyage a sufficient antagonist to this Satanic power, with whom he could ally his own
faltering, and almost routed, forces. But it was not merely
for peace that Melville set out. Beneath the obvious and inevitable retreat was possibly the hope that the old energies
would come back again, that the old Titan would re-awake
and the old challenge stir again in his bosom—that, with
some of his domestic cares relieved or forgotten, the joy
of battle would come back to him, the relish for arduous
days of creation. Hopes and fears went with Herman Melville across the Atlantic: but unless we misread his words
completely, the fears were uppermost. Perhaps life held no
answer. It was possible "after all, that spite of bricks and
shaven faces, this world we live in is brimmed with wonders,
and I and all mankind, beneath our garbs of commonplaceness, conceal enigmas that the stars themselves, and perhaps
the highest seraphim, cannot resolve."

3

Again we come very close to the external round of Melville, for, after sailing to Glasgow and making his way
through Lancaster, he arrived at Liverpool on November 8,
1856. There, at the White Bear, he began a journal which
he carried through the better part of his trip. Like his earlier
journal, it is chiefly a record of outward impressions: medi-

tation, the working of the inward eye, seems always to have followed much later. He was a good traveller. Hawthorne, whom he hunted up in Liverpool, describes him as making his long journeys with scarcely more than a toothbrush for equipment: Melville still retained the sailor's knack of stowing away a good deal in a small space, and doing without the landsman's non-essentials; and, as Hawthorne notes, he always presented the appearance of a well-groomed gentleman. More than this: he struck up acquaintance easily, and at the outset he was tempted, upon meeting an agreeable young Scot, to go east with him forthwith on the same steamer. Melville was always keen to enjoy the contrasts and suggestions of new customs; and he notes, for example, how the landlord in the ordinary of his Liverpool hotel acted as if he were presiding over a private dinner party, all thought of mercenary ends banished, although the wine he offered his guests would later be reckoned in the bill.

Hawthorne, now American Consul at Liverpool, was staying at Southport, a watering-place some twenty miles distant; and Melville sought his old friend out there and stayed with him a few days. The afternoon of his arrival, they walked together along the strand, these two men, both, alas! aging quickly, though Hawthorne was only fifty-two, and Melville was fifteen years younger. The beach was lonely; a strong wind stirred panic in the long grass and occasionally swept the loose sand in their faces; and Melville, a little weariedly, as if somehow the matter must be settled, went back again to the things he used to talk about with Hawthorne in the sunny Berkshire days, things as bleak as the sea-coast itself, and as infinite as the sky: Time and Free-Will, and Eternity, and Faith! Melville cannot believe in Christianity nor be comfortable with his doubts, torments, inner wounds. Hawthorne, as usual, was aloofly sympathetic: it was strange how Melville persisted, had persisted ever since Hawthorne knew him and probably long before, in wandering to and fro in these deserts. If Melville

were a religious man, he would be one of the most truly
religious and reverential, thinks Hawthorne to himself: for
he has a high and noble nature, and is better worth immortality than most of us.

Melville must have looked pleadingly at that grave,
heavy-browed face, with its domed forehead, which seemed
to promise so much. Did it have no answer for him? Did
those intent eyes say to one, as Plinlimmon's said to Pierre—
Vain, vain are all your struggles and endeavours? Except
when Hawthorne wrote, how little did he ever give in exchange! Did Melville feel that Hawthorne mutely understood, and had no remedy: that the mind that had seen into
Hester Prynne's heart or Chillingworth's evil spirit had retreated, hopeless, from his riled depths? If Melville did not
feel that, still he needed a confidant, and the wild screams of
the gulls over the lonely sands may have awakened to unpre-
meditated sudden declaration the wild loneliness of his own
heart. Melville might as well confess it to Hawthorne: he
had about made up his mind to be annihilated. There was
no place for him in America: his best and deepest work, his
maturest convictions, were lightly tossed aside by his contemporaries: they were interested in whale oil at so much per
gallon, not in the quest of Moby-Dick; and they wanted
stories that would tickle their vanity, like a mirror, or make
the blood course more pleasantly, like a glass of port wine.
Melville would not commit suicide: that was a weak way out:
but he might deliberately withdraw.

Perhaps Hawthorne looked doubly grave: it is doubtful if
he offered any word of countervailing encouragement; for
he probably did not have enough confidence in Melville's
genius, much as he respected his probity, to urge him to
continue the fight. Besides, he was a little embarrassed;
despite his political influence, he had been unable to get
Melville the consular post that would have relieved him so
greatly; and he felt a little responsible for Melville's financial plight, if not for his spiritual predicament—although

his failure reflected nothing upon his practical good-will, and there is no sign that Melville was even faintly reproachful. Perhaps, at bottom, Hawthorne felt guilty because he could not offer back in friendship all Melville was willing to give—and craved. Unrequited friendship is no easy state for either party to bear.

Evening fell: the wind grew raw: the waters became steel-edged at the horizon with a girder of black: the occasional lights in the town increased the sense of solitude, as the two dark figures made their way back to the huddled silhouette of houses. There was no true end to this talk, but instead of that, the consolations of the table were presently spread: stout to drink and fox-and-geese to eat. Julian had grown into a fine lad; and Una was taller than her mother. The food, the coal-fire, and the chatter of the children before bedtime gave Melville, if only for a moment, something solid to go on, something he could not find in Hawthorne's patient silences. Well, on the morrow, Melville must say good-bye and go up to Liverpool with Hawthorne to make inquiries about passage among the steamers. On a rainy night, standing on a street corner in Liverpool, he took Hawthorne's hand and said good-bye to him. Hawthorne was touched. He respected that pale, brooding spirit, that restless, adventurous, still aimless traveller. Casually, they shook hands: the night and the rain swallowed up Melville, and they never met again, and as far as one knows, they never corresponded.

For Melville this was perhaps a last desperate essay at maintaining their friendship; and in spite of Hawthorne's cordial greeting, the meeting was hollow and it had come to nothing. Each had a secret locked in his bosom; and, in a sense, each had lost the key. Yet there was something fine and true between these two men—if only there had not been the reserve and the distance between them, a reserve that Melville's old rollicking ways and easy gipsy friendliness could not break down. One can scarcely doubt that it was

about Hawthorne Melville wrote the following Monody,
included in the sheaf of poems issued just before Melville's
death:

> To have known him, to have loved him
> After loneness long;
> And then to be estranged in life,
> And neither in the wrong;
> And now for death to set his seal—
> Ease me, a little ease, my song!
>
> By wintry hills his hermit-mound
> The sheeted snow-drifts drape
> And houseless there the snow-bird flits
> Beneath the fir-trees' crape:
> Glazed now with ice the cloistral vine
> That hid the shyest grape.

The fatal cold that had struck this friendship, the only
deep one that had sprung up in Melville's life and attracted
all the members of his personality—if one omits the retro-
spective warmth of his feeling for Jack Chase—this fatal
cold did not lessen Melville's inner pangs and his feeling of
desolation.

4

On November eighteenth, Melville finally set sail, passing
Cape St. Vincent and Cape Trafalgar, entering the Straits
of Gibraltar about a week later, and skirting along the
coast of Africa. Throughout this journey, his eyes were
keen and eager: when Gibraltar stands lit up by the sun,
and casts a shadow over the rest of the scene, he thinks of
England casting the rest of the world in shade; and when
Algiers lies before him, he remembers a passage in Don
Quixote. As the boat sails out, the town in the distance
looks "like a sloping rock covered with bird-lime." In Greece,
the scene became fantastic and memorable: the pantaloons
and male petticoats, the embroidered jackets, the noble
faces and ferocious moustachios—it is the Greece of Edmond

About—and the town itself, dirty, grimly picturesque, with old men who look like Pericles reduced to a *charbonnier*.

From Syra to Salonica: at daybreak Melville came on deck to see Mt. Olympus, covered with snow, and Ossa and Pelion to the south, with Mt. Atlas, rather conical, on the opposite shore. In port, the same welter of picturesqueness, dirt, modern needs, ancient beauty. The remains of a Roman triumphal arch across a street and the fragments of a noble Greek edifice, three columns and part of a pediment, used as a gateway and support to the outhouse of a Jew's abode. The English resident comes aboard ship: he has that cockney confidence in the rights and privileges of God's Englishman that makes the English so comical and so efficient wherever they go. He tells Melville he has been for a day's shooting in the Vale of Tempe. Ye Gods! Whortleberrying on Olympus! The countryside: hot-houses and trellises. The monastery where Melville was served with sweetmeats, fruit, and coffee, under an ancient sycamore. Under all these little odd stimulations, the palate becomes less jaded and the eyes are refreshed; the spirit itself becomes eager.

When, finally, the ship sets out for Constantinople, Olympus shows in the moonlight like a ship of white cloud. On deck, the rich Turkish effendis, in their long, furred robes of yellow, attended by their harems, securely guarded in tents, give Melville other things to think about. Orientals have no hearth, no bed, and never blush! The women are pretty; for the Mohammedan religion disdains the corset, along with a good part of Western ethics and religion. These creatures are lazy, gracious, voluptuous; in Constantinople Melville finds that women with ugly faces are rare, and that every other window shows faces, Jewish, Grecian, Armenian, which in America would be a cynosure in a ballroom. Does Melville suspect that enjoyment of the rites of sex, skill and wisdom in that enjoyment, have contributed by sexual selection and general good health to this beauty? No: this is one aspect of life where, as we shall again see later, he observes the facts, but finds no clues.

As the ship approaches Constantinople, the contrasts pile up: the sail up the Hellespont is exhilarating, although spoiled a little by the mists: at night, as the ship is lying by in a fog, he hears only the bells of the neighbouring ships, and the sharp bark of the pariah dogs on the shore. The passengers endure sea-sickness, discomfort, and damp for two days. Melville turns to an old Turk and says: This is very bad. The Turk answers: God's will is good, and smokes his pipe in cheerful resignation. That is the East's answer to our Western fretfulness, to our desire to discipline the elements and remove all the natural obstacles to man's existence and happiness: but the East pays its price for it: the beauties of Constantinople are shrouded in dank, odourous streets that are unmarked and unnamed and lead nowhere: the priests in the Mosque of St. Sophia sell the precious mosaics as they fall to the floor, not endeavouring to repair the scaling walls of that superb interior: the bazaars are a wilderness of traffic. Melville loses himself and is confounded and bewildered by the din, the barbaric confusion, of the whole city. At night he does not dare to leave the hotel, for fear of being assassinated for the sake of a watch or a ring. In short, failing to struggle against God's will, the East puts up, in the same easy spirit, with every species of human roguery: that is no answer to the White Whale! Indeed, Melville scarcely dares walk the streets in the daylight without keeping his hand on his purse: for no discoverable reason whatever, he was followed about for two or three hours by an infernal Greek and his confederates, whom he could neither intimidate nor elude. He began to feel nervous, remembering that the fearful intent of Schiller's ghost scene hangs upon being followed in Venice by an Armenian; and he was thankful when he finally escaped.

But the views! The scenes from the steamer up the Bosphorous to Buykudesh: magnificent! the whole panorama is one pomp of art and nature. Europe and Asia are here shown at their best: a gallery of ports and harbours formed by the interchange of promontory and bay: porpoises sport in the blue, and large flights of pigeons overhead go through evolutions like those of armies, whilst ships anchor at the foot of ravines, deep among green basins, where the only canvas one would expect would be tents. No wonder the Czars have always coveted the capital of the Sultans: no wonder the Russian, among his firs, sighs for these myrtles, cedars, cypresses. The green minarets of the cypress contrast with the gold minarets of the Mosque: so nature and man, so death and life, intermingle, too. Kiosk and fountain, dark trees and daisies tipped with crimson, stand out with the jewelled clearness of a Persian miniature: one would think that these scenes would melt away like some castle of confectionery if the elements treated them rudely.

Nearer, Melville is in the atmosphere of the Arabian Nights: the aspect of the first bridge, coming back, is like that of a Grand Fancy Dress Ball: the air is an immense Persian rug: 1,500,000 men are the actors in a vast and endless procession, pedlars, beggars, confectionery sellers, malefactors chained together with iron necklaces and rings; porters with immense burdens, military officers, ladies in yellow slippers, black eunuchs followed by white servants, sherbet sellers, Georgians, shepherds marching in sheep's clothing, sheep, droves of donkeys followed by animated little boys poking them assiduously, boys with Arabian Nights names, Yusef, Hassan, Hamet. But if it has the beauty of some colossal London pantomime, it also has its defect: Melville cannot step over the footlights. He sees these Turks, Armenians, Georgians, Greeks: he would like to know them better: but for conversation he must turn to the captain or the English resident, or the fellow tourist. He wearies of this spectatorial attitude, these long days when he cannot talk to a sympathetic soul. Melville had got nearer to the Typees by living among them than he did with these closer brethren. After six days in Constantinople, he set off by steamer for Alexandria, via Smyrna; for, though he makes what he can of these profane diversions, the chief end of these travels is Terra Sancta itself.

The vessel stopped at Smyrna, and Melville had his first smell of the nearer East: camel-dung drying against the walls of the houses, for fuel, and the camel himself, the supercilious ambassador of this civilization, with his neck out like a tortoise, and his tail like an eel, by which the driver directed him, the swaying of the rider increasing with the motion of the camel, as in the mast of a ship, the higher one climbs. What a unique creature: he carries his neck like a clergyman in a stiff cravat, his feathery forelegs, his long lank hind ones, and his spongy hoofs, ploughing through the muddy lanes like four mops—in short, a cross between an ostrich and a grasshopper! Melville was thrilled by the curious appearance of strings of laden camels passing through the narrow, crowded ways of the bazaar—and he learned that these gorgeous Turkish clothes, many of them, were made of cotton and silk imported into Lancashire and reproduced and sent back to the native land, to the ruin of Turkish manufacturers, and the misery of the Manchester operative, just as pure copper was sent to England, and after being alloyed and cheapened was returned as unstamped coin to Constantinople.

The ship steamed out of Smyrna and passed the bleak islands that had once meant so much in history, Delos, flowery in fable, but desolate at best and now quite sterile; and Patmos, another disenchanting isle; and Timos, with its small hamlets and the little churches sticking perkily out mid the low huts of the villages. Christmas Day Melville spent at Syra again: he mentions the captain's mild observance of the feast in a glass of champagne; but he put in the notebook no private or domestic memory. Perhaps he took to heart the advice he had already framed in Pierre: "With a continent and an ocean between him and his wife— thus sundered from her by whatever imperative cause for a long term of years:—the husband, if passionately devoted to her and by nature broodingly sensitive of soul were wise to forget her till he embrace again."

Melville contrasted these bleak, desolate Aegean Islands with those of the Polynesian archipelago: the former had lost their virginity, whilst the latter were as fresh as at their first creation. Melville knew that withered feeling. To look upon the yellow of Patmos, who would believe that a god had been there; and, one may add, to look upon the sear tint of Melville's soul, during the strained years that had just passed, who would believe that a god had once reposed there, either?

At last the Alexandrian lighthouse came into view; and shortly after that Pompey's pillar, looking like a huge stick of candy that had long been sucked. Melville made a quick excursion to Cairo; and spent two nights there, wandering through the streets, where the houses seemed a collection of old orchestras, organs, proscenium boxes, or like masses of old grotesque furniture, lumbering a garret, and covered with dust: the streets, so narrow, through the projection of the upper storeys, that they seemed almost tunnels, made noon itself dim: in the lonelier parts of the city many of the houses were uninhabited and had a ghoulish look: but the city itself, for all these desolate houses and stoved-in domes and rubbish-filled alleys, was alive with bargain and chaffer and shouting camel drivers and whining blind men: desert and verdure clashed together like splendour and squalor, like gloom and gaiety: such violent chiaroscuro in all the senses bewildered one like strong wine on an empty stomach.

The Pyramids completed the effect of this exploration. Together, they made a magnificent, a terrible, an unforgettable day. From the distance, the Pyramids jutted over the sand like purple mountains. To ascend the great Pyra-

mid, there were as many different routes as there are for
crossing the Alps: precipice on precipice, cliff on cliff.
Nothing in Nature but the sea gives such an idea of vastness; the very grass that grows around the Pyramids does
not touch them, as if in awe of them. Exhausted a little with
his climb, a pain in his chest, Melville found the Arab guides
tender: as he hurried on, for none but the phlegmatic could
scale this mound deliberately, the Arabs in their white flowing robes might have been angels conducting him up to
heaven. One old man fainted halfway up and had to be
brought down: he essayed to go inside and fainted again:
it was too much for him.

Well, it was almost too much for Melville: it was not the
sense of height but the sense of immensity that was stirred:
with all other architecture, however vast, the eye is gradually inured to the sense of magnitude by passing from part
to part: but here there was no storey or stage: it was all or
nothing, not height or breadth or length or depth but unspeakable vastness, less like courses of masonry than like
strata of rocks, a long slope of crags and precipices. As
with the ocean, you learned as much of its vastness by the
first glance as you would in a month. The great Pyramid
refused to be studied or adequately comprehended. Nor had
it lost by the tearing away of its casing, though it had
scaled enough stone to build a walled town; on the contrary,
when it presented a smooth plane it must have lost as much
in impressiveness as the ocean does when unfurrowed—a
dead calm of masonry. A feeling of awe and terror gradually came over Melville: the Arabs were no longer angels,
but seemed, in their soft, imperturbable way, somehow
malign. Stooping and doubling in the interior, as in a coal
shaft, Melville shuddered at the ancient Egyptians: they
had a mixture of the cunning and the awful. Moses learned
his lore from the Egyptians: the awful idea of Jehovah was
born there. They must needs have been terrible inventors,
those ancient wise men: as out of the crude forms of the

natural earth they could evoke by art the Pyramids, so, out of the dull elements of the insignificant thoughts that are in all men, they could by analogous art rear the transcendent conception of God. Indeed, the Egyptians had outwitted mortality. The Pyramids were conceived out of an energy as mighty as Nature's: nought but an earthquake or a geological revolution could smother it up. That was something like an answer to the White Whale—albeit such a distant answer. The pyramidical energy, as well as the pyramidical scorn, were both lacking in Melville now, high though they had towered in Moby-Dick.

Back in his high-ceilinged room of Shepherd's Hotel, with its almost monkish barrenness, the Pyramids still loomed before Herman Melville—something vast, indefinite, uncomfortable, and awful. Nothing that he met in the holy ways of Jerusalem, on the Mount of Temptation or in the Garden of Gethsemane, compared with the powerful impression left on him by the Pyramids. Did his instinct at last tell him that power was necessary, but that power alone was not enough, that Power and Love must work together, harmoniously married, as in one of the oldest of mythic figures, before man's triumph is anything but evanescent? The issue of power and love, knowledge and sympathy, contrivance and imagination, is art; and the highest product of art is not a painting, a statue, a book, a pyramid, but a human personality. When power and love were divorced in the personality, love became impotent, and power became malign and unlovely; and the personality itself mouldered, mouldered into a Jackson, a Timon, an Ahab, a Maria Glendinning, a Pierre, an Isabel. The Egyptians certainly had not forgotten love; and the Nile itself, which spread greenness when its floods receded, was the symbol of its benign fertility. Did some hint of this touch Melville in Egypt or in Palestine? Apparently, yes; for in Clarel we shall see the germs of a new feeling about life, and the source of that feeling is love, a clear and unambiguous love.

5

What further impact the journey made upon Melville's mind, we shall best gather when we come to consider Clarel and some of his minor poems; and the further events of his journey home *via* Italy, the Netherlands, and England can well be condensed into scattered observations and epigrams that punctuate the account in his journals. Passing Patmos, Melville was again afflicted with the great curse of modern travel—scepticism. "Could no more realize that St. John had ever had revelations here than when off Juan Fernandez could believe in Robinson Crusoe according to Defoe." "Pompeii like any other town. Same old humanity. All the same whether one be dead or alive. Pompeii comfortable sermon. Like Pompeii better than Paris." Pisa: "Campanile like pine poised just ere snapping. You wait to hear crack. Like Wordsworth's mooncloud, it will move all together if it move at all, for Pillars all line with it." "Rome fell flat on me. Oppressing flat. . . . Tiber a ditch, yellow as saffron. The whole landscape nothing independent of association. St. Peter's looks small from tower of Capitol. . . . Dome not so wonderful as St. Sophia's. . . . Went to Baths of Caracalla. Wonderful. Massive. Ruins form as it were natural bridges of thousands of arches. There are glades and thickets among the ruins—high up.—Thought of Shelley. Truly, he got his inspiration here. Corresponded with his drama and mind. Still majesty and desolate grandeur." "Quirinal Palace. . . . The Gardens—a paradise without the joy— freaks and caprices of endless wealth . . . as stone is sculptured into forms of foliage, so here foliage turned into forms of sculpture." Florence: "Breughel's picture much pleased me. Not pleased with the Venus de Medici, but very much astonished at the Wrestlers, and charmed with Titian's Venus." "Rather be in Venice on a rainy day than in any other capital on a fine one." London: "Crystal Palace— digest of the universe. Vast toy. No substance. Such appropriation of space as is made by a rail fence." Oxford: "It was here I first confessed my gratitude for my motherland and could view her with pride. Oxford to an American as well worth visiting as Paris, though in a different way."

6

During this crowded journey, while Melville was in Italy, there happened an event, obscure, mysterious, obliquely narrated, and published only at the end of his life, which gives us a further clue to Melville's character and experience. Knowing Melville's habits of composition, one is fairly sure that some objective fact lies beneath the surface of the verse called After the Pleasure Party: all the more because he published the poem only after he had reached the serenity and safety of old age. That these verses were not merely the product of untethered imagination one suspects, too, because their theme, remorse and bitter regret after renouncing a passionate experience, is underlined by the words of another poem, Madame Mirror:

> What pangs after parties of pleasure,
> What smiles but disclosures of pain!

This long poem, After the Pleasure Party, stands out with particular boldness because it contains the only direct references to sexual passion that one finds in Melville's entire work, except for haphazard and unimportant incidents— or the plainly fictitious events in Pierre. It is a faint and intricate clue; but one must not neglect it.

Melville pictures a paradisiac garden in Italy: the upland falling behind the house, fragrant with jasmin and orange blossom, the white marble of the house itself, gleaming between the lanes of austere trees, the green terraces falling in gentle cataracts down to the starlit Mediterranean Sea: a place of beauty and an hour of balm "after long revery's discontent." The pilgrim, dusty with travel in barren lands, revels in the sensuous peace: he is not so completely the pilgrim, so thoroughly the hermit, that his heart is entirely his own: on the contrary, it is out of a desperate dryness and loneliness of soul that Melville is suddenly beset by such temptations as the hermits of the Thebaid found in the desert. We have no image of the woman who walked with Melville through these green walks, under the star-bright sky: he himself tried, in the years that followed, to forget "the glade wherein Fate spun Love's ambuscade," tempting him to flout pale years of cloistral life and "flush himself in sensuous strife." We do not know if it was she who repulsed him, as the shore repulses the hungry billows, tired of the homeless deep, or whether it was a resistance within himself that wrecked and scattered the impulses that were driving him against the warm object of his desire: but we know that, flushed perhaps by wine, and stirred by the fragrant spring night, sex asserted itself again in Melville: the "dear desire through love to sway" came over him, and when he found himself baffled, attempting to rule his passion yet not able to reign, neither conquering the woman herself nor the passion she had awakened, he was aware of a dreary shame of frustration. Blocked in his highest powers of thought, in his career as a writer, Melville found himself equally defeated—and perhaps by the same cluster of images—in that other citadel of personality. Bitterly he cries: "And kept I long heaven's watch for this, contemning love, for this, even this?"

There is the cry of the passionate man who in his marriage had kept to the letter of his pledge, and yet found himself struggling against its spirit—struggling and yet paralysed. The sudden opening of passion, that had begun at lunch this day, as the guests of the house, like the ladies and gentlemen in the prologue to the Decameron, had lain about in groups on the grass, this passion, deepening in a secluded glade under the Mediterranean night, had pulled Melville off his lonely throne: in a dream he was a king, per-haps, a lonely king—an idiot crowned with straw! That gust of passion had brought enlightenment: the fires in him were banked, not dead: but it left him bereaved. He shrank from its consequences. In this enlightenment he remembered and magnified other incidents on his journey: the barefoot peasant girl in Naples who had climbed up the hills near the wheels of his carriage and had given him the sudden impulse to fire upon her the petty hell within his own bosom. Hers was a wily innocence, and one can only vaguely guess at Melville's memories when he exclaims: "The cheat! On briars her buds were strung. . . . To girls, strong man's a novice weak." All this became part of his "sad rosary of belittling pain."

Melville might seem to others, might in opaque moments seem to himself, a pale, scholarly man, immersed solely in things of the mind: but what a caricature that apparition was of the actual man! The pallor did not mean he could not feel the sun when it shone upon him: "the plain lone bramble thrills with Spring as much as vines that grapes shall bring," and when this mood was uppermost, how gladly would he throw his arms around some radiant ninny, the first glad, willing girl he might meet, and buy the veriest wanton's rose—"would but my bee therein repose." If only he could remake himself, or free himself from this disturbance, this void tormenting urge, this feeling of disunity, this being but half of a mismatched whole: surely, there was some anarchic blunder, some rank cosmic jest, in the state that made the single self incomplete and yet set all the odds against the possibility that selves who matched should meet and mate. This was part of Melville's disillusion, that hot impetus he had felt in that fine Italian garden promised in ultimate reward no more than his marriage, equally fervid and romantic at the start, had brought him. And yet—and yet—perhaps this temporary impulse was an impulse to act upon, whether it had any cosmic justification or not: the turbulent heart and the rebel brain did not satisfy themselves so easily with abstract reasons.

For Amor so resents a slight
And hers had been such haught disdain
He long may wreak his boyish spite,
And, boylike, little reck the pain.

When Melville leaves this scene of his thwarted renewal,
and comes to Rome, confronting its pagan statuary and its
Christian churches, he has half an impulse to gather all his
doubts and difficulties together and make a sacrifice of them
to the Church, in return for the peace she gives: but something deeper in him, something reflected in the mighty statuary and art of the Roman and the Greek, prompts him to
turn to Athene herself, who united power and peace, far
from the "sexual feud" that "clogs the aspirant's life." But
no outer institution or activity could share Melville's burden: at bottom, he feels hopeless of either Church or of
Art. Never, he says, passion peace shall bring, nor art inani-
mate for long inspire. Ah, no! because the sick man turns
to these things as to a powerful medicine, to serve as a specific, once and for all; whereas in health, they must be
treated as food, to be welcomed recurrently. Melville was
sick; and he was aware of it. "Nothing may help or heal
while Amor, incensed, remembers wrong."

For scope to give his vengeance play
Himself he'll blaspheme and betray.

Then for Urania, virgins everywhere,
O pray! Example take too, and have care.

These last lines were not given to Melville by his experience but were the fruits of his ultimate reflection: and there
was wisdom in them. Sex is deep and central in every life,
and the wrongs that are committed against Amor, whether
they are wrongs of abstention or wrongs of satiety, whether
they are the weakness of a love unpolarized, or the weakness of a love whose validity is established solely in legal

277

documents and obligations, these wrongs may exact their revenge on every phase of a man's activity. There is no formula for love, except the tact and usage of lovers. Reserve, indifference, and abstention destroy that tact: the lover loses his sense of occasion, and is impassive where he should be quick, or tormented, as Melville was tormented by the peasant girl, when he should be calm. The matter of loyalty does not enter here; or rather, all these thoughts were disloyalties; indeed, Melville was disloyal to the spirit of his marriage in a thousand repugnances or indifferences that far more seriously undermined his relations with Elizabeth than the most outright liaison would have done, had it left Melville poised, collected, refreshed.

In this experience "After the Pleasure Party," Melville approached close to a central dilemma in his life: he approached it, but he was paralysed, paralysed by the habit of self-control as other men are thrust into helpless action by their lust. Melville's career, his thought, his vision demanded a singleness of purpose: to attain this singleness he was all eagerness, as he put it in Pierre, "to cast off the most intense, beloved bond, as a hindrance to the attainment of whatever transcendental object that usurper mood so tyrannically suggests. Then the beloved bond seems to hold us to no essential good; lifted to exalted mounts, we can dispense with all the vale; endearments we spurn; kisses are blisters to us; and forsaking the palpitating forms of mortal love, we emptily embrace the boundless and unbodied air. We think we are not human; we become as immortal bachelors and gods; but again, like the Greek gods themselves, prone we descend to earth; glad to be uxorious once more; glad to hide these godlike heads within the bosoms made of too-seducing clay."

This pilgrimage of Melville's, from that high talk with Hawthorne on the bleak sands of Southport and those unspeakable thoughts that welled up in him when he confronted the Pyramids, to the sting of a passing peasant girl or the

soft hints and caresses in the arboured walk by the Mediterranean, had shown Melville the extremes of his own being:
alone with divinity, in solitude, he found himself reaching,
thirstily, eagerly, towards the all-too-seducing clay. For
Melville, unlike Plato, there was no happy union between
these opposites: he had no wise Diotima to teach him how
the children of the flesh may lead to that union with the
other self out of which the children of the spirit are born:
nor did he realize that the lust of the satisfied man is incomparably more cleansing to the spirit than the tormented
chastity of the unsatisfied one. This was a misfortune for
Melville. His salvation would have been to recognize that he
had reached the limits of his own lonely excursion: that all a
man can find as a solitary being, and value, and cleave to,
exploring in utter loneliness the trackless ways of the universe, he had achieved in Moby-Dick: pride and power and
the isolated untouched self had nothing further to teach
him, and there was no dominion more sterile than that long
reign. He must withdraw from this proud isolation, not into
the disguised pride and the equal isolation of humility, but
into participation with the life around him and into what he
had inherited from the past—not scorning Plato or Goethe
because their union had been fruitful, whilst his great im-
maculacy had proved black and sterile.

In achieving his depths, Melville had missed the surface:
he had brought up fire and lava and ashes, from that deep
volcano of his being, but he had never in maturity properly
explored the woods and groves and gardens that give men
peace and untroubled love—and it was pride, a self-defeat-
ing pride, that urged him to return to those depths, prizing
"the clear intelligence alone" and disdaining a love that was
"linked and locked with a self impure." Partly, Melville
overcame this pride, and he mingled with his fellows and
widened his explorations in the region they had settled and
cultivated: but these new aims did not engross him as the
pursuit of Moby-Dick had done. Had he been able to sur-

render more easily to love, to his wife, to his family relations, at thirty-eight, he might have discovered, while his physical powers were healing, that triumphant serenity and surety of purpose which did not come to him until his old age had transmuted his rejected passions and made a fertile union with reality.

Melville left his Italian garden, with chaos still struggling in his soul. For slighting Amor he was for a while destined to know, not inner peace, but the sting and poison of every chance arrow: in Venice, floating on the canal in a "swoon of a noon and a trance of tide" like calms far off Peru, he was to hear a lattice click and see between the slats, mutely summoning him, the loveliest eyes of a girl. He who had faced peril in nature and man, who had swum between the whale's black flukes and the white shark's fin, and who had wandered in the enemy's desert, New York, warily scanning the envy and slander that followed him there, he who had faced these things cannot stand the "basilisk look" of that girl: he bids his boatman throw off his drowsiness and shoot quickly by. The wanderer discovers that sirens are real: they do in fact lie in wait for a man, wooing him by the same deadly muses. He runs from them—excusing his shame with the memory of Ulysses, "brave, wise, and Venus' son," but the very fact that he imprisons this incident in verse and publishes it more than thirty years after shows that he did not escape easily.

"There is no faith, and no stoicism, and no philosophy," Melville wrote in Pierre, "that a mortal man can possibly evoke, which will stand the final test in a real impassioned onset of Life and Passion upon him. Then all the fair philosophy or Faith—phantoms that he raised from the mist, slide away and disappear as ghosts at cock-crow. For Faith and philosophy are air, but events are brass. Amidst his gray philosophizings, Life breaks upon a man like a morning." Without conceiving Melville's philosophy as a phantom, one may still wish that it had confronted and not so desperately fled from these enlightening assaults of life and passion. He needed no further share of restrained and circumspect virtues: he needed the courage of life, the courage to be glad with the morning sun, to breathe deeply the fragrance of the air, to relax his limbs in the heat of noon, to feel again the dear inner vigour of his manliness, that vigour which a man is conscious of only in the presence of a woman who rouses him. Denying that vigour, he found that the dawn was smothered in grey clouds, and the rose had lost its fragrance, and the sun its power to heal. His journey helped him recover his interest in life and his poise: it enabled him to carry on as a man: but, though he resumed his work, that final confidence or desperation men need if they are to undertake the great labour of creation was still insufficient. The masculine attack, so bold, so deepseated in Mardi, White-Jacket, and Moby-Dick, did not wholly come back—and if one asks the reason for this one will find the answer, in part, "traced under an image of Amor Threatening."

7

Melville returned home toward the middle of 1857. Meanwhile, The Confidence Man, published by Sampson, Low and Company, and not by his old publishers, Harper's, had done little to improve his fortunes. Indeed, its English edition was so small that it for long remained unknown to the bibliographer; and in America the work, though it received occasional praise, did not fare much better. Except in the roughest political lampooning, satire did not penetrate the leathery optimism and the cast-iron self-righteousness of antebellum America; and if Melville wanted support and confidence, The Confidence Man was the wrong way to go about it. One need not be surprised that the sequel was never published, and in all likelihood, never written.

Melville's resolve to be annihilated was lessened by his journey: for though he had not been shattered with light on the road to Damascus, faith flickered and smoked occasionally, like smouldering wood before it is ready to blaze. The shearing of his head, the donning of sackcloth, the last ironic act of renunciation was still almost a decade away: with new resolution, he made a succession of attempts to regain the position he had once occupied.

The lecture lyceum gave him his first opportunity: the Civil War was the second. Between 1857 and 1860 Melville joined the politicians and the woman suffragists and the prohibitionists and the transcendentalists and the Fourierists and the travellers from strange parts of the world and distinguished foreigners, in the one corner of the marketplace where they could all get a living: the public platform. It was not an easy pill for him to swallow, for though he lectured on the sculpture of the Vatican and the sights of Rome, he was known, hailed, gaped at still as the famous author of Peedee, Pog-Dog, and Hullabaloo—the man who had lived among the cannibals. Well might he write in Pierre: "Permanently to alleviate pain, we must first dart some added pangs." He was brave enough about the whole business; in 1858 he wrote: "I should be glad to lecture there [in Baltimore] or anywhere. If they will pay expenses and give a reasonable fee, I am ready to lecture in Labrador or on the Isle of Desolation off Patagonia."

Melville showed himself; he lectured; but he stooped no further. Mid all the spellbinders and strutting celebrities of the period, with their characteristic masks, sonorities, grimaces, this quiet man, with the small, fine nose and the weary, whimsical smile, and an air of patient earnestness, could have cut no very great figure to a public that had never been used to the emphasis of under-statement. Indeed, Melville's lecture fees tell as much: they averaged around fifty dollars a lecture, and at this time Thoreau, with even a narrower reputation, got as much for a reading. The lectures gave Melville an opportunity to travel, and he must have welcomed this: he went as far afield as Montreal and

Milwaukee: but in all he gave less than thirty lectures. One wonders about his audiences. Did Thoreau meet him at the station in Concord or did Whitman listen to him in New York? Whom did he fall in with on the Ohio river steamers? What did he make of the emigrant New Englanders, Germans, merchants, farmers, roustabouts, gamblers? Had his Mississippi buffoons touched them off, or did they make his staunchest effects pallid? Did he identify himself with them, share their aims, feel a thrill of anticipation at their destinies—or did he foresee in them the final disruption of the America that had nourished him?

The record is almost a blank; but a newspaper report of one of the lectures, in the Boston Journal, 1857, shows that Melville's shrewd eye was far from being turned inward. Describing the statues in the Church of St. John Lateran, he observes that "Socrates looks like an Irish comedian, Julius Caesar so sensible and businesslike of aspect it might be taken for the bust of a railroad president; Seneca with the visage of a pawnbroker; Nero a fast young man, Plato with the locks and airs of an exquisite, as if meditating the destinies of the world under the hands of a hair-dresser." These comments prove, what all the minor documents of Melville's life during this period show, that the jocular irrepressible spirit—"bear with mine infirmity of jocularity," he exclaims to Duyckinck—the spirit who had written Omoo and White-Jacket, was not altogether Timonized or defeated. His satire still worked obliquely, touching both his own countrymen and their pragmatic contemporaries, the Romans. Nor did Melville conceal his feelings about the benefits of mickonaree Christianity and "white civilization." In another lecture, after quoting from a local English paper in one of the South Sea Islands, which suggested the propriety of not having the native language taught in the common schools, he threw down the sheet in plain disgust, and announced to the audience, in allusion to the reputed desire of the natives of Georges Island to be annexed to the United

States, that he was sorry to see it, since, as a friend of humanity, and especially a friend of the South Sea Islanders, he would pray, and call upon all Christians to pray with him, that the Polynesians might be delivered from all foreign and contaminating influences.

During this period of lecturing, Melville began to write again, with no hope of profit or fame, but for his own satisfaction; and, anticipating Thomas Hardy's example, he turned to verse. If one can date his first new essays in verse —for the poems in Mardi show that there were early efforts —one must give the time as probably 1858, and for a while only Elizabeth shared this secret with him. By 1860, before he went for a voyage with his younger brother, now Captain Thomas Melville, commander of the Boston clipper Meteor, his verses were numerous enough to make a volume. The decision to make this voyage came rather suddenly; and one finds Melville writing to Mr. Duyckinck, mid the haste of departure, to see if he will undertake to advise with Allan Melville as to a publisher, and in case of publication, be sure that the printer's proof-reader is a careful man. Melville, the author of nine books, still deferred to Mr. Duyckinck's professional experience; and, on getting a favourable reply, he told Duyckinck that "it was quite a wind from the field of old times."

From this correspondence with Evert Duyckinck—and an allusion in a letter to George about Melville's own "winter and rough weather"—one gathers that after Pierre there had been an estrangement, or at least a prolonged silence: in 1856 the Duyckincks had recorded in their Cyclopedia their conviction that Pierre was a false step, and only now, after eight years had passed, was the breach healed. As for Melville's mood in travel, he had this to say: "I anticipate as much pleasure as, at the age of forty, one temperately can, on the voyage I am going. I go under very happy auspices so far as the ship is concerned. A noble ship and a nobler captain—and he my brother. We have the breadth

of those tropics before us, to sail over twice, and shall round
the world. Our first port is San Francisco, which we shall
probably make in 110 days. Thence we go to Manilla—and
thence, I hardly know where—I wish devoutly you were
going along. I think it would agree with you. The prime
requisites for enjoyment on sea-voyages, for passengers, is
1st health—2nd good-nature. Both first rate things, but not
universally to be found.—At sea a fellow comes out. Salt
water is like wine, in that respect." The good-bye and God
bless you, with which Melville closed this letter, showed a
sort of solemn warmth. In a lonely life, even an Evert
Duyckinck might prove a comrade. . . .

The book of poetry was never published in its original
form. Mr. Meade Minnigerode conjectures that the manuscript was that of Clarel; but Melville's concern, in his
memoranda for Allan, that each piece should be printed on
a page by itself, however small the piece, shows, apart from
anything else, that it could not have been Clarel; and when
Melville told his brother, two years later, that he had disposed of his "doggerel" to a trunkmaker, who took the whole
lot off his hands at ten cents the pound, one must infer that
he himself had become dissatisfied with the bulk of his early
work, and destroyed most of it, salvaging a few pieces, like
the verse to the Captain of the Meteor, for his later volumes.
In the first flush of experiment, however, Melville's poetry
pleased him: the form of verse gave compactness to his
thoughts, and the writing of it did not inflict that long continuous drain on his vitality that the larger prose pieces
called for. Melville would pace the quarter-deck with his
brother, reciting his verses in the moonlight: the joy of
creation, even minor creation, could still stir him up, and
no doubt the cadences of the moving ship, heaving, falling,
rolling, added to the pleasure of the words themselves.

At the end of three months, when they had reached California, Melville had exhausted his supply of books and
papers, probably, and his brother's patience, and his own

capacity for boredom: by that time his health had doubtless improved again, and, urging him to break the trip and
quicken his return, his old longing for Elizabeth may have
come back with greater force. He was never quite happy in
her company, nor was he quite happy away from it. All the
difficulties of their domestic economy tended to make their
relations prosaic and commonplace, for one does not cook for
and clean and clothe four children without a considerable
amount of unflinching prose; and Elizabeth's incapacity for
domestic duties and her irritations only made matters worse.
Yet Melville, as far as one can judge, felt not merely affection for Elizabeth: on these long absences, passion would
gather within him again, like lightning in a heavy summer
sky. He might resent her obtuseness; he might be disappointed by her failure to respond to his irresponsible hilarity; he might be sobered by the fact that his love had been
unfavourably conditioned by financial burdens and a
cramped household with a scanty larder; but for all that, he
clung to her and needed her. One must take account of this
in noting Melville's moods and moves and decisions in the
decade after 1856. Although Melville, unfortunately, felt
repulsion in a tie that was so plainly rooted in physical attachment, and longed for a heaven in which there was the
marriage of true minds without the "impurities" and im-
pediments of sex, although he distrusted the solace of physical union, as he distrusted all beautiful things which hid the
truth from men's eyes, yet he found himself perpetually
driven back to this wiser folly; and, not turning easily to
any other woman, he kept his faith with Elizabeth.

The rôle was not an easy one for her to bear: make no
mistake about it. Such violence of anticipation and such
quick satiety, such tenderness and such easy disappointment, such self-absorption, and, with it all, a certain impatience and resentment of the daily round, with its claims,
ceremonies, civilities, annoyances—with all this Elizabeth
Melville was probably never to know such deep, enraptured

happiness in her marriage as Sophia Hawthorne, who had faced dire poverty, too, had known. Elizabeth was proud of her man: she had faith in him: but it was only in the closing years of their lives, when, through bitter experience, she had acquired much, and he, through bitter experience, had resigned much, that they were on a parity. There is no doubt she encouraged him in his work, and, whether she understood it or not, believed in it. While he was gone in 1860 she assiduously looked after the placing of the manuscript, and would not be put off by the publishers' flimsy excuses. Still, for all this sympathy and loyalty, on both sides, one feels that strain, depression, tenseness, must have too often marked the life of the Melville household, during these shadowed years of poverty and ill health and dwindling fame.

If Mrs. Melville stood the strain of it, with all the toughness of middle age to bear up under it, the children did not fare so well. The photograph of the Melville children, Malcolm, Frances, Elizabeth, and Stanwix, taken when the oldest was perhaps twelve or thirteen—that is, during the early sixties—tells as much: they are a little peaked and undernourished, and the eldest child's face is sullen, dour. The racking poverty of his early youth had left an indelible impression on Melville himself, and, in even more depressing circumstances, a worse image was left upon the minds of his growing children. Melville, a man of originality and penetration in almost every other department of life, was, one suspects, a commonplace father: he expected his children to be dutiful and submissive and not to annoy their mother, and he would read them moral lectures on the whole duty of children, fearful of their being corrupted by association and contact with the age, but incapable of directing their impulses into forms of growth except by desperate exhortation —the most blank and sterile of all pedagogical methods. He wanted them to be noble and courageous and honest and indifferent to money, and, dreading the effect of the mean,

bourgeois standards that surrounded them, he was too quick
to suspect the ignoble and the base, forgetting that growth
is a happier sign in childhood than the semblance of perfection. When his little daughter picked up the word "property" and aired it to her family, Melville relentlessly teased
her about it: if he handed her the butter, he would hand it
to Miss Property: if he met her on the stairs he would mimic
Miss Property: he tormented her for the sins of her elders,
forgetting the terrible sensitiveness of a child to dogging
that has such a bitter animus behind it. This incident will
stand for others: the jolly letters he would write home, with
pictures and all manner of funny printing, or the stories
he would tell in a pleasant hour, did not wipe out the acrid
taste or lessen the distance between father and children.
There was nothing to lighten the burden of these days: these
children were orphaned, even when their father sat among
them. One son ran away; another, in 1867, was found dead
in his room, of a rifle wound, under circumstances that left
doubt as to whether accident or suicide had caused the fatality; and one of his daughters could not recur to the image
of her father without a certain painful revulsion. The picture is not a happy one: but a man with high purposes does
not always leave behind earthly children to bless him. One
remembers how Milton's daughters cursed him in his own
presence, and one realizes that one can draw no valid conclusions from such conduct—except this, that a man immersed in his inner vision is a difficult man to live with, and
if he does not renounce his family and its ties at the outset
of his quest, they may live to rise up against him before he
is ended with it. And who was to blame? Milton and Melville
wanted the warmth of domesticity: but their children had
no part in the bargain that gave them cold lodgings in the
icy chambers of Heaven, and shabby clothes and insufficient
food and few opportunities for pleasure on the earth. These
children were of Melville's flesh, but not of his mind: when
he purchased a work of art, a print or a statue for ten dol-

lars, when there was scarcely bread enough to go round, who can wonder at their black memories? If they did not understand the need of a famished soul for art, their father had too quickly forgotten his own humiliation when he went to sea in a discarded hunting-jacket. Circumstances drove Melville hard; but poverty alone does not make such a breach between a parent and his children; and though one must pity Melville in this extremity of misunderstanding, one cannot but feel that he himself contributed to it.

The death of Elizabeth's father in 1860 did not relieve the strain, except by giving the family a clear title to Arrowhead; so, until 1866, the background of Melville's life cannot be painted save in dark colours. In spite of a personal interview with Lincoln in 1861, Melville was again turned down for a consular post; and two years later Melville finally decided to leave the Berkshires. To this end, he purchased a house at 104 East Twenty-sixth Street, in New York, from his brother, Allan, to whom he sold Arrowhead in part payment. But misfortune persisted. In removing his household goods from Arrowhead, the wagon was upset and he was thrown into the frozen ruts of the road. The injury was so severe that Melville was forced to lie up for many weeks in a near-by house, and in addition, to sap further his physical health, the accident left him with a fear of carriage driving. So his troubles piled up on him; and in the end, they grew so intolerable that the humour of the whaleboat would return to him, and he would smile again. I have painted in every sober and painful detail in the background; the blacks, the dingy blues, the sear browns are the dominant colours: true: but against this sordid groundwork one must not build up a blacker foreground: on the contrary, there are occasional flashes of warm colour or high light, and to leave them out would falsify the whole picture.

There is a Micawber in all of us, not unfortunately. We may find life disappointing without losing our taste for breaded veal cutlets and stout. Overwhelmed by tragic experience, we may still laugh at a hundred minor absurdities, as Melville no doubt laughed when he discovered that in 1865 a firm of Philadelphia publishers, who had taken over the rights to Israel Potter, had brought it out under the new title of The Refugee, without Melville's consent, and had set him down as the author of two wholly imaginary books, The Two Captains and The Man of the World! Through all his ailments, one infirmity helped to counteract them, the infirmity of jocularity. He had one steady comfort and mainstay which only the blackest incidents could erase for more than a brief period: he had a sense of humour. More than that, with a little encouragement, he had positive high spirits. If one were not fully assured of this from a general knowledge of Melville's character, the letter he wrote to his brother Thomas in 1862 would make this point plain: "Yesterday I received from Gansevoort your long and very entertaining letter to Mamma from Pernambuco. Yes, it was very entertaining. Particularly the account of that interesting young gentleman whom you stigmatise for a jackass, simply because he improves his opportunities in the way of sleeping, eating, and other commendable customs. That's the sort of fellow, it seems to me, to get along with. For my part I love sleepy fellows, and the more ignorant the better. Damn your wide-awake and knowing chaps. As for sleepiness, it is one of the noblest qualities of humanity. There is something sociable about it, too. Think of those sensible and sociable millions of good fellows, all taking a long, friendly snooze together, under the sod—no quarrels, no imaginary grievances, no envies, heartburnings, & thinking how much better the other chap is off—none of this: but all equally free-&-easy, they sleep away and reel off their nine knots an hour, in perfect amity."

Or again, after his accident in 1862, in a letter to Samuel Shaw, his brother-in-law, the same grave bantering appears: ". . . I begin to indulge in the pleasing idea that my life must needs be of some value. Probably I consume a certain amount of oxygen, which unconsumed might create some disturbance in nature. Be that as it may, I am going to try and stick to the conviction named above. Now I have observed that such an idea, once well-bedded in a man, is a wonderful conservator of health and almost a prophecy of long life. I once, like other spoonies, cherished a loose sort of notion that I did not care to live very long. But I will frankly own that I have now no serious, no insuperable objections to a respectable longevity. I don't like the idea of being left out night after night in a cold churchyard."

The humour and the sentiments both remind one of another black writer, a later one, the author of the Shropshire Lad: without losing his inner thoughts, Melville could nevertheless paraphrase them into a happier vernacular. Meanwhile, a deeper blackness had settled over the land, matching, patch for patch, wound for wound, scar for scar, every ill in Melville's own body and soul. That darkness was the darkness of the Civil War; and when it finally lifted, it disclosed a different country, a different age, a different series of possibilities. The Civil War was a dividing point in the life of the country, and a dividing point in Melville's life. It widened the distance between Melville and his younger contemporaries and it sealed, with finality, his own position in society. The provincial culture was overwhelmed; and what came to take its place was not a genuine culture, but a shoddy substitute, mere fustian of the spirit. He looked around him after the worst had happened; and his words must have been Bartleby's: I know where I am. That very consciousness was enough to cut him off from the new society.

CHAPTER ELEVEN: ALARUMS AND RETREATS

BETWEEN THE provincial society into which Herman Melville was born and the America in which he found himself at the time of the Civil War there was a vast difference. The Civil War may in one sense be looked upon as an attempt to preserve the ideological framework of the United States at a time when its institutions were in a state of disruption, and all its typical ways of life were being transformed. In that the Civil War preserved this framework, upholding the Constitution, confirming the union of the states, concentrating the powers of government, it was successful: the union was saved. But the very act of prosecuting the war confirmed the chaos and hastened the disruption, so that what was saved was not freedom and equality, the freedom of voluntary association and local initiative, the equality of access to an unlimited amount of utilizable land: what was left was just the opposite of these things, servility and inequality. Land and natural resources, scattered broadcast during the Civil War under the Homestead Act, and under various acts to promote railroad building, were turned into exacting monopolies; and the government itself became the principal agent for establishing and extending privilege. In less than half a generation Walt Whitman was forced to modify many of his fondest hopes for America: for with all these new agents of exploitation dominant, there was no longer any way of distinguishing the American proletariat from that of Europe, except in their independent manners— a relic of an equality that had once been real.

The disruption symbolized by the Civil War was expressed in a hundred ways; and when one examines these manifestations carefully they can all be characterized by a single figure: the failure to achieve form. One sees the difference between provincial and industrial America in the political definition of their units: New England, for example, is a natural region, like Brittany and Provence, with a mode of thought and an institutional form based upon certain common geographic features and cultural history; the new states and territories that were founded beyond the Alleghenies had no form other than that expressed by the arbitrary lines drawn by the surveyor: their content was simply so many blank square miles. The older cities of the seaboard, with the exception of Philadelphia, had a central nucleus which had grown out of local needs and habits: the size of the blocks was determined by the depth of the houses, the amount of garden space in the rear, the traffic that would pass in the streets: in the new cities no customs and habits played a part in the configuration of the city except those of realty speculation: by 1850, St. Louis, Cincinnati, and Chicago had all forfeited to the land-gambler sites originally set aside for civic centres. In architecture, the failure to achieve form was equally conspicuous: windows, doors, rooms, façades, even apart from their grotesque efforts at decoration, all became gawky and ill-proportioned.

The energies of the country went into purely quantitative achievements: their only formal equivalent was money. The production in tons of iron, miles of steel rails, bushels of wheat, went up: cities increased in size: but the iron was used for the preposterous fronts of office buildings, the railroad served to deplete the hinterland, and the cities were dingy firetraps of wood or dingier prisons of brownstone. The war itself tore up and shot to pieces vast quantities of iron and many miles of railroad, and sundry towns and villages: but that was the true destination of all these quantitative efforts even in peace: for industrialism produced only an occasional genuine form, like the Eads Bridge, and for the most part its products were fit only to be consumed hastily and replaced and destroyed again. No wonder this civilization sweated day and night, without holidays, to produce its evanescent goods; while, in the Middle Ages, the great cathedrals and town halls were erected, without labour-saving machinery, in a rude agricultural society which spent a third of its year in holidays devoted to prayer, meditation, or festival. Where there is form and culture, there is true conservation of energy through the arts: where there is only energy, without end or form, the mechanism may be speeded up indefinitely without increasing anything except the waste and lost motion. Southern society, in which a provincial system of caste and culture held together, produced factories and slave barracks, in Charleston, for example, that maintained, uncorrupted, the forms of its classic past: but outside these aristocratic backwaters, chaos was dominant—and even in the South, one feels, it was only postponed.

In this sprawling, undisciplined America, a new type of character was uppermost. Melville described this new type when he touched on Ethan Allen in Israel Potter: "Allen," he said, "seems to have been a curious combination of a Hercules, a Joe Miller, a Bayard, and a Tom Hyer. He was frank, bluff, companionable as a Pagan, convivial, a Roman, hearty as a harvest. His spirit was essentially Western; and herein is his peculiar Americanism; for the Western spirit is, or will yet be (for no other can be) the true American." It was a sign of the waning of provincial faith that before the war everybody was eagerly looking for this individual, this type, who would serve as a symbol of unity. Even Emerson and Thoreau looked wistfully toward the rough fellows of the frontier to express what was common to all Americans. A provincial culture glories in its differences: the power to mould and express them is its unique quality: a Jefferson, a Franklin, an Adams were not only as far apart as Virginia, Philadelphia, and Boston: they were as far apart, in many

ways, as London, Paris, and Weimar. But in the period
before the war, the frontier type, Jackson, Harrison, Clay,
Frémont, Lincoln, was put forward as the sum of all our
possible Americas—albeit these figures were as far from
the Swedes of Minnesota or the Germans of Wisconsin as
they were from the Gansevoorts and the Randolphs. In a
period of dissolution a false unity seems preferable to no
common bond at all; and in the uncertainty, the disintegration, the dispersion of American society, under the vast tides
of immigration and the inexorable flow of the coal-and-iron
civilization, political Union became a compensatory symbol
for all the social and cultural fragmentation that existed.

The political and social results of the Civil War, as they
have worked out during the last two generations, have made
us a little sceptical of the sacred, unchallengeable shibbo-
leths under which the war itself was fought: we see that the
prime issues of the great conflict were silenced, rather than
settled, by the decisive victory of the North. Unfortunately,
the South's political contentions, which were partly valid,
were vitiated by the issue of slavery. Mid all the decisive
statesmanship displayed south of the Mason and Dixon line,
no one was firm enough or far-sighted enough, after Jefferson's time, to see that the holding of human beings in bond-
age, without hope or means of escape, was an untenable
anachronism: even the Russian autocracy recognized that.
The French Revolution had made this particular form of
human degradation unpalatable; like incest or tribal revenge, it could not be related to a modern society. The burden of that institution, indeed, belonged to the whole country: the great mistake of the South, from 1830 onwards, was
to assume as a divine necessity or benefit what should have
been shared with the rest of the country as an intolerable
evil—to be disposed of by some direct economic adjustment.

Melville had his misgivings about current political institutions; in Mardi he pointed out that many of the boasted
freedoms of America were the product of free land and an

uncrowded domain; and though he was a republican, he recognized inequality, and had no hope of doing away with those distinctions between man and man in a functional capacity, which separate captain, mates, and crew. His own outlook was emotionally patrician and aristocratic; but his years in the forecastle had modified those feelings, and one needs some such compound word as aristodemocracy to describe his dominant political attitude. Melville may have had his moments of admiration for the gracious ways of the South; but, quite properly, he regarded the United States as a place where narrow tribalisms had been successfully dropped, where the entire blood of Europe joined together from a thousand sources, the country being not so much a nation in the old sense, as a world, a neighbourly world; and he doubtless looked upon the Southern claim to independence as a return to tribalism and narrowness.

Like most men of good will, Melville looked forward to a time when the world itself would be federated into a whole, so that the conflicts between peoples and tribes and communities, the inevitable and salutary conflicts, would not take place on the physical plane—where they are disastrous and prove nothing—but on the plane of culture. With this in view, the breaking up of a federation is a mode of political atavism: and the attempt reinforced Melville's natural repugnance to slavery. Unfortunately, the maintenance of a union by compulsive methods leads to an enthronement of the powers of the central government, and a diminution of a regional independence; the military strength of the central government and its impudence in serving special groups within the state, in turn becomes an obstacle to the pacification of the world. Melville could scarcely anticipate this result; but his philosophy had a place for the evil which dogs the footsteps of the good, and when he said that America might turn out to be the Paul Jones of nations, intrepid, unprincipled, reckless, predatory, with boundless ambitions, civilized in externals but savage at heart, he may partly have anticipated the outcome of that political supremacy he expected the United States finally to attain. By the time the war opened, there was established a certain fatalism in Melville's mind which made him lenient to the forces that seemed to him evil: they, too, in their inscrutable way were obedient to another power.

Melville's attitude towards the Civil War was, in sum, just the opposite of Hawthorne's; and if the men had been still in communication during this period, it would probably have opened a final breach between them. For Hawthorne, New England was as large a piece of earth as he had any affection for, and whatever happened next, he asserted in the early days of the conflict, he rejoiced that the old Union was smashed. "We never were one people, and never really had a country since the Constitution was founded." There spoke the shrewd, unshaken provincial. Hawthorne looked upon John Brown, moreover, as a poisonous nuisance: for Melville he was a prophetic figure, whose death made it impossible for the stabs of controversy to heal, whose streaming beard was the very meteor of war. One may sum up Melville's political character by saying that his breeding and instincts were those of a provincial; his superficial beliefs and attitudes were those of a political unionist; and during the Civil War the latter were uppermost, but not wholly so. Well might Walt Whitman describe the war itself, and the temper of the society that ushered it in, by the word "convulsiveness." There was something arcane and uncontrollable in these partisanships and antipathies: each fragment was thrown about erratically, tangentially. It was war that produced war; and when the active state at last came about, men settled to it with a sigh of relief. War polarized these fragments: it gave an appearance of high order to this chaos.

2

There is something paradoxical in the fact that Melville's concern over slavery and his fervour for the union should have come into play during a period when he had become indifferent to most of the nearest issues of life and convinced that existence itself was a form of slavery. But one must not forget the anomalous nature of war itself. In its instrumentalities, war is a denial of life: but in mood and spirit war partly achieves all the things a humane or religious mind cherishes: selflessness, contempt for creature habits and animal comforts, nonchalance in the face of death, a willingness to give up life cheerfully for an ideal end. If it is a sin, war is an heroic sin; and who, exclaims Melville in Pierre, does not feel more warmly to the Lord of Evil himself, than towards a petty shopkeeper, who daily practices all the discreet and serviceable virtues? War is a malign, ambiguous fulfilment of the things men permanently want in life—and in its first flush, men forget its sordid accompaniments and its disastrous results, and respond, not meanly, to its immediate stimulus.

There is no doubt that the prosecution of the war quickened Melville and made him feel a purpose instead of the dull, fearful hollow of an empty and respectable life. At forty-two, broken down in health, unfit for active service, he watched these young men go forth in their blue uniforms, with flushed faces and eager tread, a little enviously: comradeship was a warm thing, even among the precious rapscallions one might find in a whaler: it was an even deeper and warmer matter among these young men who had shared sport together in their village, or courted the same girl, or studied together under the same lamp at college. These happy faces might be going to a picnic, to be pelted with blossoms, not shrapnel:

Forever they slumber, young and fair,
The smile upon them as they died:
Their end attained, that end a height;
Life was to these a dream fulfilled
And death a starry night.

Unable to throw himself into battle, Melville followed the newspaper accounts and the bulletins all the more closely. One pictures him pacing the floor of his room at night, musing over Ball's Bluff or Antietam: there is no sleep in him during these racking days: the last footsteps of a straggler die away in the street: no sound comes through the air except the distant hoot of a boat on the North River; and Melville's mind plays back and forth across the days. Intermittently, all the old glow would come back to him in these dark moments: he would picture himself perhaps, borne by the tide of men at his back over an earthworks, as he was borne in a whaleboat on the back of the lashing whale. The reckless lift: the thrust: the yell of defiance: being thrown down and struggling to rise again through a tangled drift of legs and bodies: the shout of victory: the feeling of proud defiance: the knowledge that death does not matter when one is at last, with all one's senses quickened, face to face with it. The whaleman's joy: the soldier's joy: the joy of hard living and easy dying!

The war, with its heroism and defeat, was the image of Melville's own life; and, in the blackest night, the glow of its fires illumined his face. The rigid order of warfare gave Melville the sense of a cosmic purpose at work: in the working out of Dupont's Round Fight Melville saw another significance in the struggle for the Union: it was not the political bond that Melville's contemporaries alone wanted confirmed: they desired that the Universe itself should hold together! Melville's interpretation is, I think, an illusory one; but one cannot question the deep need that it expressed.

> In time and measure perfect moves
>   All art whose aim is sure;
> Evolving rhyme and stars divine
>   Have rules and they endure.
>
> Nor less the fleet that warred for Right
>   And warring so, prevailed,

In geometric beauty curved
And in an orbit sailed.

The Rebel at Port Royal felt
The Unity overawe
And rued the spell. A type was here
And victory of law.

But it was the happy fortune of youth that Melville, be-
trayed by the disasters of middle age, returned to when he
contemplated the war. Who, he asked, can remain aloof that
shares youth's ardour, uncooled by the snows of wisdom or
sordid gain? War made life again a great spectacle and a
great adventure: that defiance of the low limitations upon
which life depends, which Melville had expressed in Moby-
Dick, came back again: vanished at last were the doubts,
perturbations, speculations, cynicisms, endless grey ques-
tionings. Ten years before Melville might have been repelled
by the evil and ugliness of it: the maimed bodies, the cruelties, the infamous prison and concentration camps, the fur-
tive squads of deserters, the hospital agonies, the litany of
unknown soldiers and nameless burial spots that Whitman
gravely remembered and recited. Now Melville was armed
for the evil and ugliness of it, and even for its futility:

No utter surprise can come to him
Who reaches Shakespeare's core;
That which we seek and shun is there—
Man's final lore.

Melville was possibly in New York in 1863, when the
carnival of looting and murder and general protest took
place over the infliction of the draft. He pictures himself,
oppressed by the sultry air, climbing to the roof-top and
looking over the hushed city: in the distance, he hears the
mixed surf of muffled sound, the roar of riot and the dull
glare of fires. The city was in the hands of the mob, and
that mob had sunk "whole aeons back into nature," vin-

dictive, cruel, irresponsible, blind, bloodthirsty. Melville heard the rumble of the artillery which finally broke up the riot and exacted vengeance on the mob; and, pondering this event, he was conscious of the grimy slur upon the Republic's faith, a slur implied by the cause of the outbreak, by the outbreak itself, and by the suppression of it. Where was now the belief in life, liberty, and pursuit of happiness? Where now the conviction that man is naturally good and —"more—is Nature's Roman, never to be scourged"? With all his new enthusiasm, Melville's deeper perceptions were never altogether out of sight:

> Did the Fathers feel mistrust?
> Can no final good be wrought?
> Over and over, again and again
> Must the fight for the Right be fought?
>
> Were men but strong and wise,
> Honest as Grant and calm,
> War would be left to the red and black ants
> And the happy world disarm.

Even the supremacy of the Union, Melville finally came to see, might bring some other result than the purpose for which it was conceived. In one of the prefatory poems in his Battle Pieces, the Conflict of Convictions 1860–1861, Melville expressed his doubt: from the allusion to the Iron Dome it is plain that the verse was written later, when the Dome itself had been put into place on the Capitol at Washington, by one of those happy accidents that sometimes give an event its exact appropriate symbol.

> Power unannointed may come—
> Dominion (unsought by the free)
> And the Iron Dome
> Stronger for stress and strain
> Fling her huge shadow athwart the main;

But the Founders' dream shall flee.
　　Age after age shall be
　　As age after age hath been,
(From man's changeless heart their way they win);
　　And death shall be busy with all who strive,
　　　　Death, with silent negative.

　　Yea and Nay,
　　Each hath his say;
But God he keeps the middle way.
　　None was by
　　When he spread the sky;
Wisdom is vain, and prophecy.

Though he was emotionally at one with the war, Melville's thoughts were not entirely harmonized with his feelings: his ultimate doubts crept into his most sanguine reactions to the conflict; and at bottom, the things that quickened him were not the formal purposes of the conflict but its incidents—the flashing youths, the gallant charge, the daring commander, the spirited horse that carried Sheridan to battle. "Nothing can lift the heart of man like manhood in a fellow man," he says. The Civil War satisfied this desperate need in his own soul: but apart from its animal vigour and glory, even its solidest purposes seemed infirm and fragile. He pictures an heroic soldier, surviving the carnage, the Seven Days' Fight, the Wilderness, the field-hospital, and Libby Prison—surviving it and reflecting on his experience: "Heaven! what *truth* to him!" He himself had already drained the lees of adversity; the war had nothing to add there, except to make his own experience that of a whole generation.

3

In the break of emotional tension caused by the fall of Richmond, Melville wrote most of his verses on the Civil War. A few were printed in the magazines during the first part of 1866, and later in the year, Melville collected and published the whole volume of verse, Battle Pieces and Other Aspects of the War; with a supplement, gravely and well written, in which he counterbalanced any Unionist fervour and elation he might have shown in the battle poems, by discussing, with great sympathy and tact, the plight of the South and the psychological problems confronting the North, particularly, in dealing with it.

One of the poems in the collection, Sheridan at Cedar Creek, was long quoted as one of the memorable poems evoked by the war; but, although Melville's verses on the war are the only serious contemporary rivals to Whitman's Drum-Taps, one cannot, with the most lenient eye, put them in the same class. Melville rarely achieved form as a poet: he was often very near to it, as we shall see when we examine his poems about the sea and his travels: but although the sensitiveness, the emotional tension, the rough powers of expression, in short, the ingredients of poetry were there, he permitted himself to be conquered by the external form of line and stanza: his rhythms are broken, not by their own inner development, but because they meet a foreign object, and get shattered against it. These verses are such jewelry as a sculptor might make. Melville's mallet and chisel and sinew were of little use with a pitch block and a graving-tool.

Among these verses there are a few stanzas that give one a hint of what Melville's potentialities as a poet were: his poem on John Brown is one of them, and another occurs in a poem commemorative of a naval victory—despite the weakness of the second line, it rings like a bell.

> But seldom the laurel wreath is seen
>   Unmixed with pensive pansies dark;
> There's a light and a shadow on every man
>   Who at last attains his lifted mark—
>   Nursing through night the ethereal spark.

Elate he never can be;
He feels that spirit which had hailed his worth
   Sleep in oblivion.—The shark
Glides white through the sulphurous sea.

It is no accident that this stanza utters Melville's deepest intuition of life. Here image is symbol, and the symbol presents, without further reflection or explanation, the idea in its totality: *the shark glides white through the sulphurous sea.* There is something final in that. Melville might hope: he might be stirred up: he might join hands with his fellows: he might even achieve victory: all these things had happened in the collective excitement of the Civil War; but in the end the elation and exaltation were doomed to pass away. In the very act of achieving personal success, Melville had become aware of something in the Constitution of the Universe that fatally marred it: the shark glides white through the sulphurous sea. His demon was not deceived. It lived in the midst of chaos, and this Civil War, unified, regimented, ordered, inexorable as it seemed, was chaos, too. Order springs from within, mixing with circumstance but never carried away by it: in other words, order is art—and art was the one thing lacking in the whole plan of life that had arisen to dominate America. Raw power, raw experience, were uppermost. White sharks swam everywhere: shark ate shark, and greedily battened upon the refuse of the sinking boat. No use to fight the White Whale, if the boat that holds human culture breaks up, and the crew is killed, and only the sharks remain in the waters. I have expanded Melville's symbol, perhaps; but one cannot magnify his disillusion. As early as 1866 he noted in his Supplement that "for them who are neither partisans nor enthusiasts, nor theorists, nor cynics, there are some doubts not readily to be solved. And there are fears. Why is not the cessation of war now at length attended with the settled calm of peace?"

In his Supplement, Melville pleaded for generosity to the

vanquished, for a spirit of forbearance, for the sort of magnanimity that the Union soldiers showed at Vicksburg, when they watched the dejected Confederates file out without raising a shout of triumph. "Let us pray," he concluded, "that the terrible historic tragedy of our time may not have been enacted without instructing our whole beloved country through terror and pity; and may fulfillment verify in the end those expectations which kindle the bards of Progress and Humanity." Melville was definitely not one of the bards of progress and humanity; but in the loose sympathies of wartime, he had listened to all their righteous self-praise and their optimistic predictions; and though he did not share their philosophy, he at least joined them in their hopes, while there was still a possibility that they might be pragmatically justified.

That weak optimism came to nothing. There was a treachery that annulled these efforts—the treachery of the madness that resulted in Lincoln's death: the vindictive virtue of the Abolitionists, who inflicted military occupation and carpet-bag governments on their fallen enemies: and that very tragic topsy-turvydom of war which provides snug berths and comfortable fortunes to the profiteers and speculators, and offers a sordid routine and a share in the general bankruptcy to those who are unfortunate enough to escape a quick and early death.

The Union had perhaps been worth dying for: but nobody could confront the post-bellum scene, with its Vanderbilts and Jay Cookes and Daniel Drews, without wondering seriously whether the Union was worth living for. The heroes were dead: dead or incapacitated: incapacitated or tired. Those who had any fight left in them would fight for Civil Service Reform, as Carl Schurz did, or if they had energy, they would go into railroads, like Charles Francis Adams: it was no accident that those who sought a career less in harmony with the accepted good works of industrialism—a Henry Hobbes Richardson, a Mark Twain, a Henry

Adams, a William James, a Stanley Hall—were usually men who had by one chance or another lived during the war at a considerable distance from the struggle, and who had missed, not alone the fine heroism of that experience, but the terrible disillusion and collapse that follows such efforts; and who, like Stanley Hall, were moved to expiate their failure to risk death on the battlefield by living a little more arduously and heroically on the plane of daily life. These men might seek patiently to build up their careers; but those who had been buoyed up by the great energies and expectations of provincial America, in that Golden Day when they had grasped power and material mastery without losing hold of culture and form—those earlier writers and makers found themselves sinking helplessly out of sight, battered wrecks, submerged by the tide of industry and finance, whose waves rose higher and higher during the ten years that followed the great storm. There were no quiet waters for these men; or, if they found them, as Emerson did, as Whitman did, they lost the power to go to sea again; and, instead of being beaten to pieces on the treacherous coast, merely rotted at the wharf.

In 1866, at the age of forty-seven, Herman Melville, too, withdrew from the war, defeated. That fine "scorn of life which earns life's crown"—earns, but does not always win it—had left him with the burdens, difficulties, grievances of a returning soldier. He had fought a not less worthy fight; and now, once for all, he retreated. He did not surrender; for he kept on writing to the end of his days; but he could no more live on his writings than a veteran of the Grand Army could exchange his medals and scars for honest bread. Melville was forced to face this fact, after twenty years of writing and fifteen years of continuous, desperate struggle. He had not given in quickly or petulantly; and when he finally made this decision, one can detect in it no sign of outraged vanity or reproach. He had gauged his position: he knew the worst: he was prepared to meet it. Through the offices of an old travelling companion, he found a place as inspector in the Custom House, a post he had described in Redburn as "a most inglorious one; indeed, worse than driving geese to water."

From this time on a sweetness and serenity began to spread over the man. The dark torture of Pierre and The Confidence Man might return in weak moments; there might be hours of stormy egoism or inner defiance; but in the main there was peace. This, too, he had anticipated for himself in Isabel's words, almost half a generation before: "My spirit seeks different food from happiness; for I think I have a suspicion of what it is. I have suffered wretchedness, but not because of the absence of happiness, and without praying for happiness, I pray for peace—for motionlessness —for the feeling of myself, as of some plant, absorbing life without seeking it, and existing without individual sensation." A Hindu sage might have sought this peace in the forest: Melville, with quiet irony, sought it in the Custom House.

4

The decision was made; the door was closed: Melville's troubles and humiliations could carry him no lower. For the first time in ten years Melville had the means, the energy, the relief from anxiety necessary for the prosecution of a long work, and with indomitable spirit he set to work again. Melville's retreat was not a withdrawal from his proper self, but a withdrawal from the conditions that hampered its expression—the taste of the public and the predilections of publishers, the demand for warmed-over Peedee and Hullabaloo. "How live at all," he asks himself, "if once a fugitive from thy own nobler part, though pain be portion inwrought with the grain," and in this sense Melville was never a fugitive. His next effort was a long narrative poem—the original edition in two volumes numbers 571 pages and about 20,000 lines—based on his Pilgrimage in the Holy Land. In his Constantinople notebook, he had originally set down a suggestion for Frescoes of Travel by Three Brothers, Poet, Painter, and Scholar; and in the intervening years the conception had grown and expanded into a modern Canterbury pilgrimage of the harassed, the faithless, the doubting, the exiled. Clarel, this new work, was not published till 1876; but the book itself was probably written shortly after the Civil War: the heightened skill in verse, the reference to the Civil War in Part IV, the fact that the poem is all of a piece, and the testimony of Melville's surviving daughter, all focus on this period; and Melville's own reference to the poem's having been long in existence before his uncle, Mr. Peter Gansevoort, generously provided money for its publication, enables one to associate the beginning of this mental pilgrimage with his withdrawal into the Custom House.

Melville's short sojourn in Palestine had made a deep impression on him: the notes that belonged to those weeks were full of observations. In Jerusalem he had encountered all sorts of queer people: an old commercial man giving tracts to people whose language he did not understand; a Philadelphian turned Jew, who had married a Jewess; a fanatical American missionary going about Jerusalem with an open Bible, looking forward to the opening asunder of Mount Olivet and in the meanwhile preparing the highway for the procession of the dead; a crazy American woman who had opened an agricultural academy for the Jews without converting a single Jew to either agriculture or Christianity. Deliberately he had saturated his mind with the atmosphere of Jerusalem, "offering myself up," he noted, "as a passive subject, and no unwilling one, to its weird impression," and always rising at dawn and walking outside the city walls. In the afternoon he would stand by the Shepherd's Gate, on the spot where Christ was stoned, and "watch the shadows sliding, sled-like, down the hills of Beretta and Zion into the valley of Jehoshaphat, then, after resting awhile, creeping up the opposite side of Olivet, entering tomb after tomb, and cave after cave." The Christ-mood sometimes came over him; he felt in himself the un-recognized god, or the goaded deity, the mystic scapegoat of an inscrutable patriarchal presence; he too had climbed the way of Calvary. But the Devil's ingenuity did not impress him: the Mount of Temptation was only a black, arid mount overlooking the Dead Sea: why did the foolish fiend think any one would value the rulership of such an empire—and if it was only a vision, why take him up to the Mount? But though every rock and road had an association, it was the landscape of Palestine that overwhelmed him: the arid hills, the smell of burning rubbish in Jerusalem, the melancholy olive tree, the whitish mildew that pervaded whole tracts of landscape—bleached—leprosy—encrusta-tion of cakes—old cheese—bones of rocks—crunched, gnawed, and mumbled—mere refuse and rubbish of creation, comparing with ordinary regions as a skeleton with the liv-ing and rosy man. "Is the desolation of the land," Melville asked himself, "the result of the fatal embrace of the Deity? Hapless are the favourites of Heaven!" Palestine had dissi-pated his romantic expectation; but it had reciprocated all the aridness and emptiness of his spirit. In the antediluvian port of Joppa, just before his departure, Joppa, which was too ancient to have antiquities, he felt like Jonah himself, and only strong self-control and grim defiance enabled him to keep cool and patient. The Dead Sea had concentrated all these impressions: the foam on the beach and pebbles had been like the slaver of a mad dog: the water had been swarthy, bitter, and, carrying the bitter taste in his mouth all day, he had felt the utter bitterness of life. "Bitter is it to be poor and bitter to be reviled, and oh, bitter are these waters of death, thought I."

All these sights and experiences formed the background of Clarel; but the poem itself is far richer in detail than the notebooks: it is an imaginative elaboration of his ex-periences, and not a reproduction of them. The arid back-ground, which reflected Melville's own feeling of hopelessness

in 1857, retreated: the foreground is thronged with people
who have independent lives and motives. All the major characters, Clarel the student, Vine the wanderer, Rolfe, another
uneasy wanderer, Mortmain, the disillusioned Swedish revolutionary, and Ungar, a Baltimore Catholic with a streak
of Indian in him, all these characters, it is true, centre like
focussed rays in Melville's own being, baffled by his perplexities, and arguing, like his own doubts, among themselves. The spirit that pervades Clarel is sober, restrained,
steady-eyed: its failure as poetry is due, in part, to this
very sobriety of thought.

5

The first part discloses Clarel, a student who has abandoned his preparations for the ministry, in Jerusalem. He
has come to lay his inner questions at the gates of religion's
own city, thinking to find from an older race, the Jews, with
a remoter history, some clue to the unsettled and uneasy
state in which he lives, and some path of development which
will lead again to wholeness. Behind the crumbling faith of
Rome and Luther is the crag of Sinai—adamant! While
exploring Jerusalem, Clarel makes the acquaintance of an
American, Nathan, who has become a convert to Judaism,
and falls in love with his daughter, Ruth. Nathan's Jewish
wife and daughter, though loyal to the faith, still long for
some of the things America had given them—and they do
not altogether share the zeal of the convert. Even in Jerusalem, the story swarms with characters: Melville tells the history of each chance acquaintance, as if by a thousand
examples from the lives of other men one might find an
answer to one's own. Most of these lives, though Melville
gives them a foreign birthplace, are touched by the reflected
light of his own history. Thus in Celio's story, one cannot
help following Melville's own plight:

> Fain had his brothers have him grace
> Some civic honorable place:

And interest was there to win
Ample preferment: he as kin
Was loved, if but ill understood:
At heart they had his worldly good:
But he postponed and went his way
Unpledged, unhampered. . . .
Since love, arms, courts abjure—why then
Remaineth to me what? The pen?
Dead feather of ethereal life?
Nor efficacious much, save when
It makes some fallacy more rife.
My kin—I blame them not at heart—
Would have me act some routine part,
Subserving family, and dreams
Alien to me—illusive schemes.

Ruth's father is killed on his lonely farm by Arab raiders
and robbers, and Clarel is not permitted by Jewish custom
to enter the House of Mourning. Being cut off from his beloved, he decides to ease his loneliness by joining a cavalcade,
going across Palestine to the Dead Sea, through the wilderness where John wandered, and back again by Bethlehem.
On the journey, we are deliberately reminded of Chaucer's
Pilgrims, and the robust, full-blooded, healthy, superficial,
English Broad Churchman, Derwent—the most completely
embodied character in the whole book—is described with a
little of that soft sweet malice Chaucer knew so well how to
use.

Thought's last adopted style he showed;
Abreast kept with the age, the year
And each bright optimistic mind,
Nor lagged with Solomon in rear,
And Job, the furthermost behind—
Brisk marching in time's drum-corps van
Abreast with whistling Jonathan.

But these Pilgrims do not while away the hour with merry
tales: instead of being able to assume the faith, and take

life pretty much as it comes, as Chaucer's honest folk did, their faith is threatened and disintegrated, and even life's happiness is a problem that must be solved: it exacerbates them almost as much as their emptiness. Chaucer's people eat, drink, joke, love, quarrel, cozen, cheat, hate, envy: living in a world where these things exist, along with chivalry and nobility and chastity, they are neither saddened nor puzzled, because the framework of that world is articulated, and each part of it has its necessary place—even the sins. Among Melville's pilgrims, however, not even the virtues are safe: each man lives in a private world that trembles and dissolves at every shock.

Contrast these pious atheists, these doubtful scholars, these sobered revolutionaries, with the Mussulman, the orthodox Jew, the bland, beef-fed English clergyman, or the Roman Catholic abbot. The latter go through their daily ritual without question or loss of energy: their orthodoxy is secure and they themselves are untroubled: wrapped in an absorbing dream, their body is indifferent to the hard pallet on which they lie. The mocking Jewish atheist is happy, too; as Spinoza, blessed with a diviner illusion, was happy: but the question is: Can a Clarel, a Rolfe, a Mortmain, in short, a Melville, acquire that sort of serenity without cutting himself off from his very flesh and tissue? Once one has broken out of the orthodoxy, one can no more go back to it than a disturbed sleeper can resume the thread of a vanished dream, no more than a grown man can go back to the games of his childhood. There was once a time no doubt when he could call sand sugar and stones bread: but now stones were stones, cold, flinty—no doubt about that. "The pains lie among the pleasures," Melville noted while in Palestine, "like sand in rice, not only bad in themselves, but spoiling the good"; and this held of faith and doubt as well as pain and pleasure.

Melville's insight no longer shrivelled and blasted the very constitution of man, as in The Confidence Man; but it pierced, perhaps, even deeper. An indictment of humanity itself is a blank indictment which turns the accuser into one of the principal defendants: one suspects the morals of Juvenal and the kindliness of Swift, precisely because they see so little of these qualities in the people about them. In Clarel, Melville went through country after country, and institution after institution, as he had done in Mardi: here he points out a weak joint, there a plaster-covered crack, or in another place a false foundation. One cannot evade these specific criticisms. From the atheist who jeers at Rome— "patcher of the rotten cloth, pickler of the wing of the moth, toaster of bread stale in date"—to the reactionary religionist who attacks Derwent's belief in a Christianity blandly coupled with comfort and progress and toasted muffins and dividends, all working together for the greater glory of Mammon, scarcely any of the complacencies of Melville's age escaped: his chilly wind blew the rotten roof off every house of refuge. Blake paused at the wonder of life, which had with the same breath created the tiger and the lamb: but Melville in a mordant line said: "If true what priests avouch of Thee, the shark Thou madst, yet claimst the dove." These lines show, I think, that the consolations of transcendental religion were always far from Melville. The consolations of Progress were, alas! equally remote: Melville had small use for those who heaved contempt on "rite and creed sublime" and yet clung to their own rank fable, the "latest shame of time." In the conflict between a crumbling theology and a cocky, over-confident science, Melville could take neither side. Melville felt that the scantling of the contemporary scientific outlook was no equivalent for the massive architecture of the ancient church; nor could he reassure himself, when he found cold adverse rains beating down on his head, that the scantling was a new and finer kind of architecture.

Yea, long as children feel affright
In darkness, men shall fear a God;
And long as daisies yield delight
Shall see His footprints in the sod.
Is't ignorance? This ignorant state
Science doth but elucidate,
Deepen, enlarge. . . .
Let fools count on faith's closing knell—
Time, God, are inexhaustible.

Melville was aware of the historic parallel to his own age; and he knew what its outcome had been. Christ had followed Osiris: Jesus had indeed come out of Egypt, as the legend said; and in the time of Cicero, when Roman society was in the same state of doubt, disruption, and despair as the Western world was in Clarel's day, a new era of resolution and faith was beginning to open. Doubt and all its maladies in the moral life were no more final in society than they were in the individual: "There is," Melville said, "no steady un-retracing progress in this life; we do not advance through fixed gradations, and at the last one pause:—through infancy's unconscious spell, boyhood's thoughtless faith, adolescence' doubt (the common doom), then skepticism, then disbelief, resting at last in manhood's pondering repose of If. But once gone through, we trace the round again; and are infants, boys, and men, and Ifs eternally." Like Matthew Arnold, Melville was keenly aware of the transition; but, being an American, he could not accept the mere sense of historic continuity, of a favourable inertia, as a substitute for a new faith.

When one examines the mood of Clarel and the conclusions of one of the pilgrims, Mortmain, the Swede, who had been a prophet of the new order and a revolutionary, bent on carrying further the vast abstract programme of the French revolution, one becomes conscious of the exceptional maturity of Melville's social observation. Melville had reached by sober meditation what Herzen, for example,

had achieved only after a long kindergarten training in
ideals and enthusiasms. Men like Herzen had avoided ultimate issues. They drugged themselves with plot, conspiracy,
oratory, propaganda, every form of verbal busy work. They
ended in total disillusion, without seeing that they should
not have reached this spiritual desert had they started out
with a less abstract and barrenly subjective view of their
task. Now, Melville, too, realized that the social revolution
had already taken on a millennial character by 1848: it was
the new democratic equivalent of the older scheme of salvation by faith, and men like Bakunin and Louis Blanc and
Engels had found in it something that knit their lives together and gave them significance, as the Civil War did for
Melville, as other-worldly religion did for the orthodox.
With this in mind, Melville's comments upon Mortmain's
adventures are all the more pregnant; for Mortmain came
to doubt not so much his purposes as his instruments:

> . . . Wear and tear and jar
> He met with coffee and cigar:
> These kept awake the man and mood
> And dream. That uncreated Good
> He sought whose absence is the cause
> Of creeds and Atheists, mobs and laws.
> Precocities of heart outran
> The immaturities of brain.
>   Along with each superior mind
> The vain, foolhardy, worthless, blind,
> With Judases, are nothing loath
> To clasp pledged hands and take the oath
> Of aim, the which, if just, demands
> Strong hearts, brows deep, and priestly hands.
>   ·   ·   ·   ·   ·   ·   ·
> Wouldst meddle with the state? Well, mount
> Thy guns; how many men dost count?
> Besides, there's more that here belongs:
> Be many questionable wrongs:

By yet more questionable war
Prophet of peace, these wouldst thou bar?
The world's not new, nor new thy plea.
Tho' even shouldst thou triumph, see:
Victorious right may wild redress:
No failure like a harsh success.
Yea, ponder well the historic page:
Of all who, fired with noble rage,
Have warred for right without reprieve.

     .   .   .   .

The world is portioned out, believe:
The good have but a patch at best,
The wise their corner, for the rest—
Malice divides with ignorance.

Insight like this may be fatal to a weak man, or added poison to a disappointed one: but when a man well bottomed takes it to his bosom, he is no longer defenceless against his own inner hopes, desires, wishes: he goes armed. Such wisdom does not nullify generous efforts: a Lenin may count his guns and men and still wage revolution: he will not do this the worse for recognizing, as Lenin grimly did, all the vain and foolish people who, along with the Judases, divide place with those who have strong hands and deep brows. Life is stultified by vacuous dreams, dreams of achievement without effort, pleasure without satiety, art without discipline, or a better social order without a moral and metaphysical conversion of the very people who must bring it about. Besides these dreams, the most gritty reality is a tonic. To acknowledge these realities, instead of seeking weak consolations or empty reassurances, is the mark of a mature mind. Melville had penetrated as far as Herzen the psychological problem of revolutionary betterment: but he was almost fifty years "before his time" in stating it. We can understand Melville's social scepticism today, and we should not, perhaps, remain so long in the trough of our own wave, apathetically waiting for a dictatorship or an earthquake or a war to rouse us and focus our energies once more, had we been able to learn from Melville the necessary cost of our efforts. For every act of the wise and the good is nullified by malice and ignorance, unless the wise and the good learn to reckon these evils among the conditions of their problem. Melville had faced human nature as a whole: he was not blind to its inert or irrational elements; nor could he accept "A Reasonable Constitution" that overlooked them.

> What though Reason forged your scheme?
> 'Twas Reason dreamed the Utopia's dream:
> 'Tis dream to think that Reason can
> Govern the reasoning creature, man.

Melville's scepticism did not flinch at even the securest parts of the conceptual universe.

> Canst feel elate
> While all the depths of Being moan,
> Though luminous on every hand,
> The breadths of shallow knowledge more expand?
> Much as the light-ship keeper pines
> Mid shoals immense, where dreary shines
> His lamp, we toss beneath the ray
> Of Science's beacon. This to trim
> Is now man's barren office.

But the tentative nature of science's triumphs, and the disintegration of the great religious unity which had heretofore provided an intelligible framework, still left one possible avenue unexplored. Perhaps salvation was to be found, as André Gide has suggested in his study of Dostoyevsky, in the practice of the arts, such salvation as the great minds

317

of the Renaissance found amid similar disruption: Wren, with his multitudinous buildings that housed an empty ecclesiasticism, Leonardo and Michelangelo with the saints that had lost their ineffable powers and taken on the forms of mighty men and women, Rembrandt with those thousand enigmatic faces, gazing back, with questioning eyes, into eyes that still question. Melville did not, I believe, fully understand this solution or face its possibility: but he saw one side of it, the advance of the mechanical arts, and there, with cold acumen, he beheld no happy sequel: rather the contrary:

> . . . Arts are tools;
> But tools, they say, are to the strong:
> Is Satan weak? Weak is the wrong?
> No blessed augury overrules:
> Your arts advance in faith's decay:
> You are but drilling the new Hun
> Whose growl even now can some dismay;
> Vindictive in his heart of hearts,
> He schools him in your mines and marts—
> A skilled destroyer.

These lines were written in the time of the supremest Victorian confidence. Herbert Spencer had demonstrated, he thought, by revamping Comte's generalization, that a military and feudal order, founded upon a demonistic theology, was inevitably going to be replaced by an industrial order, inimical to militarism, and founded upon science and free contract. That the new arts of industrialism had themselves any capacity for mischief was not hinted at by the dominant prophets of the day: Ruskin's warnings were lonely ones, and he was contemptuously thrust aside as a fanatical aesthete, who understood the stones of Venice, perhaps, but not the steel of Sheffield. In the passage just quoted, Melville went quite as far as Ruskin: industrialism, to him, offered no certain pledge of happiness or welfare: it depended, rather, upon who used these tools, and how.

The ruthless sweeping away of human values, the sacrifice of the worker's welfare to profits, and of general well-being to a bleak efficiency, and, finally, the sweeping away of all the decencies of life in a bestial internecine warfare, aggravated by all the improvements in the arts: Melville saw all these things, and perceived that a good part of the routine of education, work, and patriotism could be called, not least in the "advanced" countries, a drilling of the Hun. Walter Rathenau, one of the great industrial leaders of the past generation, came to the same conclusion at the end of the World War, and he pictured its consequences: but Melville anticipated him there, as he anticipated the disillusion of the social revolutionists. He saw that unless human values were firmly established, the practice of the arts was as blind and futile as the firing of a revolver into empty air: with power and precision at command, the revolver hits nothing whatever—but in its very aimlessness, it may destroy something precious, as the blind projection of a concrete road by a half-witted road engineer may destroy a row of elms in a New England village. Melville put this thought, it is true, into the mouth of a religious zealot: but like everything else in Clarel, it belonged to his own innermost mood.

Melville, it will be seen, did not in Clarel take refuge in any of the cheap opiates of his time: his scepticisms are as inexorable, as thoroughgoing, as they had been in the most devastating pages of The Confidence Man; but, with all this dubiety, there is a difference in the mood; and though Clarel pictures the thoughts of men unfrocked in faith, and shows them wandering over many arid deserts and picking their way through the broken streets of many ruined towns, something solid, the beginnings of a new faith, kept Melville himself from slipping into hopeless indifference or more hopeless despair. Whether Melville intentionally symbolized his dilemma in the fable I do not know; and in the light of his deliberate subtlety in Moby-Dick one cannot say positively that he did not: but the unconscious significance of

Clarel's love affair is perhaps worth speculating upon; for it affected his attitude and his conclusion.

Clarel fell in love with a Jewish maid, as Melville had fallen in love with ancient Jewish thought. Christianity was at times repugnant to Melville, for the highest virtue had for him necessarily some of the Greek or Hebraic element of power, and the epicene Christ of mediaeval legend did not attract him; nor was he comforted by supernal promises of an after-life. If Melville confesses that the truest of all men was the Man of Sorrows, he added that "the truest of all books is Solomon's, and Ecclesiastes is the fine hammered steel of woe." In the period of his own discomposure, the black aphorisms of Solomon, Koheleth, and Jesus-ben-Sirach, and the bitter plaints of Job, were closer to him than anything else in literature. "There is a wisdom that is woe," Melville had found, "and there is a woe that is madness." He had come to the first, and he had stood on the brink of madness: looking in the Bible for comfort, Melville had found, in the greatest of the Jewish writers, only a confirmation of his own fears and exasperations. "Oppression maketh a wise man mad." "Man is born to trouble as the sparks fly upward." Such sayings deepened his sympathy with Jewish culture; and, in the sense that they carried the same burden as his own, they lessened his load. Ruth, Clarel's love, dies; and the fulfilment that Clarel had hoped to find there, he must now find in his own bosom, with only the memory of her spirit to comfort him.

6

Why then, with all these virtues of thought, is Clarel necessarily Melville's most neglected book? The capital difficulty, I think, is inherent in its very conception as a narrative poem: it is impossible to carry through so many pages the quick sympathies and empathies that it is in the nature of verse to give. Wordsworth probably had as much skill in blank verse as any one since Shakespeare, and

he was unable to avoid long waste tracts in his lengthy philosophic and biographic poems. Blake and Whitman, with a
surer instinct, developed polyphonic cadences for their long
poems, and this is the only tolerable alternative, I think, at
least in English, to the immeasurable variety of prose itself.
Melville's eight-syllabled lines in Clarel are monotonous,
vary the rhyme scheme as he will; they are made even more
tedious by the stale poetic airs that accompanied it. Melville's aloofness and spiritual independence, which cut him
off from his own contemporaries, not merely saved him from
their errors and superstitions: it also prevented him from
profiting by their genuine advances. With the exception of
Whitman and Emily Dickinson, scarcely any of Melville's
contemporaries had participated in that great refreshment
of poetic language, by the fuller use of the vernacular, by
discarding the powdered wig of "poetic diction," and by the
use of direct and simple word order, that had been made
possible by Wordsworth's propaganda and example. In his
lesser poems Emerson sinned in this respect almost as much
as the poetasters around him; and Poe's "tarns" and Nycean
barks of yore and his seraphim were typical of the exaggera-
tions and clichés that afflicted the American poets of his time.

In the verses of his later years, Melville largely escaped
from this fashionable prison; but in Clarel he was too
frequently the victim of his uncertain taste. He tags adjectives on to nouns to eke out the line; he uses, all too frequently, words like fane and sward and rue and twain and
nigh, and, with unforgivable recurrence, he rhymes elf and
self; above all, not relying on his ear for more subtle quantities, he fills out lines with redundant words or phrases—
or clips them off. This clumsiness in detail adds to the
clumsiness of conception: what might have been vivid prose
became dull verse: what might have been good Borrow
became bad Rogers. Mid all this poetizing there remains, of
course, a little poetry: lines that lift out of the grey pages
like a sudden sea gull from the monotonous surface of the

ocean: there are even whole passages, in particular the Dirge that comes toward the end, which are veritably moving. But although the materials for intense feeling or vivid imagism are present, they are spoiled in the mixing. All this acute observation of men, things, places, seems to clog Melville's spirit: when he achieves victory, it is a victory of thought: an idea becomes pregnant and a dozen good lines are born. But the detail over-rides the general impression, as the ingenuity of the Hindu craftsman over-rides the total effect of his wood-carving: the movement is slow: the aim is dispersed. There is a story and a climax in Clarel; but we do not feel them in passage. We miss the poignance of Ruth's death, by having forgotten her entirely.

It is unfortunate that Melville diverted into the ingenuities of a foreign versification the energies that should have gone into mastery of the theme itself. But matter and manner are always one; and because Melville did not find harmonious form for his intuitions, we are deprived of a good part of them, and those that remain we must pick, like precious shards, from the refuse heap of the poem. He was a true poet; but formal verse was not his medium; and the relentless probity of his mind, the keen reaching into the heart of a dilemma, lacked in these lengthy verses an appropriate vehicle. Melville was wrong when he thought that some of the aroma might have exhaled during the years Clarel remained unpublished: the aroma had never been there.

7

It was a long, weary pilgrimage, this pilgrimage of Melville's, as Clarel is a long, weary poem; but at the end of it, something crystallized within him, and without blunting his doubts or shutting off his conflict, at last focussed them. Something happened to Melville in Palestine, or during the years between, that was the equivalent of falling in love with a Jewish maiden. Although Clarel returned from his pilgrimage to find himself bereft, the experience of love had given him something: the love that would have redeemed the uni-

verse for Captain Ahab and kept him from his deadly
contest with the whale, now was a pledge of his own redemption for Melville. What the nature of that experience was
one does not know: one can only judge by its final effect;
and in the last pages of Clarel the whole weary strife of
debate is suddenly brought to a close, at the end of the lover's
grief, in the epilogue with its pledge and hope:

> Then keep thy heart, though yet but ill-resigned—
> Clarel, thy heart, the issues there but mind;
> That like the crocus budding through the snow—
> That like a swimmer rising from the deep—
> That like a burning secret which doth go
> Even from the bosom that would hoard and keep;
> Emerge thou mayst from the last whelming sea,
> And prove that death but routs life into victory.

The budding crocus, the rising swimmer, the bursting
secret were symbols of a new promise in Melville's own life:
in the Epilogue one sees the later Melville, who had
approached, and was slowly finding peace, rather than the
unsettled, bitter man who wandered through Palestine, and
confronted the "caked depopulated hell" of barren Judah.
There was no verbal answer, no creed, no theology, no
orthodoxy to comfort him and give a final meaning in exchange for his present soreness and perplexity. God does
not answer Job: he overawes and silences and converts him
and suddenly showers him with blessings: the relief is as
mysterious as the oppression which makes a wise man mad.
So with Melville. An animal faith, the dumb belief in all the
immediate presentations of life—this animal faith, quickened by love, knit together again. Creeds are, after all, only
the suspicious distortions of this dim, plasmal sense that
bottoms all of us. When that faith exists, life even in its
humblest aspects is neither black nor terrible, however heavy
its disappointments; without it, all that the world values is
thin, and all that the heart may contemplate is empty. There
is no rational justification for this animal faith; for it is

part of the nature of man and perhaps of all living things, and it antedates the doubts and difficulties that would disturb it.

Again and again Melville confronted this problem; and much though he admired the order and art they introduced, he could not accept the solutions offered by Judaism, Mohammedanism, Buddhism, or historic Christianity. In his preface to a poetic fragment, Rammon, Melville puts the dilemma before a son of Solomon's old age, immoderately influenced by his father's despondent philosophy. "Vanity of vanities—such is this life. As to a translated life in some world hereafter—far be that thought. A primary law binds the universe. The worlds are like apples on the tree; in flavour and tint one apple perchance may somewhat differ from another, but all partake of the same sap. One of the worlds we know. And what find we here? Much good, a preponderance of good; that is, good it would be could it be winnowed from the associate evil that taints it. But evil is no accident. Like good it is an irremoveable element. Bale out your individual boat if you can, but the sea remains the sea."

In his despair, Rammon is attracted to Buddhism by Prince Siddartha's personality and by the fact that his high rank had not hardened his heart to the lot of the mass of mankind, "nor in any wise intercepted a just view of the immense spectacle of things." But Rammon is too young to realize, with Melville, the fallacy of Buddha's very situation: it did not occur to him to conjecture "that the more spiritual, wide-seeing, conscientious and sympathetic the nature, so much the more spiritually isolated, and isolation is the mother of illusion." Melville was on guard against this error: isolated, he had refused illusion, the last comfort of isolation, and had abandoned all efforts to explain away man's helplessness and ignorance, and his corporeal extinction: he accepted this condition as a datum. And yet life went on! Far better, this, than a new illusion; for it brought self-respect and a belief in those forms of ideality which are within man's power to achieve or experience. By skilfully managing his little boat, not by pronouncing metaphysical incantations over the storm, man keeps afloat mid the vast waters that threaten him. The boat may be swamped, perhaps; but there is no other way! Life bottomed all formulas: art fended off catastrophe—if life ebbed or art ceased to be effective, well, one had faced reality and had respected necessity and one could meet the end with ironic resignation: in effect, the most dogmatic and devout could do no more.

At the end of Clarel, Melville found life, not good or bad, malicious or forbearing, true or false. Something more important had happened: he found it livable. In that mood the days that followed the Civil War were spent, quiet, chastened, subdued, temperate days. . . .

8

One may figure Melville's career as a June evening—the sun glowing in the sky, the birds darting about the trees, chattering, warbling, trilling, intensely active. The sky-gold turns to waves of salmon pink: the pink to lavender: the lavender edges into purple: suddenly dark has come. The cheerful sounds cease. A belated bird or two silently wings to his nest: there is blackness, and the hoarse croak of distant frogs alone breaks the silence. In half an hour the scene changes from the most brilliant activity and ecstasy to utmost passiveness. Bats swoop silently in the air; a chill comes up from the river: darkness is cool as well as silent. Is all over? Not yet. Presently the fireflies make a warm firmament of the fields, and in the pale rising of the moon, the earth itself takes on another glory. There are fireflies and moonlight and the domestic chirp of crickets in the night of Melville's life, its last quarter century—not silence and unrelieved blackness. After the first collapse of day into night, nature stirs again: there is movement and there is life. A little before the clock tolls the hour of midnight and the day itself passes, a shower of aerolites falls through the sky. . . . We have just seen the afterglow; and we are now to witness the final brilliance of the night.

CHAPTER TWELVE: THE FLOWERING ALOE

THE DAYS pass and one day is like another: there is comfort in monotony. The brick house in East Twenty-sixth Street, with its muddy-yellow exterior and its brownstone trim, with its old mahogany parlour furniture, its towering brown bookcases, its print of the Bay of Naples hanging in the front hall, has a calm dark gravity which sets it off from houses that make garish gestures of brightness or gaiety within. When the sun hits the rear rooms there is warmth; when geraniums and pansies appear in the yard below there is colour. Melville's house is a refuge from the city outside. Looking like every other house in the row, it has still a quiet interior of its own, an interior, like Herman Melville's, acquired before the débâcle of the Civil War. The brown wallpaper and the black iron bed in the wan north light of Herman Melville's room almost alone indicate that a day has dawned that is somewhat darker than a starless night.

The sixties have passed; the seventies have come. Heroism gives way to complacency, and courage to chicane. Even General Grant himself, type of resolute action and manly confidence and dogged devotion while the war was on, becomes in Presidential office little more scrupulous than the head of a foraging party: gambling and corruption take place before the magnanimous man who had been chivalrous to Lee and thoughtful of the conquered army. Is it any wonder that New York itself, which had been invaded and seized by people who had left Europe under stress and poverty, and were thrown into its miserable tenements and sinister streets, this Salonica of the Western world, was prey

326

to a ring of politicians as remarkable for their brazenness as for their peculations? On the edges of the city, near the gas tanks, but sometimes spilling over into the respectable sections, gangs line up on each side of the street and exchange bullets. It is worth one's life to carry a gold watch through certain parts of the East Side: Constantinople, twenty years before, was no happier place for felons and assassins. What superb triumphs offset this brutality, this degradation! In 1869, an elevated railroad is built; a little later, a cable car is attached to a cable, and goes; the human voice finds a means of travelling over an electro-magnetic circuit. Man has stolen fire from heaven again, and is conquering the world with it; but, stealing the fire, he has left the more valuable parts of heaven behind. The voice that travels so far says the same banal things. The railroad that shuttles men back and forth across the city does not improve anything except the potentialities for speculation in real estate.

Melville had foreseen all the sordid developments of "this dishonorable epoch" while they were still in the germ, thus fulfilling the Chinese philosopher's notion of what a wise man is: he had viewed the myriads playing pigmy parts, debased into equality, and "in glut of all material arts" had predicted a civic barbarism, with man disennobled and brutalized, "dead level of rank commonplace: an Anglo-Saxon China"—the very Dark Ages of democracy. He had perceived that the new democracy, fed by the smatterings of newspapers, and moved by the war-cries of demagogues, was in reality as credulous and foolish as the polity of the Middle Ages; perhaps more so, because it had lost a decent and saving sense of its inferiority. What part could Melville take in this world? How could he cope with the practical men of his time, and "mix with tempers keen and narrow like a knife"? Or how could he have any intellectual transactions with such good-hearted but mushy-minded people as Edmund Clarence Stedman? His new contemporaries were schoolboys. Howells had the optimism of a boom-town news-paper or a stock prospectus: Lanier, who deserved better of Fate, wrote a booster book about Florida for a railroad: and in the decade when Melville published his own Pilgrim-age in the Holy Land, Mark Twain achieved affluence by producing Innocents Abroad.

Melville himself had hailed the spirit of the West as that which truly reflected America; but when the spirit actually appeared, in the form of a Mark Twain or a Bret Harte, he must have had his misgivings. At thirty, Melville had grap-pled with spiritual problems that Mark Twain kept furtively locked in his bosom until his old age, and, for fear of destroying his reputation, did not publish till after his death. What did Mark Twain know of "a hell over which mere hell serves for a heaven"? These new Americans were innocents at home as well as abroad. Those who knew that darkness existed were afraid of it: they said, whistling cheerfully, that Progress would do away with darkness in a year or two: the arc-light would abolish the burglar: the long-range gun would abolish war: the ocean cable would abolish international misunderstanding: typewriters would relieve the difficulties of authorship: divorce would do away with the maladjustments of the married. Innocents indeed! Is one puzzled that Melville shrank from the post-war generation?

Melville's home was a refuge, and his shanty of an office was a refuge too. While the new parts of the city were exult-ing in the ugliness of brownstone fronts, accentuated by perverse cornices and mouldings, Twenty-sixth Street was still largely red brick, built a little too late for charm, but early enough to possess iron balconies facing south, like London in the Regency. Every morning a grave, firm, square-bearded man leaves Number 104. A little slow and reflective in gait, as if deliberately setting himself apart in pace as well as inward gesture from the world about him, Melville turns west toward Madison Square, passes

through its green, and follows Fifth Avenue, whose ranks
of trees are just beginning to be broken, down to Fourteenth Street, where already the brownstones, though only
a few years old, are being converted into fashionable confectionery stores, bakeries, jewelry shops. He follows the
broad thoroughfare clear over to Hudson Street, and then
turns to the block below, where the Gansevoort Market and
the customs office lie, touching the river. These brown buildings, these smug garish shops, these crass, dirty waterfront
hotels, are too ugly to attract his attention even if use and
want did not quiet his interest. In five years, ten years,
twenty years, the changes are not very important: the horse-
cars become fewer and the tangle of traffic at Union Square
is worse and Broadway from Fourteenth Street up becomes
"Ladies' Mill," the fashionable afternoon thoroughfare for
shopping: but on the whole the outer world does not make
any serious claims. The familiarity of everything is reassuring. The name Gansevoort, on the market at the end of
his walk, is a touch of welcome. There is a Gansevoort Hotel
on Little Twelfth Street and West Street; but when Melville inquires what it stands for, he finds that the hero of
Fort Stanwix is now only a name. Well: names remain!
Gansevoort remains; perhaps Melville will remain, too.

Melville, as customs inspector, has one of the lowest political positions open to patronage: he is an Ishmael among
Ishmaels, and a pariah among outcasts: impecunious bank-
ers, broken-down sports, bankrupt merchants, political
nondescripts, people who were fit for nothing elsewhere, in
short, as R. H. Stoddard described it, "an asylum for
nonentities." The scene itself, though mean, brings Melville
close to his element: the ships coming in, the odour of tar,
hemp, rotting wood, brine, the severe manly ways of the captains, the affable circumspection of the pursers—they remind Melville of another day and another fortune and another disguise. Best for him to do his work, to shut his mouth,
to get through the day patiently: like Rama, the Hindu god,

misplaced in human lot, discredited, abiding there in out-
lawry. "May life and fable so agree?" Melville asked in
Clarel, and he knew the answer: they did. "There is more
power and beauty in the well-kept secret of one's self and
one's thoughts," Maurice de Guérin had written, "than in
the display of a whole heaven that one may have inside one."
Melville underlined those words, and kept his heaven facing
inward.

The monotony brings quiet: the monotony brings peace.
On drizzly mornings, before the ships can drudge up the
river through the fog, there are hours of inward placidity.
Melville peers through the pall on the river outside and sees
somewhat more poignantly into his own position; perhaps
the final lines of a poem come to him then:

> Nor cringe if come the night:
>   Walk through the cloud to meet the pall,
>   Though light forsake thee, never fall
> From fealty to light.

While he must serve his sentence in this prison, there is only
one thing to fear: a new Administration; shifting to a new
post, learning new faces, having once more to battle and
struggle. Fortunately, Melville has friends in the department, clever worldly fellows like Stoddard: a word to him is
passed along to the chief; the rumour of a transfer is
quieted. Melville need never leave this cloistered street, this
melancholy examination and appraisal, this even equable
round: this is as good as another Sailors' Snug Harbor, over
which his younger brother Tom now is governor. Yes, it is
good for a lifetime—if one may call these empty hours life.

Gansevoort Pier at one end: Lizzie and the two girls at
the other. The meagre evening dinner, indifferently cooked,
the household gossip, the strain of observing an emptiness
at the table, of Mackie, who is dead, and Stanwix, who has
gone off: the sudden look of tenderness on the worn face
opposite, that stings yet sweetens everything. The customs
office is hell: this family circle is perhaps purgatory: it is

only when Melville withdraws to his room upstairs, and is by himself, that he can faintly re-enter the heaven that once surrounded him. There, with his pictures, his books, his glass of brandy to seduce sleep, the day ends in a solitude and a hush—tolerably. This is the daily round; but there are better occasions. On a warm summer night Melville might loll on the canvas steamer-chair placed on the narrow iron balcony, smoking his pipe, looking at the stars, gently holding Elizabeth's hand. Melville's passion is spent; but affection has deepened. With the slow renewal of his organic faith, he can accept his wife more fully and warmly, much more fully and warmly than when sex itself was primarily a physical irritation that left him disappointed and doubtful of the very basis of love, when he was tormented by passions at once inexpressible and unreciprocable.

When one of Melville's daughters grows up and marries, and Melville becomes a grandfather, he goes out to these children easily: he bounces them on his knee, makes noises like wind whistling through the rigging, sings a stave of an old chanty, walks with them in Central Park. This is not the tense harassed man his own children bitterly remembered from their youth: he is benign even when his thoughts are elsewhere, and occasionally downright jolly. His granddaughter still remembers his queer, literary words and the wiry feel of his beard: that bespeaks intimacy. There is a shadow between Melville and his family: they do not see him as he is, but as he is distorted by their own repulsions, their own bitterness: but when Melville's son-in-law casts eyes on Melville for the first time, buying a cigar in a hotel lobby in the White Mountains, there is something in the old man's air, like that in the man Flammonde, that captivates him and holds his attention: a distinguished man! In his family, he will remain an exile. They do not understand his jocularity and his occasional high spirits. They are offended by his inept sense of humour. In the Berkshire days he had dubbed one of the village gossips Miss Pecksniff and his mother had covered herself with mortification by addressing the good lady by this title when she called. One never could be quite sure about Herman Melville's jokes. His notion of a jolly time was to cook up a mess of crabs and sit around the table for a whole afternoon, picking at the flesh, drinking ale, telling stories, and haranguing the world in general, as if his wife and daughters and cousins were in the maintop of the Neversink. They were bored by these jokes, and indifferent to Melville's high spirits. If his daughters had not been reduced to dowdy dresses, if he had not had the wicked habit of asking belated suitors whether they preferred hominy or oatmeal for breakfast, if the family did not all feel that the high spirits of a poor man were purchased too cheaply, Melville might not have felt the hostile ring around him. These outbursts would be paid for, perhaps, by depression and inner exasperation: but they kept the too-even daily round from appalling Melville like the breath of infinity.

The age was against Melville; and his family were the mirror of the age: he knew that. They believed in work, in working and keeping up an appearance: in being respectable and tepid and unemotional and industrious. Even the nicest of his relatives, like his cousin Kate Gansevoort, with whom he maintained a desultory correspondence, rather apologized for being a person of leisure. For them all, doing, not being, was the main end of life. As if there were any merit in not being a person of leisure! They talked of the dignity of work. Bosh. True work is the necessity of humanity's earthly condition. The dignity is in leisure. Besides, ninety-nine hundredths of all the work done in the world is either foolish and unnecessary or harmful and wicked. What people needed was not work: they needed values. To recite poetry, to contemplate pictures, to write or to talk briskly or to meditate and chew one's own thoughts, quietly, on the maintop—work was good if it made these things possible, and bad if it blinded one to them, or made them impossible. . . .

2

People try to break in on Melville's even round, they seek to intrude on this cloistral quiet: they try in vain. Melville visits Pittsfield again, when the Centenary Committee asks him to write a short biography of his Grand-uncle Thomas for the Memorial Volume, and he has occasional vacations at Arrowhead or in the White Mountains, or in Albany or New Bedford, where one of his sisters lives: familiar places, familiar people. A young man who has read Melville's books awakes one morning on a wharf in New Bedford to find himself gazing at a mild-eyed old man in a blue serge suit with whom he falls into conversation: the nautical terms on the old man's tongue betray that he knows the sea; and the young man, a composer, is delighted to find that he is talking with his literary hero, Herman Melville. Contacts like these, with chance acquaintances, Melville did not repel; but those who sought him more deliberately were rebuffed. If the visitor mentions Mr. Omoo a cloud of annoyance will pass over Melville's face and perceptibly cool the surrounding air. Melville's public would not have his best: well, he is proud and will not be accepted for the sake of the least. Such interest will heal no wounds. Don't they realize Melville's contempt? Don't they feel who should be the patron and who the patronized? Doubtless not. Resentment threatened to flare up in Melville, perhaps, when he contemplated his literary contemporaries; so he did not contemplate them. The New York writers asked Melville to join the Authors' Club when they founded it: he refused. Still assiduous, towards the end of his life they gave Herman Melville a dinner of honour. A pleasant irony. Whom did they honour, these fashionable journalists, these professional diners-out, these men-about-literature? That dinner did not feed Herman Melville, that admiration did not console him. Theirs was the outward attentiveness of base neglect.

Melville breaks his own silence to hold out a hand of sympathy to that honest, hearty Englishman, his junior, Mr. W. Clark Russell; for Russell knows the sea, too, and though not a writer of equal rank, is almost a fellow spirit: in his letter of thanks he mentions Moby-Dick: a true mark of appreciation. These two writers dip flags to each other, like passing ships; and when Melville, a few years later, in 1888, publishes his Sea Poems, he dedicates them to this English novelist of the sea. James Thomson is another kindred soul: all too well Melville knew the streets and alleys of his City of Dreadful Night. Melville corresponds for a few years, between 1884 and 1888, with Mr. James Billson of Leicester, who was Thomson's friend; and writes warm words of appreciation about Thomson's poems. "As to pessimism," Melville writes, and these words should be underlined, "as to pessimism, although neither pessimist nor optimist myself, nevertheless I relish it in the verse, if for nothing else than as a counterpoise to the exorbitant hopefulness, juvenile and shallow, that makes such a muster these days—at least in some quarters." Neither pessimist nor optimist: of course: for there is a "light and a shadow on every man who at last achieves his lifted mark." We shall see that mood engraved in Melville's final verse.

Had contacts not been hard for Melville to make, he might have had a try at Elihu Vedder, too. Vedder's picture of The Redeemed Slave, shown at the Academy Exhibition of 1865, touched something in Melville; and Vedder had gone on, apparently, a little apart from the beaten track of veracious scenery and fictional illustration: he seemed to know that there was more than one level of experience, that there was, so to say, an immediate "beyond," grounded in the senses and intuitions quite as much as the direct work of one's eye. Where had he acquired this? In contrast to Vedder, there was another recluse whom Melville may perchance have brushed by on Fourteenth Street, more than once: a painter bred in New Bedford, loving the sea, too, and painting its mystery, much nearer to Melville in his loneliness,

his visions, his love of Shakespeare, his reticences and with-
drawals, than any other soul in America: Albert Pinkham
Ryder. Melville was never to meet him, or as far as one
knows, recognize his work. Not finding him, Melville turned
to Vedder, the lesser man, who at many removes was a link
between Melville and Blake.

Blake and Ryder were true fellow spirits: Russell and
Vedder were life's ironical substitutes; but, lacking knowledge of the spring, Melville slaked his thirst at the tap. He
dedicated his last book of poems, Timoleon, to Vedder; and
it is rather fortunate he died before he read Vedder's complacent answer, an answer without the faintest reference
to Melville's own works. Vedder was not the man to respond
to Melville: he was born half a generation later, and that
made a great difference. Vedder had been attracted by
Blake, and in his youth he found that he, too, had the power
of conjuring up visions, as thick and sensible as the furniture he touched: but Vedder had deliberately curbed his
power because, as he explained, "while if cultivated it would
soon enable me to see as realities most delightful things . . .
the reaction would be beyond my control and would inevitably follow and be sure to create images of horror indescrib-
able. A few experiences have shown me that that way
madness lies, and so, while I have rendered my Heaven somewhat tame, at least my Hell remains quite endurable."

What a contrast, this timid "V," with Melville, who had
let his visions open, and had risked everything to follow
them. His magnificent hell was worth all the placid heavens,
with their weak symbolisms, that Vedder achieved. That
Melville did not know Blake until 1874 at earliest, was a
real misfortune, but inevitable; like Melville, he was not
recovered until more than a generation after his death.
Blake, had Melville known him earlier, might have helped
him cast off his paralysing braces, Blake, who turned heaven
upside down, showed that God and the Devil had exchanged
costumes, felt that energy was pure delight, and had none

of Melville's haunting reluctances over sex, but delighted in his beautiful wife with the fresh naked energy of Adam's self. But pictures and books were near to Melville during this period: he collected and enjoyed prints and reproductions of pictures: he had a reproduction of one of Rembrandt's self-portraits and The Woman Taken in Adultery, and if he did not enjoy Blake's pictures, he responded to Blake's shadow, Flaxman. Melville's taste in landscape was excellent: Claude and Turner were his masters, Turner as much as anything, perhaps, for his sea-pictures, his ghostly headlands, his sun-drenched fogs. Melville reflected on the nature of art; indeed, in an unimportant set of verses called The Hostelry, he attempts, with the aid of Hals, Lippi, Spagnoletto, Veronese, Carlo Dolce, Steen, and Watteau, to define the nature of the picturesque. The verse is weak: the ideas are obscure: but the selection of characters gives a further light on Melville's tastes and interests. In a later verse, on the boors in a picture by Teniers, we see how his wakeful brain "elaborating pain" took comfort in the suggestion of the creature-brown warmth of even the lesser realists; and one may safely say that there was nothing fine in art that he was not capable of responding to. It was the accident of living in New York in the seventies and eighties that kept Melville away from the painters who might have meant more to him, El Greco, Delacroix, Goya, Daumier, Blake. These all might have had a more intimate message for him; but, with his feeling for Rembrandt, he was close to his own kind. In Holland, he had first noticed Rembrandt's shadows. Rembrandt's depth, his torment, and the warm blood of humanity beneath it all—that was Melville's, too.

3

The years passed; the dun seventies gave way to the grey eighties; and at last the prisoner was led out of his cell. In 1886, when Herman Melville was sixty-seven, his wife received a legacy from her brother, Lemuel Shaw, and the unremitting routine could at last be broken. The succour that might have saved Melville some of his worst pangs and difficulties at thirty-three, came reluctantly more than thirty years later. He shook his wings, made one or two uncertain steps forward, doubtful, after all these twenty years of regularity and servitude, if he could venture flight. A few of these warming-up exercises remain: the series of prose sketches on the Marquis de Grandvin, Jack Gentian, Colonel J. Bunkum: they have the air of juvenile compositions, done just for practice. In a very little while his hand grew more schooled; slowly, thoughtfully, he began work, revising older poems and writing new ones. John Marr and Other Sailors he printed privately, two years after his liberation; and Timoleon he published, even more privately, in 1891, the year of his death. In November, 1888, Melville began Billy Budd, the only prose work of any consequence after The Confidence Man: he started to revise it slowly in March, 1889, and did not finish it until April, 1891.

In neither the poems nor the sketches was there the furious effort of a pent-up man, desperately to finish something before his death: for he had never entirely abandoned literary effort: Bridegroom Dick is dated 1876, the year Clarel was published. Melville worked during these final years with the firm, methodical concentration of a man taking up a thread where some purely external circumstance had compelled him to lay it down. He valued these days: they were to be the crown of his life, and to give him, at least, the satisfaction of self-vindication. The hours were so precious that when an admirer, Mr. Archibald MacMechan, one of the first to revive Melville's fame in our own day (1914), asked for further light on Melville's works and his point of view, Melville did not answer him, except to express his thanks and to say that "though his vigour sensibly declines, what little is left he husbands for certain matters as yet incomplete, and which indeed may never be completed." These are the words of a man who has had retirement forced on him; not those of one who has doubted the office of literature, and has nothing to say.

Deliberately, Melville wrote his quiet coda: muted, a little lower in key than his earlier work, these poems and Billy Budd contain the earlier themes of his life, now transformed and resolved. Let us look more closely at this final testament. Melville's life has a beginning, a middle, and an end. The last twenty years, though tedious, solitary, insulated, bitter with apples of Sodom, had not been lived in vain: the verse is more skilled, certain: the poems are crystals, pure if not unflawed: here at last is that concentration, for the lack of which Clarel does not live. The prison had left its pallor on the prisoner; but it had not deprived him of the skill to use his liberty. Had he written only this handful of verses, this brief novel, Melville would still, like Stephen Crane, have left something of a mark on American literature.

4

Melville's mind continually played over the sea. As Whitman felt that Leaves of Grass must tally with the earth in its most common and universal aspects, as he confronted all doubts and perturbations with the miracle of a single blade of grass, so Melville perhaps felt that his writing must tally with the sea—that every joy and hope and lust of life must be able to face its terrible realities. Clarel is full of images of the sea. The student, in his vaulted room in Jerusalem, looking over the terraced roofs of the city, is "like some ship-boy at masthead alone, watching the star-rise"; and Melville characterized Vine's strength by saying that he had supplemented Plato with a "daedal life in tents and boats." There are a hundred other allusions and images. The sea was the source of Melville's strength, and even when his daedal life was over, its profound imprint remained.

In the prose preface to John Marr, Melville explained that Marr had left the sea, settled down in the prairie as a pioneer, had lost his wife and child through fever, and

remained a lonely soul, cut off by his roving and cosmopolitan past from the farmer-folk, the land animals, around him.
In Bridegroom Dick, a longer poem, Melville assumed the
guise of an old man-of-war's man, seated by his wife, sun-
ning himself on an October day, balmy as spring, he with his
pipe, she with her tea. The old fellow's mind goes back over
his cruises, his ships, his shipmates: the whole round of the
day, polishing the pinnacle, minding the helm, shooting the
sun, announcing the time to the quarter-deck at noon—and
all his mess-mates and superiors, Old Chuck-a-block, Commander All-a-Tanto, Orlop Bob, Rhyming Ned, Top-gallant
Harry and Jack Genteel: the old revels, the old bouts of
liquor, the old battles. The words are so salty the fish-bones
almost stick in one's throat; and in the very litany of names
Melville achieves poetry; for once, the crabbedness of his
verse increases its effect.

In another verse, To Ned, Melville seems to address his old
comrade, Toby, recalling the rich isles they roved when they
were young, and predicting that the pleasure-hunter, weary-
ing of routine resorts, would at last discover the Marquesas
and other authentic Edens in the South Seas. This poem
gives one pause. One wonders if Melville's early disillusion
with marriage and success was not, more than one can ever
definitely say, due to the fact that he had drunk such a deep
draught of beauty in the South Seas that life thereafter,
in the dusty, smoky, jangling air of America or Europe, was
insipid and brackish. No wife who wore stays and petticoats
and flannel nightgowns, and who was laden with household
cares, could be another Fayaway: no farm with a cow and a
horse and fences to repair could be another palm-grove. The
Marquesas had perhaps spoiled his taste for such dreary
fare. So delicious is this memory of the past, that Melville
even marvels if mortals may twice, here and hereafter, touch
a paradise!

In the same spirit, in his later poems, he remembers the
happy port of Syra, full of juvenile fun, reminding him of

days when trade did not exist, and toil and stress were not
overbearing, and life was leisure, merriment, and peace.
Melville never deceived himself by dismissing these things as
mythical, or by magnifying the importance of sanitation and
sound currency. This feeling of animal delight had redeemed
him from his own torments; he knew it was one of the permanent blessings of life; and a civilization that knew nothing
of it, except through the depravity of complete drunkenness,
was in a far lower stage of barbarism than its most vigorous prophets had dared to say. If there were no pleasurable
excitements, there would be murderous ones: if there were
not dances there would be wars: and, for lack of strong
sensual graces, men would become hard, vengeful, stupid,
oppressive. Melville turned to Syra, or to Naples in the time
of King Bomba, not because he was unaware of poverty,
rags, misery, but because he knew there was sadness and
misery in New York, too, without the redeeming thoughtless-
ness and careless pleasure. "A fig for Bomba! Life is fair
squandered in superabundant leisure." That was an answer Clarel had shrunk from accepting from Derwent: but
it was not an invalid one. The very virtues of Western civilization, its industry, its thrift, its willingness to postpone
present goods for future rewards, tended to degrade life
quite as much as its downright vices.

Melville's sea poems, however, were not all pieces of happy
reminiscence. The wreck of a victorious man-of-war, the
deserted raft with a signal flying, the disintegration of the
figurehead Charles-and-Emma by storm and weather, the
mad plunge of a ship against an iceberg: these are images
of a different order. Melville did not become weak and sentimental in his old age; but instead of letting the dark background of the universe dominate the composition, he paints
in a warm foreground, as in a still-life of Chardin's, with
some sensible, kindly object to capture the interest and reflect the high lights. The sea remains the sea, pitiless, echo-

less, indifferent to man's hopes and dreams: but the man in Melville is himself again.

> Healed of my hurt, I laud the inhuman Sea—
> Yea, bless the Angels Four that there convene;
> For healed I am ever by their pitiless breath
> Distilled in wholesome dew named rosmarine.

One could tell from these poems, even if one lacked the contemporary testimony of a Pittsfield acquaintance, Mr. J. E. A. Smith, that Melville, in these closing days, was no bitter, defeated old man. Mr. Smith says that in 1885, on Melville's last visit to Pittsfield, he "bore nothing of the appearance of a man disappointed in life, but rather had an air of perfect contentment, and his conversation had much of his jovial, let-the-world-go-as-it-will spirit. It would," as Mr. Smith very justly continues, "be well nigh a climatic miracle if a brief ride to Pittsfield and a few snuffs of Berkshire air should so restore to society and its enjoyment a man who had just been the recluse and almost misanthrope pictured by some of the New York newspaper writers." In his letter dedicating John Marr to Mr. Russell, Melville stresses the quality of geniality, "the flower of life springing from some sense of joy in it, more or less"; and, delicately, shyly, like a belated crocus, this flower bloomed in Melville's last years. When he wished Russell from his heart the most precious things he knew of in this world, health and content, he wished him the first because he had once known it in its miraculous fulness, and the second, I think, because he had at last found it. When on a clear day Melville would wander through the woody ravines and pastures near Fort George, or when he would take a ferryboat ride down New York Bay, shifting from one side of the boat to another, to take in every aspect of the harbour and every new ship, the old keenness, the old zest, would return. If his life was still that of the recluse—"I am an old fogy," he wrote in 1880, to excuse his staying at home—his feelings were far from Pierre's or Timon's.

There is poetry in parts of John Marr, particularly in The Haglets, not merely measured lines and rhymed endings. There is even more poetry perhaps in Timoleon, and perhaps a deeper revelation of Melville's inner convictions and strivings. The verses from which the volume gets its title shoot parallels into Melville's own life: Timoleon rescued Timophanes, but it is Timophanes who is his mother's pride. She sees herself in him and looks, through him, to become an envied dame of power, a social queen: Melville, who had once perhaps wanted his mother's generous love, realized that his lack of worldly success had stood in the way of it: a discovery he first announced when he wrote Pierre. Exiled, Timoleon ceases to hate his fellow citizens; but, cut off from common membership in the marketplace, in severance like a pale head found after battle apart from the trunk, he confronts the gods, not finding the wrong in man, but taking his quarrel to the Arch-Principals themselves. Has ideality no counterpart except in man's mind? Are earnest natures but fatherless shadows? The edges of Melville's old torment are here; and I should be inclined to date the poem from an earlier period; but in other verses one discovers that his resolution has completely knitted together. Under the title of The Enthusiast, he places the words: *Though He slay me, yet will I trust in Him.* It is a poem of brave defiance; and it tells so much about the man that I must reproduce it.

> Shall hearts that beat no base retreat
>   In Youth's magnanimous years—
> Ignoble hold it, if discreet
>   When interest tames to fears;
> Shall spirits that worship light
>   Perfidious deem its sacred glow,
>   Recant and trudge where worldlings go,
> Confirmed, and own them right?

Shall Time with creeping influence cold
    Unnerve and cow? The heart
Pine for the heartless ones enthralled
    With palterers of the mart?
Shall faith abjure her skies,
    Or pale probation blench her down
    To shrink from Truth, so still, so lone,
Mid loud gregarious lies?

Each burning boat in Caesar's rear
    Flames—No return through me!
So put the torch to ties though dear,
    If ties but tempters be.
Nor cringe if come the night:
    Walk through the cloud to meet the pall,
    Though light forsake thee, never fall
From fealty to light.

Melville did not see in post-bellum America, with its parvenus pining for distinctions and dignities, its lawmakers "taking the lawless one's fee," in all the sham and shuffle of those guilty days, any pledge for a happier society. The Age of the Antonines was far behind; and their return seemed equally distant. "Apollo's bust makes lime for Mammon's tower." This man of integrity must fortify himself from within; and when the present offers him no foothold, he must stand with Posterity or with the Ancients. This was the sort of "adjustment" that Melville achieved; and it was the only kind, in his position and day, that was worth working for. There is no notion more delusive or unscientific, in the strict biological sense, than the belief that a poet may make a happy "adjustment" to his circumstances by turning bond-salesman, or the artist by becoming an advertising expert. This course neglects the elementary fact that the relation between an organism and its environment is interacting and reciprocal: the best sort of adjustment is that which tends to preserve life with its highest values intact. The proper adjustment to a fire is not to plunge into it; and the response of a poet to an unfavourable environment is not to commit suicide but to use the most economic means for saving himself. Melville had done this —and he was saved. "Happiness," Spinoza said, "consists in a man's being able to maintain his own being." When Melville read this dictum in Matthew Arnold's essay on Spinoza, in 1871, he marked the passage: it described his own effort. In a more fruitful age, his being would have been maintained in harmony with, not in opposition to, the community: but at all events his vital duty was to maintain it.

5

We come to Melville's last verses, those which he gathered in a MS. called Weeds and Wildings, which remained unpublished until Mr. Raymond Weaver edited the definitive edition of his work in 1923.

These final poems have all the qualities one cherishes in Melville: his geniality, his humour, his lofty brooding, and that aloof satiric eye beneath which his contemporaries shrivelled from the grandeur of their reputations to the littleness of their deserts. In addition, another quality of Melville's personal life wells to the surface and confirms all one's other intuitions: a deep affection for his wife, and a warm sympathy. The "clover dedication to Winnifred"— who was Lizzie—recalls the old times together at Arrowhead, when the red clover had blushed through the fields about their house. They had not exactly lived in clover during those years or the later ones: ah, no! nor had they known anything of the four-leafed kind, except once, as he reminded her each year, "on the early forenoon of the fourth day of a certain bridal month, now four years more than four times ten ago." Melville recalls how, after a morning walk in the summer, he would return home with a handful of clover blossoms, to put on the maplewood mantel in Lizzie's south-facing room: her altar. "And in October most did I please myself in gathering them from the moist-matted aftermath in an encircled little hollow nearby, soon to be snowed upon. . . . And once—you remember it—having culled them in a sunny little flurry of snow, winter's frolic skirmishes in advance, the genial warmth of your chamber melted the fleecy flakes into dewdrops rolling off from their ruddiness. 'Tears of the happy,' you said. Well, and then whom but to thee, Madonna of the Trefoil, should I now dedicate these Weeds and Wildings, thriftless children of quite another and yet spontaneous aftergrowth, and bearing indications, too apparent it may be, of that terminating season on which the offerer verges. And for aught of the melting mood that my verses may possibly betray, call to mind the dissolved snowflakes on the ruddy oblation of old, and remember your 'Tears of the Happy.' "

There is a story of an acquaintance asking Melville for a copy of one of his books, and Melville's answering that he did not have a copy in the house. One has no reason to suspect "O. G. H.'s" veracity, or that of Melville: but one would get a false impression of Melville if one thought that this indicated he had forgotten his work, or its worth, or his old ambitions. There are a dozen references to his literary fate, pointed, sardonic, in Weeds and Wildings. One of the most obvious of these references is a poem entitled The American Aloe on Exhibition. "It is a floral superstition," observed Melville in the little introduction, "as every one knows, that this plant flowers only once in a century. When in any instance the flowering is for decades delayed beyond the normal period (eight or ten years at farthest) it is owing to something retarding in the environment or soil."

Now, after one has made due allowances for the inner obstructions to Melville's further development in the critical period of maturity, one realizes that Melville and Mr. Van Wyck Brooks are right: for even had he continued at the level of Moby-Dick—as indeed he did in Benito Cereno—there was something retarding in the American environment and soil, in the thirty years that followed the Civil War.

One cannot separate a man from his social environment: a society lives in a man: a man is a creature in society: the inner world is less private and the outer world less public than people habitually and carelessly think. These very words, inner and outer, individual and social, are merely conveniences of thought: there are no actual lines and borders, except practical ones. Melville's triumph, like that of his contemporaries in the Golden Day, was the last expression of a provincial society, and the first prophetic achievement in a newer and deeper culture. His own disaster was an emblem of the disintegration of that provincial society, and the blight of the new culture, which though fully conceived in the mind, received neither nourishment, warmth, nor protection from the narrow, mechanistic, money-bent society that succeeded the provincial one. If the inner world be not a phantasm, it must be united to an outer world that nourishes it and supports it, even when it offers oppositions and antinomies. This relationship had existed before the Civil War; and when the external milieu became impoverished, it ceased to exist—and the Aloe ceased to flower.

This poem admits no doubt of the fact that Melville was grimly describing himself. People came to see the Century Plant on exhibition, ten cents admission, but seldom more than two came at a time! This was the homage that Melville met in his old age—and what comfort, what tender comfort it was! What can the aged stem do? It moans:

> At last, at last! but joy and pride,
> What part have I with them?

> Let be the death that kept me back
> Now long from wreath decreed;
> But, ah, ye Roses that have passed
> Accounting me a weed!

When Melville touches on Captain Vere's eventual death, in Billy Budd, he adds that this spirit, in spite of its philosophic austerity, may yet have indulged the most secret of all passions, ambition, without attaining the fulness of fame:

and one cannot doubt that Melville is disclosing his own secret. The more violent the pride, the deeper the ambition, the more fiercely it guards itself. But look more closely at Melville's humility: it towers like a mountain! Listen more closely to his silence: it shouts like an army! He well knew, all the while, how little the vain roses mattered that accounted him a weed; and we, who look back upon Melville's ostensible contemporaries, Lowell, Stedman, Stoddard, Aldrich, can scarcely help sharing his contemptuous smile. For these good gentlemen, in their most tolerant mood, Walt Whitman was the Good Grey Poet, useful to be trotted ceremoniously out on the platform, once a year, to recite his oration on The Martyred President; and as for Melville— he was the queer old fellow who had once lived among the cannibals. One can fancy the superior droop of their lips when Robert Buchanan, an English writer, told them that these two men were the supreme imaginative writers America had produced.

Did Melville forget his books or think them paltry? The verses, Immolated, are an even more direct answer.

> Children of my happier prime
> When one yet lived with me and threw
> Her rainbow over life and time,
> Even Hope, my bride, and mother to you!
> O, nurtured in sweet pastoral air
> And fed on flowers and light and dew
> Of morning meadows—spare, ah, spare
> Reproach; spare and upbraid me not
> That, yielding scarce to reckless mood,
> But jealous of your future lot,
> I sealed you in a fate subdued,
> Have I not saved you from the dread
> Theft and ignoring which need be
> The triumph of the insincere
> Unanimous mediocrity?
> Rest, therefore, free from all despite
> Snugged in the arms of comfortable night.

In still another poem, called Thy Aim, Thy Aim? he questions whether mid the dust and dearth and din he may by some deed prove to be an exception, and he warns himself to beware of envy, for if striving on he win the goal, he will get only a flower of reputation, which is cut down in an hour; but if he survive that, he will still only earn a funeral flower —the belated funeral flower of fame. Melville was spared the pillory of being praised as a travel-writer and a humourist, with Mark Twain, or coupled as a poet with Aldrich; and in the bottom of his heart, there was an anticipation of his final survival, not without a feeling of satisfaction. Having prepared his own coffin, like Queequeg in Moby-Dick, he could even fancy the flowers and wreaths that a later generation would place over it. Funeral flowers, yes, but even funeral flowers may solace a man, if he contemplates them before they are cut!

The relief from Melville's dull grind had come a little too late: one must not flinch from that fact. He was conscious of his age and his physical debility; and, so far from railing at youth, he would not, "reduced to skimmed milk, slander the cream." Youth, he knew, was immortal: " 'Tis the elderly only grow old." But age brought one advantage: it taught him the wisdom of folly. When a spirit appears and asks him where he would choose to dwell, in the Paradise of Fools or in Wise Solomon's Hell, he does not pause to weigh the answer; but, ironically, he reverses his belief in Moby-Dick and demands the fool's paradise! From these sardonic snatches of Melville's verse one gets some notion of what his conversation on daily topics, the chicanes, briberies, corruptions, social follies and stupid observances of his contemporaries must have been. Melville's wit was meant for keen society: small wonder he created Jack Gentian to keep him company.

In The Rose Garden, verses written during the first days of Melville's release, one finds him asking himself whether he should turn to verse or to prose. The question was an important one: he must have known that his strength lay in prose, if only the theme were big enough to enlist all his energies; but Melville delayed and dallied, hesitating to commit himself to an impossible task. In his dilemma, he consults a friend, asking him whether it is better to have a heap of posies or a few drops of attar; and his friend tells him that his time has gone by. To which Melville answers that, unfortunately, he had come into his roses late; but first he wants to settle this little matter—poetry or prose? Not being able to decide, he tried his hand at both. His old eagerness was there; but something had happened. "Age, dull tranquilliser, and arid years that filed before" had unfitted him for flowers. Here one feels the final pathos of Melville's position—the last foul thrust of fate. In his maturity, he had been cheated of outer sustenance, and when it finally came to him, he found himself cheated of inner support. That brambly garden, that sour soil, needed energy to bring it back into a state of cultivation, and energy, not the will or the skill or the delight, was the one thing that Melville, at sixty-seven, lacked. "My dear Sir," he had once exclaimed to Mr. Duyckinck, "the two good things to be yet discovered are these—the art of rejuvenating old age in men, and old-ageifying youth in books." He had not altogether failed in the latter: but the first need was beyond him.

But when energy fails, skill may partly make up for it; and there is a simplicity and directness in these poems which shows greater control of his medium: the annoying inversions are fewer, and among the wildings of Melville's old age, there is still a rose or two left over from a more cultivated garden. The poem that fittingly closes this ms. volume, The Lake, is perhaps the finest Melville wrote: it is a colloquy between his own spirit and the spirit evoked by the Lake of Pontoosuce. Melville here faces death and emptiness of being, and he draws his faith from that spectacle in which the great religions have found their sustenance, in the march of the seasons, the rhythmic cycle of life, the ecstasy, the

agony, the tragedy of the dying god, and his annual resur-
rection and renewal.

> "All dies! and not alone
> The aspiring trees and men and grass;
> The poets' forms of beauty pass,
> And noblest deeds they are undone,
> Even truth itself decays, and lo,
> From truth's sad ashes pain and falsehood grow.

All dies!

> The workman dies, and after him, the work;
> Like to those pines whose graves I trace,
> Statue and statuary fall upon their face:
> In every amaranth the worm doth lurk,
> Even stars, Chaldeans say, fade from the starry space,
> Andes and Appalachee tell
> Of havoc ere our Adam fell,
> And present nature as a moss doth show
> Of the ruins of the Nature of the Aeons long ago.

.   .   .   .

> Dies, all dies!
> The grass it dies, but in vernal pain
> Up it springs and it lives again;
> Over and over, again and again,
> Who sighs that all dies!
> Summer and winter and pleasure and pain,
> And everything everywhere in God's reign,
> They end and anon they begin again;
> Wane and wax, wax and wane:
> Over and over and over again,
> End, ever end, and begin again—
> End, ever end, and forever, and ever begin again!"
> She ceased and nearer slid, and hung
> In dewy guise; then softlier sung:
> "Since light and shade are equal set,
> And all revolves, nor more ye know;
> Ah, why should tears the pale cheek fret

For aught that waneth here below?
Let go, let go!"
With that, her warm lips thrilled me through,
She kissed me, while her chaplet cold
Its rootlets brushed against my brow,
With all their humid clinging mould,
She vanished, leaving fragrant breath
And warmth and chill of wedded life and death.

That peace and oneness with Nature, which Isabel had prayed for, came at last to Melville in the closing years of his life. He had renounced much; but he had gained much. What is life? the king in Mardi had asked the philosopher; and the philosopher had said: That question is more final than any answer. After much doubt, exacerbation, searching, after a long weary pilgrimage through books and lands, and not a little intercourse with men, Melville was back to the view of his youth: he now accepted its finality. What power and heroic defiance had not accomplished, love, which has its philosophic equivalent in the desire to merge oneself with the universe and surrender to it, and accept its purposes, as one accepts the desires and whims and aims of one's beloved—love had achieved this. It was no accident that Melville's warm attitude toward Elizabeth coincided with this last warm acceptance of the universe. Melville surrendered to his wife, and he surrendered to his rough old mother, the earth, owning the primacy of that ceaseless urge which begets the Ahabs and Babbalanjas and Medias and Jack Chases and Pierres and Clarels, recognizing that intelligence, power, virtue, are not prime movers themselves, but derivative mechanisms that transmit and utilize the energy of life. If one spurn that energy and deny its sources, one's dreams are futile and one's hopes empty: but when one accepts life itself as the primary fact, then the dying year brings no grief, and all that fades and decays is but a pledge of what shall again, one day, live and flourish: the very universe itself, and space and time, are but modes of being,

351

no more eternal than the senses that react to them and project upon them the forms that make them useful and significant to man. Whatever be the ultimate nature of things, the universe man conceives is still held together at his own centre: its significance is part and parcel of his own. And at the centre of that centre is a fertilized ovum. Out of the egg comes not merely man but his world: the mightiest constellation is but the ectoderm of man's original plasm. There is a greater energy than Moby-Dick's. The seed that in its growth pries open the rock has more power than the inert and brutal elements that oppose it, and there is a seed in man whose growth cannot be denied, a seed that binds him to all life, and causes him to direct his energies, despite frustrations, despite warring elements in his own being, towards a fuller existence marked by love and understanding. The ideality, which Melville could not find in a cold "external" universe metaphysically separated from man—and falsely so—is embodied in the common instincts of animals: it was when he ceased to draw upon these sources that the world became black and painful and hostile, and ideals seemed ghastly disembodiments. When the roots of his animal nature were nourished once more, he leafed again, as the trees leaf in Indian summer, and courage and faith returned. Melville had faced the colourless, unintegrated, primal world that underlies and antedates that which we know through our senses, our feelings, our experiences: he had touched the bare, unkind beginning of things, that chaos which existed when darkness reigned over the face of the waters, and only Moby-Dick had stirred in the deep: he had beheld the white unrefracted truth which exists before it passes through man's being and is broken up into the colours of art and thought and custom and ritual and organized society. But Nature paints like a harlot, not without reason: she desires to attract the passions of men, to attract and use them for her own end: life. Melville's consciousness of a more primal world made him see more exhaustively, I think, into the nature of existence: but it was bare rock-truth, unweathered into soil, still less worked over by plants, insects, moulds, and the tools of man: and it gave him nothing that his spirit could feed on. At last he escaped from that bleak ultimate revelation, and, participating in the ancient cycle of life, he found his own life renewed once more.

6

Melville's last poems gain by comparison with his earlier work: but his prose inevitably loses a little. One does not miss his lack of energy in a quatrain; it is plain and perceptible even in a short novel. One notes this falling off of Melville's prose in the sketches on the Marquis de Grandvin: it comes out again in the little addition to Rip van Winkle that he wrote. In his prime, writing about Hawthorne, Melville had little use for the tepid quality of Irving's prose, so genteelly lymphatic; but now, in 1890, he went so far as to dedicate his addendum to the Happy Shade of Sunnyside. The torrid tropical sunlight, the violent gold and purple of Melville's earlier prose vanished: what was left was the mild pale sunshine cast on the bronzed oak leaves of a winter landscape. These graceful but diminished energies properly link Melville's spirit with Irving's. The immediateness of the old narratives was gone. Billy Budd, his final novel, is not a full-bodied story: there is statement, commentary, illustration, just statement, wise commentary, apt illustration: what is lacking is an independent and living creation. The epithets themselves lack body and colour: Billy Budd has nothing to compare with the description of boiling whale-oil in Moby-Dick—"a wild Hindoo odour, like the left wing of the Day of Judgement."

Billy Budd, which was dedicated to Jack Chase, wherever he might be, alow or aloft, lacks the fecundity and energy of White-Jacket: the story itself takes place on the sea, but the sea itself is missing, and even the principal characters are not primarily men: they are actors and symbols.

The story gains something by this concentration, perhaps: it is stripped for action, and even Melville's deliberate digressions do not halt it. Each of the characters has a Platonic clarity of form. Captain the Honourable Edward Fairfax Vere, "starry Vere," is a man of superior order: humane, reserved, free from cant, fortified by an equal knowledge of men and books. After the mutiny of the Nore, the time when this story takes place, the command of a British naval vessel is no easy one: the officers are tense and expectant, though outwardly indifferent: mutiny may break out any minute among the "people." Billy Budd, a seaman taken over by impressment from The Rights of Man, stands out from the rest of the crew: one of Nature's innocents. A fine frame, yellow hair, an open, almost girlish face, set him off with angelic beauty: and he is a natural favourite among the crew: the Handsome Sailor of eighteenth century balladry.

Without overt act, merely by being what he is, the personification of strength, health, beauty, innocence, Budd incurs the enmity of Claggart, the master-at-arms. Claggart, with a suspicious past at his back but with soft humid ways and obsequious intelligence, has quickly won promotion: he is now the evil agent of discipline, prowling over the ship, watching for disorder—a sea-bag not stowed away, a sailor evading work, or a hint of mutiny. It is as natural for Claggart to hate goodness as it is for Budd to personify it: the evil in the man is apparently causeless in any immediate sense, like the venom in a snake: it simply is there. With a benign, ambiguous exterior, he secretly contrives in small ways to make Billy's lot miserable; and when Billy, perplexed, brings the matter before a trusty wizen-mouthed old sailor, the old fellow tells "Baby Budd" that Claggart has it in for him. In his simpleness, Budd cannot believe it. How could he?—for he had given no offence. So Claggart plots more deeply against Budd; through confederates in the crew, tale-bearers and spies, he tries to bribe Budd into mutiny. Budd, not realizing the meaning of the suggestion when it is made to him, still flushes with anger, like a fresh girl spattered by an obscenity. Then Claggart goes further. He takes advantage of Budd by wakening him from a sleep and getting him into a compromising position before he is sufficiently awake to withdraw. Now Claggart thinks he has Budd in his power. He appears before Captain Vere and humbly submits his report of Budd's attempted treachery.

Captain Vere, being a firm man and a sound one, is not greatly impressed by Claggart's tale: it looks too thin: but for the sake of form and discipline, since the customs of the navy make it necessary to employ such fellows as Claggart, he summons Budd to his own cabin to confront the master-at-arms, instead of airing the matter by a public inquiry. When Budd comes, Claggart repeats his lie to Budd's face. This poor lad has only one physical blemish: in moments of stress he stammers, and now, confronted by this sudden, horrifying suspicion, he can for the moment give no answer. His mouth makes an effort: no words come forth: the blood mounts up to his head. Captain Vere wisely attempts to soothe him: "There is no hurry, my boy, take your time." These kindly words have just the opposite effect to that intended, for, touching Billy's heart to a mighty effort at release, he answers Claggart's lie with a cannon-blow from his fists. Budd's first and only act of rebellion is fatal: Claggart is instantaneously killed.

Vere has no belief whatever in Budd's guilt; but this act swiftly alters the case. The perjurer has been struck dead by an angel of God; but in this world, the angels must hang. A swift deck court-martial is held in the captain's cabin, and Vere is caught by the dual nature of his position. He is commander of the ship, a captain, a disciplinarian, responsible for the safety of all aboard, committed by the terms of his commission to the Articles of War and all that they imply. As a man, with fatherly feelings toward this innocent boy, he would be merciful: as commander, he acts against his innermost wishes and urges his subordinates not to be swayed by motives of compassion. His fellow officers reluctantly respect their superior's probity: they sentence Billy Budd to be hanged for murder. Privately, as man to man, as father to son, Vere announces the sentence to Budd. Justice done, pity, magnanimity, stir Vere to the bottom: the feelings of the judge and the judged are transferred; for the burden now lies on Captain Vere rather than on the victim; and Vere, in turn, is the instrument of an institution. When the hemp is placed around Billy Budd's neck, Billy turns to the quarter-deck and cries out: God bless Captain Vere. He dies happily, in the first vapoury glory of the dawn—dies, and becomes a legend among the sailors, and the spar from which he was hanged is followed through its vicissitudes, and ballads are sung and tales are told about him.

Billy Budd is the story of three men in the British Navy: it is also the story of the world, the spirit, and the devil. Melville left a note, crossed out in the original manuscript, "Here ends a story not unwarranted by what happens in this incongruous world of ours—innocence and infirmity, spiritual depravity and fair respite." The meaning is so obvious that one shrinks from underlining it. Good and evil exist in the nature of things, each forever itself, each doomed to war with the other. In the working out of human institutions, evil has a place as well as the good: Vere is contemptuous of Claggart, but cannot do without him: he loves Budd as a son and must condemn him to the noose: justice dictates an act abhorrent to his nature, and only his inner magnanimity keeps it from being revolting. These are the fundamental ambiguities of life: so long as evil exists, the agents that intercept it will also be evil, whilst we accept the world's conditions: the universal articles of war on which our civilizations rest. Rascality may be punished; but beauty and innocence will suffer in that process far more. There is no comfort, in the perpetual Calvary

of the spirit, to find a thief nailed on either side. Melville
had been harried by these paradoxes in Pierre. At last he
was reconciled. He accepted the situation as a tragic necessity ; and to meet that tragedy bravely was to find peace, the
ultimate peace of resignation, even in an incongruous world.
As Melville's own end approached, he cried out with Billy
Budd: God bless Captain Vere! In this final affirmation
Herman Melville died. September 28, 1891, was the date
of the outward event.

EPILOGUE

EPILOGUE

WHY DOES Herman Melville mean so much more to us than he did to his own contemporaries? What has his thought done for us, and what has his vision given?

The change that has come about is not merely a change of style, so that the things which amused Mr. Stedman or Mr. Lowell are now old-fashioned, like hooped skirts, while the things that concerned Melville are, like the cubist quilts and coverlets of the 1850's, distinctly modern. Typee is still as good a book as Mr. Arthur Stedman thought it; but we see now that it belongs to a more common order of literature, whereas Moby-Dick, the more closely we consider it, mounts to that lonely wind-swept plateau in whose rarefied air only the finest imaginations can breathe. Distinctly, Moby-Dick belongs with The Divine Comedy and Hamlet and The Brothers Karamazov and War and Peace; and if it does not establish its right to this company, it must occupy a lower place than the successful novels of its period, a David Copperfield or a Pendennis, books written with a complete acceptance of the current limitations and provincialities.

Melville's work, taken as a whole, expresses that tragic sense of life which has always attended the highest triumphs of the race, at the moments of completest mastery and fulfilment. Where that sense is lacking, life shrivels into small prudences and weak pleasures and petty gains, and those great feats of thought and imagination which transform the very character of the universe and relieve human purpose from the scant sufficiency of toiling and eating and sleeping, in a meaningless, reiterative round, shrivel away, too.

361

John Ruskin saw the truth of this when, in spite of his pacifist convictions, he praised the art of war, for its effect upon the human spirit: life is intensified and purposive when the battle with the inimical forces that surround us, like Ahab's battle, is a deliberate pursuit and challenge, and not merely an apathetic waiting for a purely physiological end.

The tragedy of life, its evanescence, its frustrations, its limitations within physical boundaries almost as narrow as a straitjacket, its final extinction, becomes, in a day that consciously embraces its fate, the condition of an heroic effort. Death, which biologically is merely the terminus of a natural process, acquires significance for man because he anticipates it and modifies his activities so as to circumvent it: by memory and foresight, by choosing his ends, dreaming of immortality, erecting monuments and statues and museums, and above all, by transmitting the written word, man creates a destiny beyond his life's physical span. It is just because the worms lie in wait that man defies the gods, cherishes the images he has created and the relations he has solidified in custom and thought, and centres his efforts on those things which are least given to meaningless change. Though the sensible world is not derived, as Plato thought, from the heaven of ideas, the opposite of this is what every culture must strive for: to derive from the sensible world that which may be translated to a more durable world of forms.

Within the world of these forms there is Life, a thing of value, and not merely living, a matter of fact and habit and animal necessity. Whether one develops this tragic sense of values on a battlefield, like Sophocles, or in a whaleboat, like Melville, it is a precious experience: for living, merely living, as every profane writer from Petronius Arbiter to Theodore Dreiser has shown, brings boredom, satiety, despair: whereas Life is eternal, and he who has faith in it and participates in it is saved from the emptiness of the universe and the pointlessness of his own presence therein. Living, for man, in all but the most brutish communities, like those of the savages of the Straits of Magellan or the outcasts of a Liverpool or New York slum, includes and implies this Life; and when Melville summons into his whaler the several races of the world, he is expressing the universal nature of that effort which caps nature with culture, existence with meaning, and facts with forms. Ahab's tragic struggle is the condition of every high endeavour of the mind, even though Death be its tragic reward; while adjustment, acquiescence, accepting outward conditions as inward necessities, though they may prolong living in the physical sense, effectually curtail Life: this attitude, the attitude of Melville's contemporaries, the attitude of the routineers and Philistines of all times—and they have never perhaps been so numerous as today—disrupts life more completely than illness and death do; for it brings about a deliquescence of forms, such as the nineteenth century showed in all its common arts, and a disintegration of human purposes. When that happens, the White Whale of brute energy reigns supreme: Life itself is denied: living produces no values, and men hide their emptiness by embracing dull counterfeits of purpose.

Melville's younger contemporaries, who fought in the Civil War, knew Life and Death; but those who prospered in the years that followed knew something more dreadful than simple death: they knew chaos and purposelessness and disintegration, such chaos and purposelessness, mixed with a wan, reminiscent hope, as Henry Adams pictured in his Education. Herman Melville portrayed a human purpose, concentrated to almost maniacal intensity, in Moby-Dick; and in Pierre and The Confidence Man, he showed the black aftermath, when the purpose was not sustained and carried out in art, and when he himself was deserted in his extremity, by contemporaries who neither understood nor heeded nor shared his vision. No single mind can hold its own against all

that is foreign to it in the universe: Shakespeare's solitary
heroes issue their brief defiance only to be blotted out: such
unity of spirit as one may possess, as philosopher or poet,
must be sustained in the community itself. Now, a new culture, the product of two hundred and fifty years of settled
life in America, had produced Walden, Leaves of Grass,
Emerson's Notebooks, and Moby-Dick; but that culture,
instead of supporting and carrying forward the integration
of man and nature and society shadowed forth in those
books, was completely uprooted by the Civil War, and a
material civilization, inimical in many aspects to the forms
and symbols of a humane culture, was swept in by the very
act of destruction.

Two generations of that material civilization have shown
us its lopsidedness, its aimlessness, its grand attempt to
conceal its emptiness by extending concrete roads and
asphalted streets and vacuum cleaners to more and more
remote terrains. Our most humane writers, like Mr. Sher-
wood Anderson, have proved how mercilessly the whole
human being is crippled by this one-sided triumph; and
even our most bewildered writers, who have exulted in all
these maimed energies, have shown in their very act of
deification how brutal and aimless they are. We realize that
the effort of culture, the effort to make Life significant and
durable, to conquer in ourselves that formidable confusion
which threatens from without to overwhelm us—this effort
must begin again. And in thus making a beginning we are
nearer to Whitman with his cosmic faith and Melville in his
cosmic defiance than we are to a good part of the work of
our own contemporaries. It is not that we go back to these
writers: it is, rather, that we have come abreast of them; for
in creating that new synthesis, in lieu of the formless
empiricisms and the rootless trancendentalisms of the last
three centuries, the writers of our own classic past were
nearer to the contemporary problem than almost any of the

Europeans have been—since the physical remains of another culture in Europe give the mind a false sense of stability and security.

Herman Melville's world is our world, magnificently bodied and dimensioned: our synthesis must include and sublimate that very quest of power which Melville portrayed with such unique skill, as a combination of science and adventure and spiritual hardihood, in Typee, Mardi, and Moby-Dick. Melville's life warns us not to stop here: men must test their strength in surrender as well as in lonely conquest: he who knows neither social union nor sexual passion nor love is indeed an Ishmael, who finds himself an outcast because he has cast out that which was most precious to his own nature: there is love in the universe as well as power: the sun warms and the rain slakes the thirst: the whales dally and the first song of creation is the song of sex.

The synthesis that Melville foreshadowed in his ideas is not simply a logical structure: the search for such an abstract solution of life's problems is one of the idola of the closet. Melville's synthesis was embodied in acts and deeds. During the years of his early manhood, as he wandered about the world and contemplated existence under the stars and bore a hand in working the ship, his environment, his experience, and his vital relationships were an integer. He did not lack what libraries and cities and the social heritage of man gives: indeed, he enjoyed fully the resources of a sound literary and philosophic scholarship; but he mixed this with activities that gave back to books the subtle properties that cannot be transmitted to the printed page, but must be derived directly from living. The reviewers in London might well have been shocked by the spectacle of a common sailor writing Typee or White-Jacket. Melville had bridged in his life that great gap between the respectable, learned professions and the common trades that had hitherto been crossed, with rare exceptions, only by those who definitely had lost caste, or who, like Burns, had risen with a sense of uneasy, sullen pride to acceptance among people of high rank.

Melville was an American—and that implied the dissolution of spiritual frontiers. America had taken all the established castes and classifications of Europe and left them to sort themselves out according to nature and ability: this was the true and beneficial result of eighteenth century thinking and its political accompaniments. By a singular dissociation of ideas, which involved the destruction of an old social tissue, it had permitted a free and disinterested creature, a man, to emerge from a conglomeration of classes and practical interests. Melville was not primarily a sailor; he was not an adventurer; he was a man sailing, a man adventuring, a man thinking, proving in his early manhood that a whole and healthy life may involve many functions, without sacrificing its wholeness and health to any one of them. Whitman with his carpentering and his nursing, Thoreau with his pencil-making and gardening, were Herman Melville's brothers in the way and the life. They did not disdain practical life: they faced it manfully: but instead of neglecting every other activity for "business" they saw that what was called business was only a small part of the totality of living: they behaved toward it *as if it were real*, as Whitman said, with the knowledge that merely getting a living was not a sufficient contribution to Life. Brutal though Melville found whaling to be, it communicated, nevertheless, a sense of Life: there was astronomy and natural history and art and religion within the bulky hold of a whaler, as well as technics and business and the daily log-book.

The vision that grew out of this experience was a whole one, not, like the science of its time, subordinated to practical interests or even narrower metaphysical schemata. Through its dissociation from inherited values all things began at scratch: no one element in life, except sex, carried a handicap. Melville's settling down was inevitable, inevitable and difficult: but the difficulty was not due to the inability of a restless adventurer to accept a tamer and more even existence: it was due to the fact that, having known a rounded and cultured life, however savage and exacting, he could not submit to the desiccated routine of Western civilization, with its contempt for art, its gross disregard for the higher manifestations of science, its dislike for meditation, its subservient religion, its frank subordination of all other values to that of Comfort. Melville's contemporaries, with chance exceptions, neither lived as full a life as he had lived in the South Seas, nor were able to understand it, even as a theory. For these contemporaries, Melville's vision was an example of Bedlam literature: they did not realize that Bedlam was precisely the world they lived in, and that Melville's vision, like Emerson's, like Whitman's, like Thoreau's, was a part, and a great part, of a new cultural synthesis.

The stripping down of Herman Melville's ego, which he began in Mardi and finished in Pierre, was a sloughing away of labels, nicknames, party war-cries, habits, conventions, and acceptances; it was, necessarily, a prelude to that building up of a new ego, a surer and more central, a social and participating self, which is the task of our own time for both men and communities. Melville was crippled in the work of reconstruction by a hiatus in his own career, which was followed and made final by the social hiatus of the Civil War: though he sought to carry the work further in Clarel, one cannot pretend that he did anything but give a hint of this mended psyche, this more richly integrated self: one of his last poems, The Lake of Pontoosuce, perhaps approaches nearer to the goal than any other work of his. Had he built up that ego, his vision might have fully complemented Whitman's—land and sea, day and night, sunlight and shadow, triumph and tragedy. That union was latent: it is for us to effect it. It is useless, however, to speculate upon what might have been. The accidents that befell Melville, as he rounded his own Cape Horn, were part of that malign doom he himself pictured in Moby-Dick, and they do not affect the essence of his work. Whatever Melville's life was, his art in Moby-Dick exhibits that integration and synthesis which we seek. Through his art, he escaped the barren destiny of his living: he embraced Life; and we who now follow where his lonely courage led him embrace it, too. This embrace was a fertile one; and in each generation it will bring forth its own progeny. The day of Herman Melville's vision is now in the beginning. It hangs like a cloud over the horizon at dawn; and as the sun rises, it will become more radiant, and more a part of the living day.

NOTE ON BOOKS

THE COMPLETE and definitive edition of Melville's works is that published by Constable and Company, London, 1923-1924. With the exception of Israel Potter, The Confidence Man, Pierre, and the various volumes of verse, all of Melville's work can now be obtained in contemporary popular editions. Mr. Raymond Weaver's edition of The Shorter Novels of Herman Melville (Horace Liveright, 1928) and Mr. Henry Chapin's edition of the Apple-tree Table and Other Sketches and of John Marr and Other Poems (Princeton University Press, 1922) make almost all of Melville's significant minor work available. Mr. Meade Minnegrode's Some Personal Letters of Herman Melville and a Bibliography contains extracts from some of Melville's Letters to Evert Duyckinck. The bibliography covers in detail all of Melville's writings, giving both American and English first editions. The first biography of Herman Melville was that of Mr. Raymond Weaver: Herman Melville, Mariner and Mystic (Doran, 1921). Mr. John Freeman's brief critical biography belongs to the new English Men of Letters Series (Macmillan, 1926); Mr. Freeman has the distinction of being the first to deal patiently and critically with Melville's poetry. Various other volumes on Herman Melville are now in course of preparation. Among the critics whose studies of Melville have contributed to his revival and to a proper evaluation of his work I would mention especially Mr. Frank Jewett Mather, Jr., Miss Viola Meynell, Mr. Percy Boynton, Mr. J. W. N. Sullivan, Mr. E. L. Grant Watson, and, not least, Mr. Van Wyck Brooks.

INDEX

INDEX

372

tion, 18; moved to Bleecker Street, 18; melancholy situation, 19; relatives, 20; influence of Manhattan, 21; ambitions, 22; father's death in 1832, 23; fixation of father's image, 24; struggle for existence, 25-26; Grand Tour, 27; an infant Ishmael, 28; bitterness of youth, 28; disappointment in Liverpool, 33; exploration of city, 34; first view of misery and degradation, 34-35; essential education, 35; return to Lansingburgh, 36; slow growth, 36; early sexual life, 36-37; first literary effusions, 37-38; beginning of self-consciousness, 39; preparation for literature, 38; attraction to sea, 40; departure from New Bedford, 41; leaves ship at Nukuheva, 46; lives among Typees, 47-52; is rescued by the Julia, 52; makes friends with Dr. Long Ghost, 52; participates in mutiny, 53; is confined in British jail, 54; becomes a rover, 54-55; enjoys idle life, 55; works in Honolulu, 55; becomes sick of adventure, 56; ships on U. S. Frigate, United States, 56; homeward bound, 56-62; discovers abuses in Navy, 57; makes friends with Jack Chase, 57; is influenced in literary taste by ship's library, 57-58; is condemned to flogging, 58; has impulse to assault Captain, 58; resents "massacre of beards," 59; falls from yard-arm, 59-60; beginning of manhood, 61; lands at Boston, 62; writes Typee, 67; habit of documentation, 69; accuracy, 70; effect of censorship on, 77; successful author, 78; writes Omoo, 81; marries Elizabeth Shaw, 86; honeymoon, 87; daily routine, 87-89; has weak eyes, 88; writes Mardi, 91; tightening of domestic responsibility, 108; necessity for potboilers, 108; writes Redburn, 108; writes White-Jacket, 114; goes to Europe, 119; becomes acquainted with English society, 122; steady growth and development, 131; return to America, 131; moves to Arrowhead, 136; meets Hawthorne, 142; correspondence with, 144 ff.; discovers Hawthorne's sentiments, 147; apprenticeship over, 150; intensity of effort in Moby-Dick, 151; ruin of eyesight, 152; feeling of desolation, 154; is damned by dollars, 155; contempt of fame, 155; swift development, 156; exaltation and terror from Moby-Dick, 156; situation after Moby-Dick, 196; culmination of powers, 197; disclosure of weaknesses, 196; his wilful defiance, 199; mood of defeat, 200; betrays himself in Pierre, 218; terrific pressure leads to retreat of, 220; dilemmas as writer, 107, 220; anticipation of defeat, 221; failure to mature in marriage, 222; draws near spiritual Cape Horn, 223; alienation from humanity, 227; scorn of critics, 228; Timonism, 230; meets successive misfortunes, 235, 236; weakened health, 236; writes Piazza Tales, 236; Israel Potter, and The Confidence Man, 236-255; recoils from painful experience, 259; goes on voyage to Holy Land, 261; visits Hawthorne in England, 261; discusses withdrawal from literature, 263; fails to renew friendship, 265; sails for Near East, 265; explores Constantinople, 267, and Cairo, 270; has passionate encounter in Italy, 274-281; returns home, 1857, 281; seeks to gain living in lecture lyceum, 282; voyage to San Francisco in 1860, 284; longing for Elizabeth, 286; commonplaceness as father, 287; sells Arrowhead, meets carriage accident, moves to New York, 289; interest in Civil War, 292-303; eventual disillusion, 303; withdraws from literary struggle, 306; gets inspectorship in Customs House, 307; writes Clarel, 307-308; is indifferent to "recognition," 333; is released from Customs House, 336; re-

INDEX

sumes literary work and writes Billy Budd, 337; publishes John Marr, 338; publishes Timoleon, 342; writes Weeds and Wildings, 344; expresses warmth of love for Elizabeth, 345; finds peace, 351; expresses ultimate resignation in Billy Budd, 357; death, 357

Melville, Malcolm, 92

Melville, Maria, mother of Herman Melville, comparison with Mrs. Glendinning, 14

Melville, Stanwix, 287

Melville, Thomas, ambition to become sailor, 67

Men-about-literature, 333

Metcalf, Eleanor Melville, v

Milton, 191

Minnigerode, Meade, 285

Misinterpretation of Melville, 224

Missionaries, 74

Moby-Dick, writing of, 147-157; summary of, 158-176; criticism of, 176-195; symphonic quality, 182; organic conception of, 182; its meaning as story of sea, 183; as parable of evil, 184; as tragedy of man, 187, as contrast of practical and ideal life, 188

Modern vision of life, 194

Mohi, 95

Monody (to Hawthorne), 265

Mortmain, 310

Murray, Dr. Henry A., Jr., vi

Murray, John, 73

Mythology, Moby-Dick as first modern, 193

Nathan, 310

Nature, oneness with, 351; paints like a harlot, 352

New York, in 1819, 15-16; after Civil War, 326; its brutality, 327

New Bedford, centre of whaling industry, 42, 158

No Trust, 249

O'Brien, Fitz-James, 198

Olympians, English, 124

Omoo, 81-84

Orthodox illusions, Melville's rejection of, 324-325

Out of the Cradle Endlessly Rocking, 191

Palestine, effect on Melville, 309

Paradise of Bachelors, 130, 236

Paradox of morality, 216

Passion, reawakening in Italy, 275; frustration, 276-281

Parrington, Vernon, 199

Peace, Melville's ultimate, 357

Pequod, The, 161

Personal disappointment and bitterness, 109; an Ishmael, 109

Physical characteristics, Melville's, 119

Physical weakness, 225

Piazza Tales, The, 243

Pictures, Melville's favourite, 130, 336

Pierre, 196-206

Pilgrims, Melville's and Chaucer's, 311-312

Pip, 170

Pittsfield, 135, 341

Plotinus Plinlimmon, 215

Political institutions, Melville's misgivings over, 295

Post-bellum America, 343

Primal world, Melville's consciousness of, 353

Progress, its illusory nature, 313-314

Prose-sketches, 337

Provincial society, 9; its economic foundations, 10; mixture of nationalities, 10; reality of family, 11; idealized in Pierre, 13; destruction, 292

Psychological truth, in Pierre, 211

Pyramids, the, effect on Melville, 271

Queequeg, 160

Rama, 330

Rammon, Introduction to, quoted, 323

Realism, 5

Recoil from black experience, 255

Redburn, 108-114

Refugee, The, 290

Rembrandt, 336

Resignation, on point of, 259

375

INDEX

Whale ship, Melville's College, 46
Whaling implements, 45
White, as symbol of elemental truth, 168
White-Jacket, 114-118
Whitehead, A. N., 191
White Whale, incarnation of malicious agencies, 166; symbol of external universe, 167; Ahab's defiance of, 167
Whitman, Walt, 4, 5

Woman, her absence in Melville's work, 201
Woodberry, George, 80
Work, dignity of, 332
Wulf, Uncle John de, 20

Yillah, 94; symbol of spiritual quest, 51; beckons Melville, 52
Yoomy, 95
Young Goodman Brown, 203